CW01460411

Law's Sources

Law's Sources

NEIL DUXBURY

Professor of English Law, London School of Economics

OXFORD
UNIVERSITY PRESS

OXFORD
UNIVERSITY PRESS

Great Clarendon Street, Oxford, OX2 6DP,
United Kingdom

Oxford University Press is a department of the University of Oxford.
It furthers the University's objective of excellence in research, scholarship,
and education by publishing worldwide. Oxford is a registered trade mark of
Oxford University Press in the UK and in certain other countries.

Published in the United States of America by Oxford University Press
198 Madison Avenue, New York, NY 10016, United States of America.

British Library Cataloguing in Publication Data
Data available

Library of Congress Control Number: 2025937520

ISBN 9780198981152

DOI: 10.1093/9780198981183.001.0001

Printed and bound by
CPI Group (UK) Ltd., Croydon, CR0 4YY

FSC
www.fsc.org
MIX
Paper | Supporting
responsible forestry
FSC® C013604

The manufacturer's authorised representative in the EU for product safety is
Oxford University Press España S.A., Parque Empresarial San Fernando de Henares,
Avenida de Castilla, 2 – 28830 Madrid (www.oup.es/en or product.safety@oup.com).
OUP España S.A. also acts as importer into Spain of products made by the manufacturer.

Preface

The book's title, with its nod to Ronald Dworkin's *Law's Empire*, invites perplexity from the outset, particularly given the book's length. The whole of the law? Every source? The book is not a compendium of sources but rather an examination of conundrums and controversies that sources raise. Central to the project—this sentence might help you decide whether to read on—are two topics which lawyers know to be both intellectually and practically significant: how law connects to sources, and how sources are used by legal actors, particularly judges. The point of my addressing the first topic is to try to show how modern legal philosophy attests to a shift in perspective—a shift which appears to have been somewhat unappreciated by legal philosophers themselves—whereby arguments and controversies about sources of law have come to coalesce increasingly around the notion that sources are to be understood not, primarily, from the standpoint of citizens *qua* subjects to whom the law applies but rather from the position of those who, given that their decisions are enforcements of law, have to make determinations as to how the law is to be applied from one instance to the next. The bulk of the book, in so far as it has a bulk, is taken up by the second topic—how legal decision-makers reckon with sources, particularly with sources which they need not countenance, and how they put them to work. Plenty has been written on this topic. As with the first topic, some of my conclusions put me in disagreement with others. Much of what I have to say is prompted by previous research of my own, some of which, I now think, is insufficiently attentive to the ways in which sources are negotiated by (as distinct from how they bind or influence) judges.

The book isn't about a specific jurisdiction, and it doesn't belong to any particular area of law or legal analysis. Roman law and civil law briefly feature—have to feature—when attention turns to the source-status of juristic work, but the focus is otherwise entirely on the common law, and especially the United States and England (I do mean England). Inevitably, I tread a delicate line between trying to capture commonalities between jurisdictions while remaining sensitive to the fact that these jurisdictions, though bonded by common law, have their own mentalities and conventions. The approach I've taken draws not only on material and illustrations from numerous legal systems but also on various methods of legal inquiry—legal history, constitutional theory, snippets of comparative law, applied legal philosophy, even some good old-fashioned case law analysis. Some of the excursions into unfamiliar fields and jurisdictions inevitably involved a degree of method acting. If my performance comes up short it's nobody's fault but my own, especially since various judges and academics were kind enough to provide me with very detailed feedback on rehearsal-stage typescripts. To this end, I record my thanks to Charles Barzun, Jacco Bomhoff, Ross Cranston, Nicola Lacey, Mark Leeming, George Leggatt, John Murphy, Richard Re, and Emmanuel Voyiakis for their appraisals and advice. I'm also very grateful to the four referees who read draft chapters for Oxford University Press—parts of the text were revised considerably in light of their feedback—and to John Roper at the University of Virginia Law Library for assisting me in tracking down some of the materials that feature in chapter 8.

Contents

Introduction   xi

1. Source(s)   1

2. The source-law distinction   7
   a) *Statute as source*   7
   b) *Refining the distinction*   9
   c) *Custom*   16
   d) *Custom and constitutions*   21

3. The tenacity of the sources thesis   27
   a) *The sources thesis*   28
   b) *Interpretivism and sources*   29
   c) *Source appropriateness*   34

4. The concept of the secondary source   37
   a) *The contours of secondary sources*   38
   b) *Non-legal and upgraded sources*   41

5. Secondary sources as sources of law   44
   a) *Juristic authority in the civil law tradition*   47
   b) *The common law*   51

6. Code source   60
   a) *The US Restatements*   62
   b) *The sliding scale of authority*   68

7. Source identification: some difficulties   74
   a) *Hazards of identification*   76
   b) *The void* ab initio *conundrum*   79
   c) *The* sua sponte *reliance conundrum*   83

8. Scholarship as a secondary source   92
   a) *Judges on scholarship*   94
   b) *Judges using scholarship*   102
   c) *Coda: judges and attribution to scholarship*   118

Conclusion   129
Index   133

Introduction

Everybody knows that with some forms of discourse there is an expectation that claims bear a relationship to sources. Claims do not become unassailable just because the expectation has been met. Anyone unconvinced by them—by your pronouncements as a scholar, journalist, exam candidate, or whatever other source-oriented enterprise happens to engage you—might want to scrutinize just how it has been met. What do you understand sources to be? Are they fit for purpose? How have you used them? Is your use of them objectionable? These questions have their variants in the realm of legal discourse. Actors in this realm use sources of law. But what are sources of law?

Law students learn early on in their studies that there are, broadly speaking, two types of source: primary sources, which pertain to actual, applicable law, as distinct from secondary ones, which are essentially information and opinion about law. The distinction is a valid one—or so I shall contend in this book—though it can certainly be made to look fragile on close inspection, and those legal scholars (there's no shortage of them) who maintain that there is no meaningful distinction to be drawn have multiple arguments to which they can resort. *Numerus clausus* doesn't apply to primary sources; the door is always open to newcomers.[1] A source could be primary in one system and secondary in another (and, of course, *vice versa*). Not only are sources never paradigmatically primary in the sense of yielding laws that bind as fetters bind, moreover, but secondary source-materials, such as *dicta* and Restatement provisions, are now and again applied by judges as if they were legal authority.

Distinctions aside, just what it means to speak of a source—primary or secondary—is difficult to ascertain. The names that are given to some of the primary sources of law are also the names of types of law. A constitution would seem to be simultaneously law and source, though if an original constitution is (or contains elements of) law, there arises the vexed question—addressed in

---

[1] Even when 'legal systems . . . provide, in some constitutional or legislative provision, a detailed list of their various sources of law', there is still the 'possibility that new (non-codified) sources emerge from the sheer practice of the law-applying officials'. Giorgio Pino, 'Sources of Law', in *Oxford Studies in Philosophy of Law: Volume 4*, ed. J. Gardner et al. (Oxford: OUP, 2021), 58–92 at 70, 72, and see also 88–89.

Law's Sources. Neil Duxbury, Oxford University Press. © Neil Duxbury 2025.
DOI: 10.1093/9780198981183.001.0001

chapter 2—of whether a constitution (or its legal content) could ever be ascribable to a source of law, given that this source would have to exist anterior to the very phenomenon which marks the beginning of the legal system. Legal philosophers, we will also see in that chapter, are sometimes adamant that what is commonly understood to be law is actually only a source. One of the objectives of this book is to demonstrate that, in the twentieth century, positivist legal philosophers abandoned a figurative or historical conception of primary sources, as locations from which laws originate, in favour of a test-based or analytical conception of primary sources—sources as criteria enabling the identification of the rules of a legal system. Although this modern positivist approach to primary sources has redoubtable explanatory value—we will see that even the best-known rejection of it, Dworkinian interpretivism, seems never entirely to escape its reach—it sets aside the question of what citizens identify as law and asks instead what it is that legal officials, particularly judges, recognize to count as law when they make legal decisions about citizens' actions. One curious consequence of this jurisprudential makeover is the revival and reconfiguration of an early-twentieth century argument—an argument which eminent legal positivists discredited—which has it that judicial resort to statutes is not the application of law but the derivation of law from a source (or, as some who advance the argument prefer, of legal norms from a text).

The first three chapters of this book might be summarized as an attempt to capture the various dimensions to the concept of a primary source of law, as well as to illustrate how there was a mid-twentieth century turn in legal philosophy—commonly associated with something we will encounter under the name of the sources thesis—which fundamentally reoriented the question of what it means to speak of a source being a primary source. The principal, somewhat underestimated implication of this reorientation was that primary sources came to be understood not, first and foremost, as sources of directives binding on citizens, but rather as criteria enabling judges to identify what qualifies as applicable law when making legally binding decisions.

When judges make these decisions, they might also take into account material—prime examples are judicial *dicta*, foreign judgments, legislative history, and legal scholarship—which they do not identify as law but which provides, say, the context to, or a perspective on, or an appraisal of, the law that they identify. The fact that this material is not itself held up as law makes it, by default as it were, secondary source material. This rather suggests that secondary sources are easy to ascertain: that they are sources yielding material which judges might take account of as information or argument, but which they don't identify as applicable law. When, in chapter 4, we start to consider secondary sources, it will very quickly become clear that the picture is more complicated. Intuitively it seems wrong, first of all, to maintain that any material whatsoever that does not derive from a primary source must therefore be secondary source material; with much of the output that bears upon people's everyday lives, it is difficult to conceive how it might ever inform or influence reasoning about law-application. Yet there are no criteria for ascertaining what count as secondary sources. Any source that informs or persuades judges when they decide how to apply the law is a secondary source.

Judges, moreover, will sometimes follow a proposition drawn from a secondary source much as they would a rule binding on the court. In some instances, this simply amounts to reclassification: what was previously not law now is. But there are also instances when judges are not conferring primary source status on secondary source material but rather are opting to treat secondary source material—usually specific secondary source material, and in specific circumstances—as if it did have primary source status. These instances—there is no denying that they exist—concern propositions which do not formally bind as law but which, given judicial willingness to countenance them much as they would if they were binding law, seem somehow to rank above the types of legally informative or persuasive pronouncements that are routinely classified as secondary source material.

Most of the discussion of secondary sources in this book concerns one secondary source in particular. Perhaps only a legal scholar with an outsized ego would consider legal scholarship to be a secondary source deserving of special attention—though we will see in chapter 8 that quite a few common-law judges seem to have been similarly minded. Counsel and judges quite regularly turn to one type of scholarship, the legal treatise, and quote it alongside—occasionally even instead of—applicable authorities because it better expresses what, in the authorities themselves, comes across as convoluted or elliptical. Rarely, however, are common lawyers—in the case of judges it may well be accurate to say that they are never—receptive to the notion that legal scholarship may yield *de facto* binding legal propositions of its own, that it may perform the role of a primary source. There are common-law judges, especially in the United States, who have denounced certain types of legal scholarship as being of little or no practical value even as a secondary source. In the English legal system, judicial views on the capacity of scholarship to influence their reasoning tend to be more positive and placatory. In an earlier book, I analysed judicial attitudes towards scholarship in both countries.[2] Various judges subsequently improved on the

---

[2] Neil Duxbury, *Jurists and Judges: An Essay on Influence* (Oxford: Hart, 2001), 23–46, 61–115.

analysis.[3] The final chapter of this book is, in essence, another attempt at improvement.

How so? To date, studies of scholarship as a secondary source have tended to focus on the extent to which the work of academics assists judges when they formulate decisions, the areas of law most amenable to academic influence, and the types of academic work (and types of academic lawyers!) most likely to prove influential. In major common-law jurisdictions, there emerged in the twentieth century something of a mantra, detectable still, to the effect that the judge-jurist relationship is basically symbiotic: that the writings of academic lawyers can be influential on the courts much as the judgments of courts can inspire the reflections of academic lawyers. This argument makes an appearance late on in this book—as, too, does its distinctly more dour cousin, the not-uncommon claim that, in the eyes of many judges, too many academic lawyers are high plains drifters, intent on producing scholarship that is of no value whatsoever to anyone contributing to the work of the courts. Judges and academics have had lots to say about both these perspectives, so they receive only minimal scrutiny here. Far more attention is paid to a more complicated question: that of how scholarship—which, we will see, need not be legal scholarship—is actually used in judgments.

Even though judges are not always as transparent as they ought to be when making use of scholarship (see the coda to chapter 8), there is plenty of evidence throughout common-law court systems that scholarship assists them as a source of legal information and legal argument. These systems—certainly the court systems of England and the United States—also yield evidence of another, less clear-cut, possibly less common phenomenon: judges discovering in scholarship modes of reasoning which help them develop their legal perspectives and pronouncements in ways that other secondary sources do not. Judicial efforts to shape existing law are sometimes driven by scholarship not in the straightforward sense that judges can be seen to be receptive to information or persuaded by arguments set forth in scholarly work, that is, but rather because reasoning contained in that work serves a heuristic or provocative purpose—because it challenges them to finesse, and contributes to how they formulate, their own thoughts on how some aspect of the law should be shaped.

---

[3] Lady Justice Carr, '"Delicate Plants", "Loose Cannons", or "A Marriage of True Minds"? The Role of Academic Literature in Judicial Decision-Making' (2023) 23 *Oxford Univ. Commonwealth L. J.* 1; Lord Burrows, 'Judges and Academics, and the Endless Road to Unattainable Perfection' (2022) 55 *Israel L. Rev.* 50; Richard A. Posner, *Divergent Paths: The Academy and the Judiciary* (Cambridge, Mass.: Harvard UP, 2016), 24–28; Lord Neuberger, 'Judges and Professors—Ships Passing in the Night?' (2013) 77(2) *Rabels Zeitschrift für ausländisches und internationales Privatrecht* 233.

Readers might have picked up on an unarticulated admission. This book pursues two disparate lines of enquiry. Primary sources go to the question of how norms come to be (and cease to be) identified as laws. It will become clear in chapters 5 and 6—which examine transformations of non-binding material into law—that this question is relevant to secondary sources, too. Secondary sources, however, go primarily to the question of what lawyers and legal decision-makers do with—how they interpret, overrule, distinguish, cast doubt on, make the case that they are providing the best renditions of— the norms that they identify as law. The ontology of primary sources—what they are, how they yield legal norms, how they are to be distinguished from those norms—is the province of legal philosophers. Secondary sources tend to engage legal philosophers only to the extent that some instances in which non-binding material is drafted into service, but not formally re-categorized, as binding law are at least *prima facie* out of line with the thesis that a norm binds as law because it is an offspring of a primary source. Since the designation of sources as secondary has to do with the fact that they are understood to yield information about and perspectives on—but not actual—law, secondary sources aren't of central relevance to the philosophy of law.

Secondary sources come into their own—are more likely to feature significantly (which doesn't necessarily mean that they will be acknowledged)—in judicial opinions, and in arguments made before the judges who deliver them. In so far as this book concerns primary sources, it is mainly a disquisition on a type of legal philosophy. But the greater portion of the book, while never entirely moving away from legal philosophy, is basically an essay on secondary sources and the roles they can be seen to have played in common-law courts. Considered as a whole—and to be clearer about the implied admission—the book not only explores two different paths but also speaks (or purports to speak) to two overlapping but, ultimately, different audiences: a) legal philosophers, the majority of whom will probably consider the ins-and-outs of source-negotiation to be of little, if any, intellectual significance, and b) judges and lawyers (including doctrinally-minded academic lawyers), most of whom will seek no philosophical tuition on identifying applicable laws, but who will likely be interested in the many different ways in which secondary sources have been used to interpret and fashion the laws on which legal arguments are built and according to which cases are decided.

Underneath all the detail that is about to follow, there runs a fairly straightforward collection of claims. It does no harm, at the outset, to try to set these claims out tersely. Primary sources yield norms that are authoritative as binding law. Secondary sources yield material (it isn't always normative) that is authoritative in a non-binding sense: as trusted knowledge or compelling argument, say, rather than as binding law. It matters that lawyers and judges think about primary sources, because arguing cases, and deciding cases according to law, means identifying the laws relevant to the facts that cases present. Of course, lawyers and judges, once they have identified the law applicable to the facts of a case, are hardly likely to be done with sources. For there is also that second layer of sources, yielding the many types of material that help lawyers to formulate their legal submissions to court, and help judges to decide on how the law applies to facts. Sometimes, these secondary source materials are promoted to primary level. Sometimes, they aren't promoted but are made to work at that level anyway. Often, consideration of secondary source material will lead, or be part of what leads, a court to read the law in a way that has it apply differently from how it had been thought to apply. Secondary sources play to what, in due course, will be called law-fashioning instincts. Though the ways in which these sources are brought to the service of such instincts is—as is especially clear from the use of scholarship in courts—not always as might be predicted.

1

Source(s)

Sources substantiate claims. Sometimes they will not, of course, because we will have misread or misunderstood a source, or failed to spot that the source we have identified is not the relevant one. A phenomenon might have multiple sources, and behind one source there might be another. The sun is not the only source of Vitamin D, and while it is the source of the natural light across my desk, I think of the source of that light as my office window. We aren't always good at identifying sources, and our interpretations of them can be unreliable.

Sources themselves can be unreliable. Reliance on an unreliable source could be the cause of our undoing. Conversely, we might make a claim more compelling by distancing our position from sources which we know, which we might be able to show, are unreliable. When a source is especially valued, there might be conventions or rules endowing with it elevated status or perhaps even granting it a distinct form of protection, as when accreditation rules enable journalists to preserve source-anonymity.

Law yields variants on these anodyne observations. It also generates issues of its own. The most immediate of these is the question of what sources of law actually are. 'So', Marcus asks Atticus early in Cicero's *Laws*,

> what do you want me to do? What are your instructions? That I should write little handbooks about the regulations for gutters and shared walls? Or list the rules for contracts or court procedure? Such things have been diligently compiled by many writers, and I think they are less significant than what you expect from me.[1]

In the *Republic*, Cicero had already formulated a version of the question which Atticus encourages Marcus to address: '[w]hat is the source of law, either the law of nations or this civil law of ours?'[2] In the *Laws* (and later, in *On Obligations*), Cicero's preferred answer to this question derives from a Stoic

---

[1] Cicero, *de Legibus* I. 14.
[2] Cicero, *de Republica* I. 2.

Law's Sources. Neil Duxbury, Oxford University Press. © Neil Duxbury 2025.
DOI: 10.1093/9780198981183.003.0001

conception of nature. '[T]he source of law and justice' is not 'the praetor's edict', but rather 'has to be deduced from the nature of man'.[3] To 'have been endowed by nature with reason' is to 'have also been endowed with right reason, and therefore with law'.[4] '[S]ince the whole human race is seen to be bound together'[5]—since 'there is a bond of fellowship which in its widest sense exists between all members of the entire human race'[6]—we 'share the knowledge of justice amongst ourselves and ... impart it to all people'[7] through 'principles of right living' ('friendliness, generosity, and an appreciative mind which remembers acts of kindness').[8] '[L]aw'—meaning 'that highest law which came into being ... before any law was written down'— 'is a force of nature, the intelligence and reason of a prudent man, and the criterion of justice and injustice'.[9]

Note that it is *the* law that has *a* source. Though Cicero maintained that individual laws are not truly laws if they offend against right reason,[10] the dialogue that he constructs is not about those laws—the regulations for gutters, the rules of court procedure, and the like—but rather about the idea that nature, or natural law, is the source of the legal order. 'Cicero and his ideal interlocutors pose ... the question ... of "sources of law", as ... [one] of the nature of law'; 'the search for the nature of law turns out, it seems, to be a search for the source of law'.[11] But Cicero of course understood, and occasionally observed, that regulations and rules have *sources*—that they are attributable to legislative action and, most of all in Cicero's day, custom.[12] Post-Ciceronian Roman lawyers—as is evident from both Gaius and Justinian—would explicitly acknowledge from time-to-time that laws originate in a range of sources.[13] The more popular

---

[3] *de Leg.* I. 16–17.
[4] Ibid. I. 33.
[5] Ibid. I. 32.
[6] Cicero, *de Officiis* III. 69.
[7] *de Leg.* I. 33.
[8] Ibid. I. 32.
[9] Ibid. I. 19; see also ibid. II. 10; and *de Off.* III. 72 ('nature is the basis of law').
[10] *de Leg.* II. 13 ('What ... if a gang of criminals agreed to make some rules? ... In a community a law of just any kind will not be a law, even if people ... have accepted it').
[11] Lanfranco Mossini, 'Fonti del diritto. Contributo alla storia di una metafora giuridica' (1962) 74(1) *Studi Senesi* 139 at 160, 165.
[12] See *de Leg.* III. 12; and (on custom as a source of law) *de Inventione* II. 22; also *de Oratore* I. 212 (though custom, for Cicero, is confirmed as law because it accords with nature: Peter Stein, 'The Sources of Law in Cicero' (1978) 3 *Atti del III Coloquium Tullianum (Roma 3–5 Oct. 1976)* 19, 23).
[13] See e.g. Gaius, *Institutes* I. 2 ('The rights [*iura*] of the Roman people are established by statutes [*legibus*], plebiscites, ordinances of the senate, imperial constitutions, edicts of those entitled to issue them, and answers of the learned [*sc.*, unanimous juristic opinion: ibid. I. 7]'); Justinian, *Code* I. 17. 1. 6 (the opinions of Papinian and jurists who complemented his labours are 'as if their studies were derived from imperial constitutions'); *Digest* 1. 3. 32. 1 (Julian) ('Inveterate custom is not undeservedly preserved as if it had statutory force, and this is the kind of law that is said to be established by behaviour; for given that statutes themselves bind us for no reason other than that they have been accepted by the judgment of the people, it is fitting also that what people have approved without any writing should bind everyone').

modern predisposition, as will become clear, has been to examine a legal system's sources rather than seek to identify an overarching source.

To presume a division in juristic speculation—between those who purport to identify law's source and those who enquire after sources for legal rules—would be a mistake. Common-law and civilian legal perspectives yield evidence of jurists simultaneously asking after both. Early-modern English lawyers regularly referred to legal maxims as an elevated source of law. 'Maxims are the Foundations of the Law, and the Conclusions of Reason', Edmund Plowden pronounced in 1550, 'and therefore they ought not to be impugned'.[14] In the early seventeenth century, Edward Coke expressed much the same view: a maxim—capturing a legal argument or proposition which has been regularly scrutinized by judges and which stands as tried and tested reason—is 'a sure foundation or ground of art, . . . a principle . . . common ground, *postulatum*, or an axiome'.[15] He was quick to add, nonetheless, that maxims are but one of 'several fountaines or places' from which the common law emerges.[16] Coke's great rival, Francis Bacon, advanced a similar, albeit more granular, line of argument. Though he occasionally maintained that maxims must themselves derive from legal sources,[17] his preferred position was at one with that of Coke and many other jurists of the time: that 'Maxims are the Foundations of the Law, and the full and perfect conclusions of reason'.[18] Indeed, much of Bacon's juristic writing is devoted to providing ever more sophisticated formulations of maxims as sources of law—as 'fountains of justice, whence all civil laws are derived but as streams'[19] and which 'the unjust judge . . . corrupteth'.[20]

Yet Bacon was also inclined to write about law as derived from one or another ultimate source: from 'God . . . the praetor and revenger',[21] or from the

[14] *Colthirst v Bejushin* (1550) 1 Plowd. 21, 27.

[15] Edward Coke, *The First Part of the Institutes of the Laws of England; or, A Commentary upon Littleton* (London: printed for E. and R. Brocke, 1794 [1628]), 11a.

[16] Ibid. 11a–11b.

[17] See e.g. Francis Bacon, 'Maxims of the Law' (1597), in *The Works of Francis Bacon*, 7 vols ed. J. Spedding et al. (London: Longmans, 1876–1883), VII, 307–387 at 322–323 (While it is 'preposterous to prove . . . maxims', there are 'reasons . . . whereupon they depend').

[18] Francis Bacon, 'A Brief Discourse upon the Commission of Bridewell' (*c.* 1587), in *The Works of Francis Bacon* (n 17) VII, 509–516 at 509. See also John Fortescue, *De Laudibus Legum Angliæ* (Cincinnati: Clarke & Co., 1874 [1599]), 20; John Doderidge, *The English Lawyer* (London: More, 1631), at 38, 124–125, 152–153, 164, 196–197, 216, 261–262, 270.

[19] Francis Bacon, 'Advancement of Learning' (1605), in *The Works of Francis Bacon* (n 17) III, 253–491 at 475; see also his 'Example of a Treatise on Universal Justice or the Fountains of Equity, by Aphorisms' (from *De Augmentis Scientiarum* (1623), book 8), in *The Works of Francis* Bacon (n 17) V, 88–110 at 105–106 (aphorisms 82–83).

[20] Francis Bacon, 'Of Judicature' (1612), in *The Works of Francis Bacon* (n 17) VI, 506–510 at 507.

[21] Francis Bacon, 'Aphorisms on the Greater Law of Nations or the Fountains of Justice and Law' (*c.* 1614–1622), trans. Mark S. Neustadt in his *The Making of Instauration: Science, Politics, and Law in the Career of Francis Bacon* (Ph.D. dissertation, Johns Hopkins University, 1987), 272–299 at 288 (aphorism 16).

'supreme and commanding power' of the Crown,[22] or from 'the ancient and original power of the people'.[23] In Germany in the nineteenth century, the last of these assertions was turned into a serious juridical proposition. A legal system's grounds of origin (*Entstehungsgründe*), Friedrich Carl von Savigny argued, is the character, experiences, and consciousness of a nation's people. 'If we ask . . . about the subject in which and for which positive law subsists, we find the people. . . . Positive law lives in the common consciousness of the people, and we therefore have to call it peoples' law'.[24] But Savigny was careful to draw a distinction between identifying the people as the primordial source of law and locating 'our sources of law [*Rechtsquellen*]',[25] viz., 'the . . . origin of legal rules . . . in the pure territory of law'.[26] Just as Roman law had its sources (Savigny identified them as 'legislation, customary law, and legal science'),[27] there is, he maintained, a circle of sources (*Quellenkreis*)—'Justinian's laws, canon law, imperial laws, and the scientifically-derived common law'—which forms the material basis of Germany's legal system.[28] Law has its source, he claimed, and laws have their sources. The history of both common-law and civilian legal thought yields plenty of evidence of jurists upholding both these assertions at one and the same time.

Although it can seem somewhat mystical to speak of law's source, the proposition as often as not stands for something straightforward, such as that a legal system's cardinal source of law is, say, another legal system, or a person or organ with ultimate law-making authority. And while it is easy to form the impression that legal philosophers, particularly positivist legal philosophers, have predominantly been concerned with explaining law in terms of a master-source, the reality is more nuanced. Early positivists—who maintained that legal authority is located in the sovereign *qua* ultimate source[29]—certainly lent credibility to this perspective. Yet the principal proponent of classical legal positivism, John Austin, did not quite fit the role of the out-and-out source-monist.

---

[22] Ibid. 281 (aphorism 12). In other contexts, he argued that this power is limited by law: see e.g. his argument before the Exchequer Chamber in the *Post-Nati* (i.e., *Calvin's case* (1608) 7 Co. Rep. 1a), repr. as Francis Bacon, 'In the Case of the Post-Nati of Scotland', in *The Works of Francis Bacon* (n 17) VII, 641–679 at 646.

[23] Bacon, 'Aphorisms on the Greater Law of Nations' (n 21) 286 (aphorism 15).

[24] Friedrich Carl von Savigny, *System des heutigen Römischen Rechts*, 8 vols (Berlin: Veit, 1840–1848), I, 14.

[25] Ibid. I, 65.

[26] Ibid. I, 61.

[27] Ibid. I, 66.

[28] Ibid. I, 264.

[29] Jeremy Bentham, *The Limits of Jurisprudence Defined*, ed. C. W. Everett (New York: Columbia UP, 1945 [1782]), 111; John Austin, *Lectures on Jurisprudence or the Philosophy of Positive Law*, 2 vols, 5th edn, ed. R. Campbell (London: Murray, 1885), II, 510.

The sovereign, he insisted, is law's originating or 'fountain' source; but there are also legal 'reservoirs' or subordinate sources of law—courts, legislatures, and custom—which should be thought of as 'fed . . . and . . . emitting . . . borrowed waters . . . from' the sovereign, from the 'Fountain of Law'.[30] There were jurists writing in Austin's wake who would have had him make more of this concession to source-pluralism.[31] One of them, John Salmond, sought to rise to the challenge by distinguishing the 'formal source . . . from which the authority of the law proceeds' from 'legal-material' sources (such as court judgments supplying the content of legal rules) and 'historical-material sources' (such as *obiter dicta* and juristic opinions supporting the creation of particular rules).[32] Hans Kelsen professed to be neither a source-monist nor a source-pluralist, but simply exasperated. What, he wondered, was the point of these exercises? If 'sources of law' is defined in such a way that it encapsulates all laws and law-making institutions, as well as 'all those ideas which . . . influence the law-creating organs', the definition 'seems to render the term rather useless'.[33] A source could be a practice or a phenomenon that comes to acquire the status of law, or a lawmaking agent or agency, or whatever authorizes—or, for that matter, whatever provides the impetus for or shapes the content of—a law-maker's legislative action.[34] 'The ambiguity of the term "source of law"', Kelsen maintained, 'makes it rather unsuitable for scientific discussion'.[35] From his perspective, a taxonomical approach to the concept—an approach that Salmond's typology seemed to validate—could only compound the ambiguity.

Salmond's contribution to sources discourse is, in fact, subtle and prescient. It is true that he was mainly interested in cataloguing law's sources. But he also sketched a new way of thinking about them. To 'talk of legal sources', he maintained, is to assume there to 'be already in existence some law which establishes them and gives them their authority'.[36] This type of law, or 'rule', enabling courts to identify binding legal authority, must be 'legally ultimate and underived'.[37] A binding authority 'is recognised and administered by the

[30] Austin, *Lectures on Jurisprudence* (n 29) II, 510.
[31] See e.g. Carleton Kemp Allen, *Law in the Making*, 3rd edn (Oxford: Clarendon Press, 1939), at 3, also 58 ('[T]he study of the sources of law cannot be approached with the preconception that they are derived from a single origin').
[32] John Salmond, *Jurisprudence*, 9th edn, ed. J. L. Parker (London: Sweet & Maxwell, 1937; 1st edn publ. 1902), 193–197.
[33] Hans Kelsen, *General Theory of Law and State*, tr. A. Wedberg (Cambridge, Mass.: Harvard UP, 1945), 132.
[34] See Norberto Bobbio, 'Kelsen et les sources du droit' (1982) n.s. 27 *Archives de Philosophie du Droit* 135, 136–138.
[35] Hans Kelsen, *Pure Theory of Law*, 2nd edn tr. M. Knight (Berkeley: University of California Press, 1967 [1960]), 233.
[36] Salmond, *Jurisprudence*, 9th edn (n 32) 200.
[37] Ibid. 201.

Courts, and no rules are recognised and administered by the Courts which are not rules of law'.[38] It is in the nature of an ultimate, authority-establishing rule that it enables courts and other law-enforcing organs to recognize what is and is not applicable law.

> Every legal system contains certain rules determining . . . that all . . . principles which conform to such and such requirements are to be recognised as . . . principles of law, and applied accordingly. . . . Rules such as these establish the sources of the law. A source of law, then, is any fact which in accordance with the law determines the judicial recognition and acceptance of any . . . rule as having the force of law.[39]

Sources, on this account, are to be understood not as points of origin but rather as formalized or structured 'facts' or social practices—*stare decisis*-governed judicial decision-making, enactment of statutes by legislatures in accordance with a legislative process, ascertainment by a court that a custom has prescribed—which yield the rules that law-applying organs identify as having the authority of (judge-made, enacted, customary) law. The best-known critic of the legal philosophy underlying this account preferred to call these facts or practices not sources but 'grounds' of law (see chapter 3, section (a)). Celebrated positivists writing in Salmond's wake persisted, as Salmond had, with the language of sources. More significantly, they persisted with his methodology. Or to be more precise, they detected in his jurisprudence the rudiments of their own argument: that sources supply the criteria of validity which facilitate the identification of what counts as applicable law.[40] This argument is explored throughout the next two chapters.

---

[38] Ibid. 49. For an earlier formulation, see John W. Salmond, *First Principles of Jurisprudence* (London: Stevens & Haynes, 1893), 87–88.

[39] Salmond, *Jurisprudence* 9th edn (n 32) 196–197; see also Salmond, *First Principles of Jurisprudence* (n 38) 228. The first legal theorist to spot that Salmond was breaking from, rather than merely finessing, Austin's argument was probably Roscoe Pound, 'Sources and Forms of Law' (1946) 21 *Notre Dame Lawyer* 247, 248–249.

[40] See H. L. A. Hart, *The Concept of Law*, 3rd edn (Oxford: OUP, 2012; 1st edn publ. 1961), 292; Joseph Raz, *The Concept of a Legal System*, 2nd edn (Oxford: Clarendon Press, 1980), 190–191.

2

The source-law distinction

One virtue of the modern positivist argument, the argument first sketched by John Salmond, is that it distinguishes sources of law from law. This distinction poses no insurmountable difficulty for legal philosophers when laws are traced to non-legal sources, as when customary law is said to originate in custom. Difficulties arise, however, when the same term is used to describe both a source and a type of law. Rather aptly, the botanist-turned-jurist, Roscoe Pound, distinguished laws as species from sources as genera: law is a 'body of authoritative materials prescribed or received as the basis of judicial decision',[1] and one might (Pound accepted that one need not) think of sources of law as 'the literary shapes, official or otherwise, in which the authoritative materials are to be found'.[2] Pound's contemporary, John Chipman Gray, famously placed statutes in the genus rather than the species column.

a) *Statute as source*

Gray's approach, in doing this, was to take a simple observation regularly made by jurists of the era—that laws are dead instruments until courts animate them[3]—and to tweak it: rather than being laws not brought to life, statutes untouched by courts are not laws—and are still not laws even once courts lay hands on them—but are mere sources of law. Pound's literary shapes in enacted form are 'only words that the legislature utters',[4] 'the sources from which the courts draw the Law'.[5] Statutes depend on 'the will of the judges for their

---

[1] Roscoe Pound, 'Hierarchy of Sources and Forms in Different Systems of Law' (1933) 7 *Tulane L. Rev.* 475, 476.

[2] Ibid. 478.

[3] See e.g. Frederick Pollock, *A First Book of Jurisprudence for Students of the Common Law* (London: Macmillan & Co., 1896), 226 ('[L]aw without interpretation is but a skeleton without life, and interpretation makes it a living body'). For the classic critique of this view as applied to statutes, see James McCauley Landis, 'Statutes and the Sources of Law', in *Harvard Legal Essays Written in Honor of and Presented to Joseph Henry Beale and Samuel Williston*, ed. R. Pound (Cambridge, Mass.: Harvard UP, 1934), 213–246.

[4] John Chipman Gray, *The Nature and Sources of Law* (New York: Macmillan, 1921), 124–125.

[5] Ibid. 170.

Law's Sources. Neil Duxbury, Oxford University Press. © Neil Duxbury 2025.
DOI: 10.1093/9780198981183.003.0002

effect';[6] they 'are ... not ... part of the Law itself', for there is no such thing as 'legislative law'.[7] '[I]n truth, all the Law is judge-made law', and 'legislative acts, statutes, are to be dealt with as sources of Law'.[8]

H. L. A. Hart, the twentieth-century's pre-eminent analytical legal philosopher, considered Gray's refusal to accord statutes the status of law to be an 'interesting form of rule-scepticism'.[9] Gray's contemporary, Leon Green, purported to subscribe to a more uncompromising, stereotyped-realist version of the argument. Judges, on this version, not only make law but are the source of it as well. In a judge's hands, what lawyers uphold as sources—Green was thinking about precedent rather than statute— are easily cast aside: past decisions are 'no more law than the light from last night's lamp is electricity'.[10] Gray's rendering of the argument was not so close to Green's as it was to that of the eighteenth-century English cleric, Benjamin Hoadly, who resisted locating legal authority in, without entirely discounting, the past. Hart spotted the affinity.[11] 'He, who is truly the Law-giver' is 'not the person who first wrote, or spoke' the law, Hoadly maintained, though he immediately added that the true law-giver 'hath an absolute authority to interpret', rather than the right to disregard, what was originally written or spoken.[12]

Gray might have sidestepped the extreme version of rule-scepticism, but his argument is hardly robust. His principal error rests in his claim that statutes are sources 'to be dealt with'. Judges, he maintains, are the ones who do the dealing. 'The shape in which a statute is imposed on the community as a guide for conduct is that statute as interpreted by the courts. The courts put life into the dead words of the statute.'[13] But citizens also deal with statutes in so far as they reckon with them as part of the law of the land. Laws, not sources from which laws are derived, guide citizens. If statutes were only a source of law, a ruling that a defendant is liable for breach of a statutory duty would not be a decision according to law. Action contrary to an unanimated statute—one from which no court has yet derived a legal norm—could not, at the point of acting, be unlawful. For the statute would not, as convention has it, be law operative with

[6] Ibid. 177–178.
[7] Ibid. 125.
[8] Ibid. Within a decade of Gray advancing the argument, it was adopted chapter-and-verse in one of the classics of American legal realist literature: Jerome Frank, *Law and the Modern Mind* (Gloucester, Mass.: Peter Smith, 1970 [1930]), 131–137.
[9] H. L. A. Hart, *The Concept of Law*, 3rd edn (Oxford: OUP, 2012), 141.
[10] Leon Green, 'The Duty Problem in Negligence Cases' (part 1) (1928) 28 *Columb. L. Rev.* 1014, 1015.
[11] Hart, *The Concept of Law* (n 9) 141.
[12] Benjamin Hoadly, *A Sermon Preach'd before the King at the Royal Chapel at St. James's on Sunday March 31, 1717*, 3rd edn (London: printed for James Knapton, 1717), 12.
[13] Gray, *The Nature and Sources of Law* (n 4) 125.

prospective effect but rather a source of *ex post facto* law—law carved out of the statute by a court and applied to conduct retrospectively. If statutes were but sources of law, and all law judge-made law, then a core principle of the rule of law—that citizens should be able to discover the law governing their actions at the time that they act[14]—would be undermined, for discovery of the law on any particular matter would depend on the courts having already pronounced on it.

For Hart, Gray's thesis runs up against other objections. That there is indeed such a thing as legislative law is clear from the fact that the enactment of a statute may have the immediate effect of negating the binding force of a precedent; the statute's abrogation of the judge-made law at which it is directed precedes any interpretation of the statute by a court. Moreover, if legislators were not lawmakers but source-creators and the sources, once created, had to be judicially activated, courts would somehow have to acquire source-activating authority: if there are courts there must already be legal rules, after all, vesting courts with activating power.[15] To 'go the full length of denying that the status of law can belong to any statute . . . before the courts have actually applied it' is, Hart maintained, 'surely quite absurd'.[16] Kelsen was of a similar view. A legal norm is authorized by, and so derives its validity from, a higher legal norm. Casually speaking, therefore (Kelsen, we know, eschewed the description), the higher legal norm is a source. But this source, this higher legal norm, is no less law than is the legal norm that it validates. The statutes which courts interpret, and from which they derive legal norms, are themselves legal norms: 'Gray does not see that these "sources of law" . . . are legal norms, are really law. He . . . is right in maintaining against traditional doctrine that the courts create law. But he errs in his belief that law is created only by the courts.'[17]

b) *Refining the distinction*

Kelsen and Hart pronounced starkly on Gray, but their verdicts aren't a *coup de grâce*. For there has emerged, in the past half century or so, a line of argument

---

[14] '[I]n a civilised society which acknowledges the rule of law individual members of that society are entitled to know when they embark upon a course of conduct what the legal consequences of their doing so will be, so that they may regulate their conduct accordingly.' *IRC v Joiner* [1975] 1 WLR 1701 (HL), 1714 (Lord Diplock).

[15] See Hart, *The Concept of Law* (n 9) 137.

[16] Ibid. 65–66; see also H. L. A. Hart, 'Kelsen's Doctrine of the Unity of Law', in *Ethics and Social Justice*, ed. H. E. Kiefer and M. K. Munitz (Albany: SUNY Press, 1970), 171–199 at 195.

[17] Hans Kelsen, *General Theory of Law and State*, trans. A. Wedberg (Cambridge, Mass.: Harvard UP, 1945), 153.

affirming the gist of Gray's thesis. There are, with some overlaps, two broad groups of legal theorists invested in this line of argument: analytical legal philosophers, and critics of what is referred to in the United States as 'textualist' interpretations of statutes.

There are versions of the argument advanced by the analytical legal philosophers which bear some resemblance to Gray's.[18] By no means, however, are these philosophers simply replicating his thesis. Their core claim is that statutes—and, indeed, precedents and customs—are sources of law, but that 'sources of law should not be confused with legal norms ... which can be derived from sources ... and by which judges are guided in arriving at ... decisions'.[19] Legal norms are derived from sources of law through interpretation, broadly conceived.[20] Interpretations 'bring us from a legal text (a source of law) to the meaning(s) *expressed* by that text (a legal norm)'.[21] 'The norm is a particular meaning conferred on a statement ... analysed' by legal actors 'as the source of the legal norm' and 'derive[d] from texts which these actors consider to be formal sources of law (constitution, statue ...)'.[22]

This modern analytical argument is more subtle than Gray's. A statute is understood to be a source in the sense that it provides norm-formulations or norm-sentences—typically, statutory provisions[23]—which legal decision-makers interpret so as to produce statutory norms: there is a source (the statute) containing norm-formulations (statutory provisions) from which, through authoritative—which does not necessarily mean correct[24]—interpretation, judges derive valid legal norms. The distinction between source and norm is not always readily discernible, proponents of the analytical argument tend to observe, because in some non-controversial cases there will be no linguistic difference between the legal norm derived from a statute and the relevant norm-formulation contained in it. In cases of this kind, '[t]he plain meaning of the applicable legislative text reveals a norm which determinately solves the case at issue',[25] and so the source provides judges with definitive guidance, regardless of their preferred method of statutory interpretation, from the

---

[18] See e.g. Riccardo Guastini, 'Fragments of a Theory of Legal Sources' (1996) 6 *Ratio Juris* 364.

[19] Fábio Perin Shecaira, 'Sources of Law Are not Legal Norms' (2015) 28 *Ratio Juris* 15, 17.

[20] Ibid. 19 ('any attempt to derive the meaning of a source of law').

[21] Paolo Sandro, *The Making of Constitutional Democracy: From Creation to Application of Law* (Oxford: Hart, 2021), 208. (Emphasis in original.)

[22] Pierre Brunet and Véronique Champeil-Desplats, 'La théorie des contraintes juridiques face aux théories des sources du droit', in *Les sources du droit revisitées. Volume 4: Théorie des sources du droit*, ed. I. Hachez et al. (Brussels: Presses de l'Université Saint-Louis, 2012), 385–425 at 398.

[23] See Sandro, *The Making of Constitutional Democracy* (n 21) 229–230.

[24] See ibid. 230.

[25] Shecaira, 'Sources of Law Are not Legal Norms' (n 19) 18.

moment of enactment. Gray insisted that judges extract 'laws' from statutes, but the modern analytical preference for 'legal norms' is more precise because some norms derived from statutes are judicial rulings binding only on the parties to a case (for example, decisions of first-instance courts) rather than legal rules capable of repeated application. And while Gray calls statutes sources but not laws, the modern analytical position seems to entail the concession that a statute is both source and law, but is law only in the sense that the statutory text has been approved by a legislature.

But if, the analytical philosophers maintain, by 'law' one means 'legal norm'—it is here that their argument aligns with Gray's—a statute categorically is not law. '[W]hat exists before the [court pronounces] judgment is not a norm, but . . . a legislative text. . . . The legal norm is not this text, but only its meaning. Before issuing a judgment, it is up to the court to interpret the text, to determine its meaning.'[26] 'Sources do not produce, and even less are, legal norms. Sources . . . are . . . texts, and only through interpretation of these texts may we know what legal norms they convey. Strictly speaking, then, a legal norm is not itself produced by a source, but rather by the interpretation of a source.'[27]

One minor difficulty with the analytical argument is that the idea of norm-sentences occupying some sort of intermediate position between the source and the legal norm doesn't quite fit with common-law interpretive convention. According to this convention, when judges make decisions based on statutes they interpret—or certainly, when the enacted language yields controversy, ought to interpret—not individual norm-sentences, but rather norm-sentences as understood in their statutory context.[28] But this is small beer as compared with the primary difficulty attaching to the analytical argumenta: the depiction of enacted text as legally authorized but having no legal-normative identity of its own. Statutes, once brought into force, have their own *sui generis* legal-normative dimension not the least because, in those instances where they are applicable, they speak normatively to law-applying officials—judges and other law-enforcers must engage with them (which is not to deny that the terms of

---

[26] Michel Troper, 'Fonction juridictionnelle ou pouvoir judiciaire?' (1981) 16 *Pouvoirs* 5, 9.

[27] Giorgio Pino, 'Sources of Law', in *Oxford Studies in Philosophy of Law: Volume 4*, ed. J. Gardner et al. (Oxford: OUP, 2021), 58–92 at 68, and see also 81–82.

[28] On statutory interpretation as interpretation of statutes as a whole, see *R (Quintavalle) v Secretary of State for Health* [2003] UKHL 13 at [8] (Lord Bingham) ('[T]he controversial provisions should be read in the context of the statute as a whole . . .'); *K. Mart Corp. v Cartier, Inc.*, 486 US 281, 291 (1988); *United States v Morton*, 467 US 822, 828 (1984) ('We do not . . . construe statutory phrases in isolation; we read statutes as a whole'); *Composers, Authors & Publishers Assn. of Canada Ltd v CTV Television Network* [1968] SCR 676 (SC Can.) at para. 13; *A-G v Prince Ernest Augustus of Hanover* [1957] AC 436 (HL), 463 (Viscount Simonds); *Nolan v Clifford* (1904) 1 CLR 429 (HC Aus.), 453 (O'Connor J).

engagement may allow an interpreter a considerable degree of discretion). It is certainly possible for a legislature simultaneously to enact a statute and render all or part of it normatively inert, as when a commencement regulation determines that an enacted law or legal provision will not take effect until some point after enactment.[29] But the point of taking this course of action is precisely to accord a statute, or an element of the statute, provisional status as text (approved by law-makers, but not yet binding on law-enforcers), typically so as to allow would-be litigants time to prepare before the text is rendered legally normative.

In the United States, there are critics of textualist interpretive theory who not only maintain that enacted text is not law but who react with incredulity to the claim that it is. Their argument is nothing if not forthright. 'Text is not law, for they are different sorts of things. A text is an assemblage of signs and symbols; a law'—note how, in this regard, the analytical-jurisprudential and counter-textualist perspectives align—'is a normative entity'.[30] The text offers up formulations of norms, but actual legal norms have to be created out of the text. Courts do not apply statute law—there's no such thing—but rather interpret the text in order to produce the law to be applied. 'The myth that "text is law"'[31] entails 'a category mistake',[32] a 'platitude'[33] (peddled by those 'in the business of spreading falsehoods');[34] it 'feeds . . . tired clichés about judges illicitly legislating from the bench'[35] and belongs in a jurisprudential 'hall of shame'.[36]

Although the anti-textualist position might seem to lack finesse compared with its analytical variant, the reasoning underpinning it is nuanced. A legislature could amend the wording of a statute to make it clearer without the amendment making any difference to how the statute is interpreted by courts. Legislatures belonging to distinct jurisdictions could enact identical statutory norm-formulations and courts in each jurisdiction, on interpreting the texts, might arrive at different normative conclusions. The legislatures of those jurisdictions could enact differently worded texts and their courts, interpreting

---

[29] To take an example from English trusts law, the equitable presumption of advancement has it that transfers of property or money from husbands to their wives and from fathers to their children are not held on resulting trust—this being the standard presumption—but rather take effect as gifts. The Equality Act 2010, s 199(1), was enacted to abolish this presumption. But the sub-section has never been brought into force (and will only operate prospectively if ever it is). It floats as text in a sea of legal norms.

[30] Mitchell N. Berman, 'Judge Posner's Simple Plan' (2015) 113 *Michigan L. Rev.* 777, 804 n 113.

[31] Erik Encarnacion, 'Text is Not Law' (2022) 107 *Iowa L. Rev.* 2027, 2067.

[32] Ibid. 2037.

[33] Ibid. 2033.

[34] Ibid. 2064.

[35] Ibid. 2067.

[36] Ibid. 2068.

their respective statutes, might reach the same normative conclusions. Legal norms arrived at through statutory interpretation float free of the statutes themselves. The semantic meaning of a legal text and the legal meaning ascribed to that text—the content of statutes and the norms that courts derive from that content—are analytically distinct.

That there is a difference, however, between the normative language of a statute and the norms arrived at through interpretation of that language does not serve to establish that only the norm generated by interpretation can be a type of law. The default setting with statutes—that they apply prospectively— entails the presumption that statutes are enacted norms rather than texts containing sentences which are not themselves norms but which yield norms on judicial interpretation. When a court interprets a statute, it seeks to settle the meaning of existing law rather than make law *de novo*; on the basis of a legal (statutory) rule, the court issues a legal (judicial) ruling (which may itself stand as a legal—precedential—rule).

Making a stronger case for treating statutes as but sources of legal norms seems to depend—certainly in the counter-textualist literature—on instances in which a court is not interpreting, but rather is actively departing from, statutory text. If judicial negotiation of a statutory provision has the court rejecting the provision's wording, the argument runs, how can the provision be law? The defendant who, in the English case of *Adler v George* (1964), was successfully prosecuted for acting contrary to section 3 of the Official Secrets Act 1920— which provided that any person who obstructs officials carrying out their duties 'in the vicinity of any prohibited place' (in this case, an army station) 'shall be guilty of a misdemeanour'—did nothing covered by that particular norm-sentence: he obstructed an official on the grounds, rather than in the vicinity, of an army station. Parker CJ found him guilty all the same, ruling that '[i]t would be absurd if an indictable offence was . . . created when the obstruction took place outside the precincts of the station, albeit in the vicinity, and no offence at all was created if the obstruction occurred on the station itself'.[37] The legal norm that the judge applied was nowhere to be found in the text of the statute. For the proponent of the thesis that statute is merely text, judicial reliance on doctrines presuming against absurdity is 'logically incompatible with the thesis that text is law, since those doctrines license courts to ignore or depart from the text'.[38] Any textualist judges who are not averse to presuming

[37] *Adler v George* [1964] 2 QB 7, 10.
[38] Encarnacion, 'Text is Not Law' (n 31) 2051–2052.

against absurdities 'should deny that text is law. Apart from being false, the claim invites misunderstandings of their views.'[39]

The problem of logical incompatibility certainly arises if applying the interpretive presumption against absurdity leads a court to rule in a way that undermines a statute or some of its content. And judicial resort to the presumption can certainly have that effect. But it need not do. Note that, in *Adler v George*, there was no logical incompatibility. The norm applied by the judge didn't override the normative force of the statutory provision; it remained an offence to obstruct officials in the vicinity of a prohibited place. Note, too, that even scholars who advance the thesis that statutes are only texts tend to concede that accepting text as law need not confine statutory interpretation to statutory language—that a court might domesticate a repugnant statutory provision, for example, by noting its incompatibility with other parts, or the general scheme, of the statute. '[T]he content of the law is primarily constituted by linguistic (or mental) contents associated with the authoritative legal texts', Mark Greenberg maintains, but he is careful not to discount the 'peripheral ways in which law can be determined other than by the linguistic content of authoritative pronouncements . . . such as filtering out or modifying absurd or immoral legal norms.'[40] Yet more notable for the purposes of this study—and further evidence of correspondence between the analytical and counter-textualist perspectives—is his observation regarding the status of the text: though statutory 'text cannot be the same as law',[41] it must be regarded as 'authoritative legal text.'[42]

In chapters 5 and 6, we will encounter arguments which trade on the protean qualities of 'authority' and 'authoritative' to make the case that there are legal texts—iconic treatises and particular non-legislative codifications—which are accurately described as law even though they were not created as law. The notion that a statute is an authoritative legal text pushes in the other direction: even though the statute was enacted as law, categorizing it thus is inaccurate. Theorists who subscribe to this notion obviously must know (and presumably are unperturbed by the fact) that it runs counter to many commonplace observations about legal practice and systems. Legislatures—the

---

[39] Ibid. 2047.

[40] Mark Greenberg, 'The Moral Impact Theory of Law' (2014) 123 *Yale L. J.* 1288, 1296 n 17; also Mark Greenberg, 'The Standard Picture and its Discontents', in *Oxford Studies in Philosophy of Law: Volume 1*, ed. L. Green and B. Leiter (Oxford: OUP, 2011), 39–106 at 53–54.

[41] Mitchell N. Berman, 'Our Principled Constitution' (2018) 166 *Univ. Pennsylvania L. Rev.* 1325, 1385 n 94.

[42] Greenberg, 'The Moral Impact Theory of Law' (n 40) 1309; Mitchell N. Berman, 'The Tragedy of Justice Scalia' (2017) 115 *Michigan L. Rev.* 783, 787.

clue is in the name—are law-making assemblies. They typically vote on the texts of bills, which, depending on how the votes go, might then be passed into law. The bills, if passed, are not enacted with the status of source or text from which laws can then be derived.[43] Constitutions and bills of rights abjure against legislatures passing laws, not sources or texts, with unconstitutional attributes. Should whatever is passed by a legislature be adjudicated upon and declared unconstitutional, the constitutional court strikes down a law, not a source or a text.

Statutes indeed are legal texts, but the nature of their legality seems to be obscured if they are designated authoritative without further ado. The text of a bill might differ significantly from the statute that was enacted. Or the statute that was enacted might subsequently have been repealed. To think that the text of the bill, or of the repealed statute, must have no authority is a mistake. Judges interpreting the law as now enacted, for example, might rely on un-enacted or repealed texts as authoritative sources of pertinent legal history (as information about the rules of what Joseph Raz called the 'non-momentary' legal system).[44] The authority of currently valid legislation is different, however, from that of texts that never were, or no longer are, legally valid. A valid statute is authoritative because it establishes an authority to create law; it still makes sense, in other words, to describe the statute as an authoritative legal text so long as it is understood that the text is not a secondary but a primary source of law.

Analytical and anti-textualist legal theorists certainly clarify how the text of an enacted statute is only a starting point in the process of law application, and that litigants have reason to care more about the legal norm derived from the text—this being the law as it bears upon their litigation—than about the text itself. But the text still has a normative life of its own: 'the text of the statute controls',[45] it must be reckoned with as binding law by, the organs that interpret and apply it. Ambiguous statutory language, according to John Gardner, 'often needs to be interpreted to find out which of two rival norms it formulates'.[46] The observation looks to fit with the thesis that statutes are sources or texts rather than legal norms. His point, however, was not that statutes offer up only

---

[43] For a rejection of this proposition see Encarnacion, 'Text is Not Law' (n 31) 2078 ('Congress makes law, it seems, by voting on texts, which the President signs. So, it must follow, it also seems, that texts are law. The problem is that, even if the meanings of statutory texts are law ... the texts themselves are not').

[44] Joseph Raz, *The Concept of a Legal System*, 2nd edn (Oxford: Clarendon Press, 1980), 34–35.

[45] A judicial *dictum* employed by any number of US judges (and certainly not only by textualist judges): see e.g. *Central Bank of Denver v First Interstate Bank of Denver*, 511 US 164, 173 (1994); *Szehinskyj v Att.-Gen. of United States*, 432 F.3d 253, 261 (3rd Cir. 2005).

[46] John Gardner, 'Some Types of Law', in *Common Law Theory*, ed. D. E. Edlin (Cambridge: CUP, 2007), 51–77 at 54.

norm-formulations as distinct from legal norms but rather that the meaning of ambiguously formulated statutory norms is established by authoritative interpretation. Any such interpretation may well alter or modify the law. But the crucial point is that the interpretation bears upon already-existing law—upon 'a legislated norm,'[47] 'paradigmatic law,'[48] 'law created by the statute'.[49] An interpretation might have other consequences besides altering or modifying the law—as when it 'binds successor interpreters,' say, or ensures that 'the legal norms created by the statute are rendered more determinate'.[50] But one of the consequences is not that there now exists a valid legal norm where previously there was only text. Statutes aren't precluded from having the status of law by virtue of being sources of law. The source of a legal norm can be another legal norm.

c) Custom

There was a time when the predominant positivist legal-philosophical position was that the source of a legal norm is *always* another legal norm. Kelsen epitomized this stance with his depiction of a legal-normative 'chain of creation'.[51] But Kelsen also appreciated that the position does not easily reconcile with the proposition, which he accepted, that some legal norms originate in custom.[52] When the source of law is custom, proponents of the distinction between sources of law and legal norms are, certainly in one respect, on solid ground: the source is patently distinguishable from the norm. 'Saying that custom is a *source* of law is not the same as saying that custom *is* law'.[53] The popular seventeenth-century English legal refrain that decided cases are

---

[47] Ibid.
[48] Ibid. 51.
[49] Ibid. 54.
[50] Ibid.
[51] According to which judges create specific legal norms by choosing how to interpret (while accepting that they must apply) more general legal norms: see Hans Kelsen, *Introduction to the Problems of Legal Theory*, trans. B. L. and S. L. Paulson (Oxford: Clarendon Press, 1992 [1934]), 56–57, 63–64, 68, 80; *Pure Theory of Law*, 2nd edn trans. M. Knight (Berkeley: University of California Press, 1967 [1960]), 238–239, 354; *General Theory of Law and State* (n 17) 135.
[52] See Kelsen, *Introduction to the Problems of Legal Theory* (n 51) 57 ('Law creation by way of custom . . . is . . . a special case'). Note that Kelsen is ultimately able to accommodate custom within his legal science because he understands custom to be created law: the determination that a custom has become law is attributable to non-customary, positive law which stipulates what must happen for a custom to become law. We will see in a moment that, as regards the English common law, the picture isn't so straightforward.
[53] Lloyd A. Fallers, *Law Without Precedent* (Chicago: University of Chicago Press, 1969), 66. (Emphasis in original.)

evidence of the customs of the realm, for example, rests on a distinction between custom as a source of legal norms and customary legal norms.[54]

Custom, nevertheless, highlights a difficulty with one element of the thesis distinguishing sources of law from legal norms: the assertion that deriving the legal norm from the source depends on interpretation. More careful expositors of the thesis can be found conceding that custom poses a challenge for anyone who maintains that the source only ever yields the legal norm by virtue of being interpreted.[55] The difficulty is not that a custom need not offer up any text for interpretation; a custom may be interpreted, and indeed be the subject of interpretive disagreement, even when it takes the form of non-documented social practice. Rather, the difficulty is that custom as classically understood (in Roman and canon law as well as in common law)[56] is not a source from which courts derive meaning in order to settle on a legal norm. English legal history shows that when the source is custom—particularly, we will see in a moment, when it is local custom—interpretive questions primarily pertain not to the meaning of the customary practice but rather to whether it is possible to identify within the practice all the elements essential to declaring that the custom is law. A determination that the custom is law depends, certainly in English common law doctrine, on certain facts about the practice of the custom having obtained.[57] The custom is declared to be law not because of what it is understood to mean, but rather because it has *prescribed.*

---

[54] See Edward Coke, *The First Part of the Institutes of the Lawes of England. Or a Commentarie upon Littleton* (London: Societe of Stationers, 1628) at 254ᵃ; Matthew Hale (d. 1676), *The History of the Common Law of England*, ed. C. M. Gray (University of Chicago Press, 1971).

[55] See Hafsteinn Dan Kristjánsson, 'Elements of Precedent', in *Philosophical Foundations of Precedent*, ed. T. Endicott et al. (Oxford: OUP 2023), 75–88 at 77; Pino, 'Sources of Law' (n 27) 67; Greenberg, 'The Standard Picture and its Discontents' (n 40) 52–53.

[56] On the Roman law idea of immemorial custom, see Friedrich Carl von Savigny, *System des heutigen Römischen Rechts*, 8 vols (Berlin: Veit, 1840–49), IV (1841), 481. On the canon law idea (custom which exceeded human memory (*consuetudo quae excedit hominum memoriam)* and which conflicted with laws of the church), see *Corpus Iuris Canonici*, 3 vols, ed. J. P. Gibert (Lyon: Brothers Deville, 1737), I, 481. The medieval civilian perspective was more relaxed: customs tended to be recognized as legally binding after the passing of decades (just how many decades depended on the type of custom). The period appears never to have been fewer than ten years, and never more than forty. See John Gilissen, *La coutume* (Turnhout: Brepols, 1982), 29–30; J. W. Tubbs, *The Common Law Mind: Medieval and Early Modern Conceptions* (Baltimore: Johns Hopkins UP, 2000), 26–27; T. F. T. Plucknett, *A Concise History of the Common Law*, 5th edn (Boston: Little, Brown & Co., 1956), 307–308. Repeated judicial opinion was custom, and, in the absence of written law, could be cited as authority. ('When something is done [i.e., decided in the same way by a court] twice', one thirteenth-century civilian claimed, 'this makes a custom'. Pierre de Fontaine (d. *c.* 1289), *Le conseil, ou Traité de l'ancienne jurisprudence française*, ed. M. A. J. Marnier (Paris: Joubert, 1846), 492.) This thinking clearly reflects Roman law: although Justinian's *Corpus iuris civilis* eschewed precedent following (*Code* 7. 45. 13), it was accepted that 'customs and usage' should guide judicial rulings 'where we have no applicable written law' (*Digest* 1. 3. 32 (Julian)).

[57] The test is different from that which applies in international law. Article 38(1) of the Statute of the International Court of Justice provides (*inter alia*) that the Court shall apply 'international custom, as evidence of a general practice accepted as law'. So, if an international custom is to apply as law, there has

Prescription, at common law, is a test of validity that courts apply to identify a custom as having the force of law even though there exists no evidence of this force ever having been conferred on the custom by a law-making authority.[58] A typical medieval scenario would be where, each year, inhabitants of a village hold summer solstice festivities in a field that X has inherited. When X asserts that the villagers have no legal right to do this, they point out—to X and to a court—that not only can nobody attest to a time when inhabitants of the village didn't hold summer solstice festivities in the field but that, before X inherited it, no owner of the field ever objected to the practice. It's as if, at some point in the distant past, a law was passed authorizing villagers to hold summer solstice festivities in the field. At common law, prescribed custom cannot be demonstrated but is nevertheless presumed to have been legally validated because it has been practised regularly and openly, and tolerated without demur, for longer than anybody alive can remember. Some customary practices which are adjudged to have prescribed do not entirely meet these criteria but still have the force of law because they satisfy a different, enacted test: England's 'modern' prescription rules on long-running use and enjoyment of neighbouring land, for example, were set down in the Prescription Act of 1832.[59] Customs of this kind are made law by positive law—are customs with statutory legal validity—rather than customary law. Custom that is declared to be law because it meets the common-law test of prescription is an altogether different beast.

The common-law test of prescription is unique to English courts; later common law systems are simply not old enough to accommodate it.[60] Before the emergence of *stare decisis*—the doctrine of precedent did not properly

to be a practice that States have freely converged on, and those States must also believe (the so-called *opinio iuris* requirement) that this practice is legally binding. The test is one of generality or substantial uniformity, rather than unanimity, among States. A State might be found to have contravened customary international law even if it can present evidence of States not always having acted in accordance with the custom. *Nicaragua v USA*, 1986 ICJ Rep. 14 at para. 186.

[58] Not all common-law customs must conform to the test in order to have the force of law. Historically, the test for the enforceability of commercial customs has been whether, as a matter of fact (until the First World War, the question was a for a civil jury), the custom was well known in the locality or market sector where the dispute before the court arose. Ross Cranston, *Making Commercial Law Through Practice, 1830–1970* (Cambridge: CUP, 2021), 48.

[59] Section 2 of which provides that the enjoyment of the neighbouring land becomes a matter of legal right once it has persisted openly and uncontested for a period of at least twenty years.

[60] Sometimes, their courts explicitly reject it. See e.g. *Golding v Tanner* (1991) 56 SASR 482 (SC South Aus.), 487 (Debelle J) ('[T]here is no room for the operation of prescription at common law in South Australia'); *Gibbs v Grand Bend* (1989) 71 OR (2d) 70 (Ontario SC) at paras 166–167; *Weidler v Arizona Power Co.*, 7 P.2d 241, 244 (Ariz. 1932) ('If an act is not an official duty, private custom, no matter how long continued, cannot make it such'); also *Brace v Shaw*, 16 B.Mon. 43, 55 (CA Ky 1855); David J. Bederman, *Custom as a Source of Law* (Cambridge: CUP, 2010), 105; and Stephen E. Sachs, 'Finding Law' (2019) 107 *California L. Rev.* 527, 547 ('[U]nwritten law … derives its content from usage today, not from whatever happened a long time ago').

make its way into English law until the eighteenth century[61]—a custom was considered to be already-existing law when:

a) some pattern of behaviour converging around a norm had prevailed for a long time,

b) nobody could testify to a time when things were otherwise (the custom had persisted 'for a time beyond the memory of man'),[62] and

c) there had not been, within memory, any custom-revoking enactment or other event contradicting the assumption that the custom had persisted since a time when it originated lawfully.

After the Norman Conquest, the idea of a custom having existed throughout and beyond human memory came to be understood according to a distinct legal definition: the custom having persisted since 'before the beginning of the reign of Richard I'.[63] Thirteenth-century attorneys and judges started to use the date specified in the first Statute of Westminster (1275) limiting the recovery of possession of land (seisin) —3 September 1189, the coronation date of Richard I—as the date marking the outer limit of the prescription period for the acquisition of easements and other incorporeal hereditaments.[64] The use of this date to mark the beginning of time within memory—any custom pursued openly, regularly, and without dispute since before Richard I's coronation was treated as law the creation of which was no longer discoverable—was attributable to the fact that it became a practice of the courts and the legal profession to apply an enactment concerning the negation of rights owing to the passage of time to disputes over whether a right had been acquired owing to the passage of time. Judges chose to rely on the Statute of Westminster for the purpose of identifying prescribed custom. The Statute did not require them to do so.

What amounted to prescribed custom differed depending on whether the custom was general or local. X, in the scenario above, was arguing from general custom—because general custom would have it that when you hold summer

---

[61] See Gerald J. Postema, 'Philosophy of the Common Law', in *The Oxford Handbook of Jurisprudence and Philosophy of Law*, ed. J. Coleman and S. Shapiro (Oxford: OUP, 2002), 588–622 at 589.

[62] John Cowell, *The Interpreter* (Cambridge: printed by John Legate, 1607), unnumbered pages, fol. 3E2r (s.v. 'Prescription (*praescriptio*)'); see also (1305) YB 45 (Bereford J) ('du temps dount il ny ad memorie'); (1305) YB 431; (1306) YB 206–207; (1308) YB 29 ('du temps dount etc'); (1308–09) YB 129.

[63] See e.g. *Coventry v Grauntpie* (1308–09) YB 71, 73; *Noyers v Colwick* (1312) YB 141, 142–143.

[64] See Paul Brand, 'Lawyers' Time in England in the later Middle Ages', in *Time in the Medieval World*, ed. C. Humphrey and W. M. Ormrod (York: York Medieval Press, 2001), 73–104 at 103 (citing a case from 1247 in which a limitation statute is used to fix the outer limit of the prescription period for the acquisition of an easement). The association of a statutory limitation date with the limit of legal memory starts to become especially evident from around 1300: see e.g. *De La More v Thwing* (1308–09) YB 176, 178; *The King v Wickham Breaux* (1313) YB 179, 180.

solstice festivities in a field without the landowner's consent, you're trespassing. But the villagers were arguing that there was a custom of the locality that diverged from and prevailed over general custom. There was no need to prove a general custom.[65] Indeed, judges were inclined to consider it bad form when attorneys attempted to prove one, because if a custom was general—immemorial custom of the realm—then it was common law. Since common law was, by definition, within the knowledge of the judges, the oracles of the law, there was no reason for lawyers to mention it in writs or pleadings.[66]

When the source of law was a local custom, the judicially enforced legal norm could not be said to originate in an interpretation placed on the source by the court. A local custom would be enforced by a manorial court—so as to bind within a locality as customary law in derogation from the common law—when its persistence since time immemorial was successfully pleaded and proved to the jury.[67] When lawyers and judges referred to an immemorial local custom, they originally meant that there was no evidence contradicting testimony that the custom had continued without interruption since 1189. But from around the second half of the fourteenth century, this test was gradually abandoned in favour of a more relaxed one: manorial court juries were ever more regularly instructed to infer the existence of a local custom since 1189 if there was evidence of the custom having been practised openly and undisturbed throughout actual living memory.[68]

Note that, at all times, there *was* a test. If a local custom was to prevail, its immemorial character—its antiquity—had to be established and could not be merely asserted. Indeed, it was not only the antiquity of the local custom that had to be pleaded and proved: one had to be able to show what the custom was (a fluid or uncertain custom was no custom at all), and a court would have to be satisfied that the maintenance of the custom was not unreasonable.[69] Custom found to have satisfied the test, and so to have prescribed, was declared a legal

---

[65] See *Beaulieu v Finglam* (1401) B. & M. 557, 558; F. A. Greer, 'Custom in the Common Law' (1893) 34 *LQR* 153, 157.

[66] See Henry Finch, *Law or a Discourse Thereof* (New York: Kelley, 1969 [1627]), 77. (A law-French version of the book was first published in 1613.)

[67] The distinction between common and (local) customary law was not always straightforwardly negotiated. Judges struggled with questions such as whether a custom widely replicated among localities was a custom of the realm, and whether local customary privileges extended to people from neighbouring boroughs as well as to the borough's inhabitants. See H. E. Salt, 'The Local Ambit of a Custom', in *Cambridge Legal Essays* (Cambridge: Heffer & Sons, 1926), 279–294.

[68] See e.g. (1291) YB 420; (1304) YB 264 (Bereford J) ('[T]hey have laid an interruption to your continuance [of the practice which you allege to be local custom], to which . . . you must answer'); *Mabile v Bishop of Lincoln* (1311) YB 117; also Samuel Carter, *Lex Custumaria* (London: Walthoe, 1696), 30–31.

[69] See William Blackstone, *Commentaries on the Laws of England*, 4 vols (Chicago: University of Chicago Press, 1979 [1765–1769]), I, 77–78. A party asserting a custom was not required to prove its reasonableness, since the reasonableness of a custom is not a matter of fact.

norm. Determinations to this effect were not without interpretive dimensions; a court could refuse to uphold a prescribed custom because it facilitated extortion,[70] for example, or because it was pleaded in vague terms.[71] But the determinations were, first and foremost, findings of fact—indeed, judges can be found demurring to juries' findings regarding prescribed custom even when they knew those findings to be incorrect.[72]

Legal norms are not derived from local customs by applying the common-law test of prescription. To find that a custom satisfies the test is, rather, to determine that what was thought to be but custom is actually a legal norm. I ought not to obstruct neighbouring landowners or their successors in title from putting cattle on my land, a court might rule, because the evidence shows not only that neighbouring landowners have used my land in this way regularly, openly, and (until now) without objection, but also that no-one alive can attest to a time when those landowners didn't use my land in this way.[73] Friedrich Hayek wrote of how, in a scenario of this kind, parties in my position are being told by a court 'that this . . . was the established custom which they ought to have known'.[74] In fact, the court is ruling not just that this custom was established, but that it was already law. When the source is prescribed local custom, a legal norm is not derived from the source through the excavation of meaning from text or social practice. The norm is a legal norm because it has passed a threshold of validity and, consequently, is adjudged to have been law since time out of mind.

d) Custom and constitutions

Is custom ever the source of constitutional validity? The idea that a constitution could be traced to a source of law of any kind meets with the objection that constitutions do not equate to law. Granted, they are quite regularly referred

---

[70] See (1430) YB 44 ('Et tout le court tient que ceo ne puit estre un custome car ceo est encontre commen droit et est extortion').

[71] See *Wilkes v Broadbent* (1745) 1 Wils. 63 (a custom purportedly supporting the overseer of a coal pit depositing earth and coals on land 'near' the pit held to be invalid for, *inter alia*, want of precision).

[72] '[As to the objection that] there cannot be a prescriptive right for coaches and chariots time out of mind, because coaches and chariots are of modern invention, . . . the jury [has] . . . found that there has been a way for coaches and chariots time out of mind . . . [W]e . . . must take it to be as the jury have found it'. *Chichester v Lethbridge* (1738) Willes 71, 72–73 (Willes CJ).

[73] For the argument that it is not custom, but rather the land over which customs emerge, that is understood to be the source of law, see C. F. Black, *The Land is the Source of the Law* (London: Routledge, 2011), 25, 45, 76, 99–101, 184.

[74] F. A. Hayek, *Law, Legislation and Liberty*, integrated 3 vol. edn (London: Routledge & Kegan Paul, 1982), I, 87.

to, might even refer to themselves, as—supreme, higher, fundamental—law. But even a written constitution is more than its legal content, and there will be constitutional law—such as constitutional court precedent—which is not contained in the text of the constitution itself. Much of the legal content of the United Kingdom's so-called unwritten constitution is actually written—enacted—law: 'constitutional' statutes such as the Bill of Rights 1689, the Judicature Acts of 1873 and 1875, the Statute of Westminster 1931, the Scotland Act 1998, and the Government of Wales Act 2006.[75] These statutes owe their validity to a source of law just as do ordinary statutes (indeed, a constitution is itself a validating source in the sense that it regulates all law making, up to and including constitutional amendment).[76] But the statutes are not the constitution. They are only fragments of it.

Constitutions become more difficult propositions when one conceives of them, not just elements within them, as a type of law. For if a constitution is law, there must be a source, or sources, endowing it with legal validity. But the first constitution precedes the legal system, so its status as law cannot be attributable to anybody legally empowered to accord it this status. Kelsen famously struggled with, indeed was defeated by, the quandary. For most of his life, he argued that the validity of a legal system presupposes a foundational systemic norm: citizens 'ought to obey the prescriptions of the historically first constitution'.[77] Near the end of his life, he conceded the flaw in his argument: 'the assumption of a basic norm . . . represents the authorization of a supreme moral or legal authority, and hence it issues from an authority lying beyond that authority'.[78] If a constitution is law, from where did its framers derive their law-making authority? 'We cannot discover, or even sensibly inquire, how its framers came to have the right to frame it. We bump our heads against an un-normed norm.'[79] The difficulty is not unique to written constitutions. The constitutional arrangement that emerges in Britain in the seventeenth century originated in a revolution associated with a king who did not have a good claim to the throne, whose parliament was not a lawful parliament—who, in short, had no legal authority to devise a new constitutional settlement.

Since the eighteenth century, constitutional doctrine has been dominated by the idea that the creation of a new constitution is, by necessity, an extra-legal

---

[75] See Farrah Ahmed and Adam Perry, 'Constitutional Statutes' (2017) 37 *OJLS* 61.

[76] See Kent Greenawalt, 'The Rule of Recognition and the Constitution' (1987) 85 *Michigan L. Rev.* 621.

[77] Kelsen, *Pure Theory of Law* (n 51) 204.

[78] Hans Kelsen, 'The Function of a Constitution' (1964), trans. I. Stewart in *Essays on Kelsen*, ed. R. Tur and W. Twining (Oxford: Clarendon Press, 1986), 109–119 at 117.

[79] Tony Honoré, *Making Law Bind* (Oxford: Clarendon Press, 1987), 103.

act: the exercise of revolutionary power by the (representatives of the) people. The source of the constitution's legal validity, from this perspective, has no legally recognized credentials—there are no laws enabling the identification of such credentials at the point when the constitution is created—but rather is the people's original constitution-making ('constituent') power. The authority of the first constitution cannot be ascribed to an actual source of law. Logic appears to dictate as much. Would anyone seriously maintain otherwise?

It has often been argued that constitutions are to be understood as borne not of revolutionary episodes and the exercise of constituent power but as the culmination of tried reason and customary practice. A constitution is best thought of not as a distinct act of creation, G. W. F. Hegel maintained, but rather as bound up with a nation's history.

> What is . . . called *making* a constitution, has . . . never occurred in history. . . . A constitution has *only developed* . . . and has run through . . . the conceptually necessary alterations and stages of formation. It is history . . . by which constitutions have been and are made.[80]

'Man cannot make a constitution', according to Hegel's contemporary, Joseph de Maistre, for 'the fundamentals of political constitutions exist before all written laws'.[81] 'Man cannot bestow rights on himself; he can only defend those which have been granted to him by a superior power; and these rights are good customs, good because they are not written and because no beginning or author can be assigned to them.'[82] Edmund Burke had already written, apropos the English constitution, of how 'it has been the uniform policy of our constitution to claim and assert our liberties, as an *entailed inheritance* derived to us from our forefathers, and to be transmitted to our posterity'.[83] The revolution of 1688, in Burke's eyes, was not so much the forging of a new constitutional settlement as the reaffirmation of a 'collected reason of ages',[84] evidence

---

[80] G. W. F. Hegel, *Philosophy of Mind*, trans. W. Wallace, A. V. Miller, and M. J. Inwood (Oxford: OUP, 2007 [1817]), 240 (§ 540). (Emphases in original.)

[81] Joseph de Maistre, 'Essay on the Generative Principle of Political Constitutions' (1810), in de Maistre, *The Generative Principle of Political Constitutions: Studies on Sovereignty, Religion and Enlightenment*, ed. J. Lively (London: Routledge, 2011), 147–181 at 161, 151. (Emphasis removed.)

[82] Joseph de Maistre, 'Study on Sovereignty' (1794–1795), in ibid. 93–129 at 108. (Emphasis removed.)

[83] Edmund Burke, *Reflections on the Revolution in France, and on the Proceedings in Certain Societies in London Relative to that Event*, ed. C. C. O'Brien (Harmondsworth: Penguin, 1968 [1790]), 119. (Emphasis in original.) On Burke's influence on de Maistre, see John D. Upton, *The Constitutional Thought of Joseph de Maistre* (Ph.D. dissertation, London School of Economics (Law Department), 2008), 126–130.

[84] Burke, *Reflections on the Revolution in France* (n 83) 193.

of a 'powerful prepossession towards antiquity',[85] of 'that *antient* constitution of government which is our only security for law and liberty'.[86] The feature common to all of these arguments is that the constitution is not a document or settlement but rather the history and customs out of which the document or settlement emerges.

None of these arguments equates to the idea that constitutional authority is attributable to custom as a formal source of law. Burke alluded to this idea, but he didn't endorse it.[87] But there were other, less lauded Whig constitutional historians who found the idea attractive. There emerged, in the seventeenth century, a strand of historical inquiry which purported to show that at least one feature of the English constitution was not simply customary but, more specifically, satisfied the common-law test of prescription.

Central to this inquiry was the notion that parliament's legislative power had existed uninterrupted since a time before the outer limit of legal memory. 'Our government by a king and estates of parliament', Thomas Hunt asserted in 1682, 'is as ancient as anything [that] can be remembered . . . a long succession of kings have recognized it to be such'.[88] Hunt made no mention of Richard I's coronation date. But others did. James Tyrrell, for example, ventured in 1684 that if 'time of memory in a prescription was from the time of King Richard I',[89] and 'time out of mind . . . extends beyond' that date, then the uninterrupted existence of the commons as a distinct estate can be traced not only throughout the prescription period, but beyond it.[90] Prescription, from this perspective, explained the legislative authority of the commons in parliament as an element of the unwritten constitution: this authority must have been conferred on the commons (how, and by whom, was anyone's guess) some time before legal memory began.

But if legal memory began in 1189, there was a problem. Although 'it indisputably appears, that parliaments, or general councils, are coeval with the kingdom itself', William Blackstone observed, it 'has been a matter of great dispute among our learned antiquarians . . . whether the commons were summoned at all; or, if summoned, at what period they began to form a distinct

---

[85] Ibid. 118.

[86] Ibid. 117. (Emphasis in original.) See also de Maistre, 'Essay on the Generative Principle of Political Constitutions' (n 81) 150 ('The real English constitution is the public spirit . . . which . . . protects all—what is written is nothing').

[87] See Burke, *Reflections on the Revolution in France* (n 83) 261, also 276.

[88] Thomas Hunt, *Mr Hunt's Postscript for Rectifying Some Mistakes in Some of the Inferiour Clergy* (London: printed for the author, 1682), 2.

[89] James Tyrrell, *Bibliotheca Politica: Or, an Enquiry into the Ancient Constitution of the English Government*, 2nd edn (London: Darby, 1727 [1st edn 1694]), 423.

[90] Ibid. 425.

assembly'.[91] That the lords shared legislative power with the king in parliament was, William Prynne argued in *A Plea for the Lords* (1648), beyond doubt. 'This right of theirs is confirmed by prescription and custom from the very first beginning of parliaments in this kingdom till this present'.[92] The scope of his argument, however, is indicated by the title of his essay: the lords alone shared this power with the king.[93] Not until the thirteenth century did parliament (a term which was not commonly used to describe large assemblies until around 1230) begin to meet regularly and in the same place; only then did it start to become something more than an elite gathering of bishops, earls, and barons.[94] Before the thirteenth century, the commons simply did not exist as a representative body of the kingdom. The idea that it was a genuinely co-ordinate third estate at the time of Richard I's reign has no basis in reality.[95]

Even if it is conceded that the commons did not take shape as an actual representative body till the thirteenth century, some Whig historians countered, there had long been borough representatives—burgesses—who represented freemen at parliamentary (and, before the time of parliament, conciliar) assemblies. As early as the tenth century, William Lambarde contended, 'in every quarter of the realm, a great many ... boroughs' were 'send[ing] burgesses to the parliament'.[96] '[T]he [Anglo-Saxon] assemblies' which 'the king convened', according to William Dugdale, 'include[d] the representatives of the people, or commons', with some English counties and boroughs 'having ever since prescribed to be privileged from sending burgesses to parliament'.[97] Parliamentary representation was a prescribed constitutional right, in other words, whatever the provenance and status of the commons as an estate. '[I]t cannot be concluded' that, 'because sometimes the lords are only remembered to have met', the 'commons were not parties to what passed in th[e] great [Anglo-Saxon] assemblies', Roger Twysden insisted, for if it is accepted that 'no custom can

[91] Blackstone, *Commentaries on the Laws of England* (n 69) I, 145. It was a dispute in which he wanted no part: ibid. ('... it is not my intention here to enter into controversies of this sort').
[92] William Prynne, *A Plea for the Lords* (London: Spark, 1648), 3. (Emphases removed.)
[93] See also Corinne C. Weston and Janelle R. Greenberg, *Subjects and Sovereigns: The Grand Controversy over Legal Sovereignty in Stuart England* (Cambridge: CUP, 1981), 124–148, 318–325.
[94] See J. R. Maddicott, *The Origins of the English Parliament, 924-1327* (Oxford: OUP, 2010), 157, 161–164, 226–228.
[95] 'To apply "prescription" in this very technical sense, to the claims of the House of Commons, would strip them of all privilege. The House cannot be shown to have existed, as a separate branch of the legislature, at that remote period.' *Cassidy v Steuart* (1841) 2 Man. & G. 437, 467 n 52.
[96] William Lambarde, *Archeion, or, A Discourse upon the High Courts of Justice in England* (London: Seile, 1635), 257. The manuscript of *Archeion* was completed by 1591 and may well have been completed earlier: see Paul L. Ward, 'William Lambarde's Collections on Chancery' (1953) 7 *Harv. Lib. Bull.* 271 at 274, 288. Lambarde (sometimes spelt 'Lambard') died in 1601.
[97] William Dugdale, *Origines Juridiciales, or, Historical Memorials of the English Laws* (London: Warren, 1666), 15.

begin since 1 R[ichard] 1' it follows that 'the sending [of] ... burgesses to parliament'—which began 'before that king's time'—must be a 'common custom
of the realm'.[98]

Twysden was—all these antiquarians were—clutching at straws. '[I]n the
time of Ri[chard] I', Nathaniel Bacon observed, 'the truth is, that ... although ...
it was ordinary for kings to make a show of summoning parliaments, ... properly they were but parliamentary meetings of ... lords, clergy, and others, as
the king saw most convenient to drive on his own design'.[99] The case for the
immemorial sovereignty of parliament could never be properly established
because the commons had not endured adamantine since before 1189, and
there was no strong basis for inferring—and definitely no hard evidence—
that the commonality enjoyed a prescribed right to representation.[100] Even
in the seventeenth century, the case for customary sovereignty was nothing
more than an eccentric, marginal, unconvincing contribution to English constitutional discourse. By the end of the eighteenth century, it had been all but
forgotten.[101] Yet, in the context of this study, it makes for an intriguing episode.
For this peculiar endeavour to connect parliament's legislative power to the
doctrine of prescribed custom might be the closest that constitutional theory
has ever come to identifying components of a constitution by reference to a
primary source of law.

---

[98] Roger Twysden, *Certaine Considerations upon the Government of England*, ed. J. M. Kemble
(London: Camden Society, 1849 [1683]), 126.

[99] Nathaniel Bacon, *An Historicall Discourse of the Uniformity of the Government of England*
(London: Walbancke, 1647), 278.

[100] See William Atwood, *Jus Anglorum ab Antiquo* (London: Berry, 1681), 42–43.

[101] For honourable mentions, see e.g. Edmund Burke, 'Speech on the Reform of the Representation
of the Commons in Parliament' (7 May 1782), in *Select Works of Edmund Burke: Miscellaneous Writings*,
ed. F. Canavan (Indianapolis: Liberty Fund, 1999), 15–30 at 18–24; *Reflections on the Revolution in
France* (n 83) 276 ('... prescription, which, through long usage, mellows into legality governments that
were violent in their commencement'); William Paley, *Principles of Moral and Political Philosophy*,
2 vols (London: Faulder, 1791), II, 122. Other eighteenth-century political philosophers invoked
antiquity—as David Hume did, for example, when he made the case for government founded on an
ancient unwritten contract—but their arguments were not based on prescription.

3

The tenacity of the sources thesis

The argument distinguishing sources and laws seems to be based on the idea that primary sources are to be thought of as binding not on ordinary citizens but on legal officials, especially judges. Gray emphasized the judicial power to extract law from the source: a statute, he insisted, is 'at the mercy of the courts'—it 'has to be interpreted by the courts before it becomes a part of the Law'.[1] He struggled to maintain this position. 'If there is a statute recognized by the courts forbidding the sale of wine, and yet wine is sold publicly ... it seems ... that the Law against the sale of wine is disregarded'.[2] Even when he kept to his preferred line, holding out that statutes are not law, he acknowledged that they 'have power as a source of law',[3] that they 'are binding on the courts'[4] in the sense that judges 'derive' legal rules not from 'their own whims, but ... from sources ... to which they are directed ... to apply themselves'.[5]

Note Gray's reference to statutes being judicially recognized. We have seen already how Salmond accorded significance to the notion of source-recognition. But it was really only with the emergence of post-classical positivist jurisprudence—the jurisprudence identified first and foremost with H. L. A. Hart—that the concept of a binding source of law was invested with this new layer of meaning. A legal system's law-applying agencies, principally its courts,[6] recognize sources—Hart mainly had in mind enacted legislation,[7] 'judgments of the courts',[8] and 'long customary practice'[9]—to be '"mandatory" or ... "formal"'[10] sources of law by virtue of the fact that they embody accepted

---

[1] John Chipman Gray, *The Nature and Sources of Law* (New York: Macmillan, 1921), 181, 267–268; see also 124–125, 170, 177–178.

[2] Ibid. 106.

[3] Ibid. 162.

[4] Ibid. 161.

[5] Ibid. 84–85.

[6] See H. L. A. Hart, 'Kelsen's Doctrine of the Unity of Law', in *Ethics and Social Justice*, ed. H. E. Kiefer and M. K. Munitz (Albany: SUNY Press, 1970), 171–199 at 191–195.

[7] H. L. A. Hart, *The Concept of Law*, 3rd edn (Oxford: OUP, 2012), 64–66.

[8] Ibid. 97.

[9] Ibid. 95.

[10] Ibid. 294n.

Law's Sources. Neil Duxbury, Oxford University Press. © Neil Duxbury 2025.
DOI: 10.1093/9780198981183.003.0003

criteria establishing the legal validity of each kind of rule: the enacted legislation having passed through the legislative process, the judgment having an ascertainable holding (*ratio*) which stands unchallenged by any superior jurisdictional authority, the customary practice having prescribed according to common law or statute. When the criteria of validity are met, 'a court in deciding a case is bound'[11] to consider a rule to 'count as law',[12] to be the '*reason and justification* for' the court's decision.[13]

a) *The sources thesis*

For Hart, then, a legal system's primary sources of law equate to the criteria of validity accepted and employed by judges (and other legal officials): laws are laws—legal philosophers would come to refer to this as 'the sources thesis'[14] (or 'social sources thesis')[15] —because they emanate from sources which law-applying officials recognize to be sources of law. Courts are bound by rules that derive from recognized sources, and the decisions that courts make on the basis of these legal rules are applications of already existing law.

There is no guarantee, however, that whatever are the facts before a court, recognized sources will yield law applicable to them. Judges, now and again, have to decide on what are essentially unregulated disputes: cases not covered by any rule that can be traced to a primary source.[16] When, in such cases,

---

[11] Ibid.

[12] Ibid. 105, and see also 108.

[13] Ibid. 11. (Emphasis in original.) See also Joseph Raz, *The Authority of Law*, 2nd edn (Oxford: OUP, 2009), 51–52.

[14] For Hart's explicit equation of sources of law with criteria of legal validity, see *The Concept of Law* (n 7) 106 ('a criterion of legal validity or source of law') and 294n ('. . . when it is said that a "statute" is a source of law, the word "source" refers . . . to one of the criteria of validity accepted in the legal system in question'). The sources thesis is not confined to general jurisprudence; judges quite regularly invoke it. We know that statutes are law and that legislative history is not, Lord Hobhouse once observed, because there are 'rules for the proper recognition of what are and are not sources of law'. *Robinson v Secretary of State for Northern Ireland* [2002] UKHL 32 at [65]. See also *R (Miller) v Secretary of State for Exiting the European Union* [2017] UKSC 5 at [223].

[15] See Hart, *The Concept of Law* (n 7) 269. On the thesis as a 'social' sources thesis, see Scott J. Shapiro, *Legality* (Cambridge, Mass.: Harvard UP, 2011), 271–273. The word 'social' is used to emphasize the claim that a norm counts as law only when it is rooted in social facts or practices (see the final paragraph of chapter 1, above) and is ascertainable without resort to moral or practical reasoning. Since primary sources are explained as socially embedded rather than derived from law, the thesis purports to avoid infinite regress (see ibid. 39, 80). Whether it succeeds in this regard is open to question, given that a norm is identified as law by a legally empowered official. As Shapiro puts it, 'in order to *get* legal power, one must already *have* legal power'. Ibid. 37. (Emphases in original.) For a defence of the thesis against the accusation of circularity, see Neil MacCormick, *H. L. A. Hart*, 2nd edn (Stanford: Stanford UP, 2008), 136–141 (a defence which is notably less diffident than the one set forth in Neil MacCormick, *H. L. A. Hart* (London: Arnold, 1981), 108–111).

[16] Raz, *The Authority of Law* (n 13) 54, 181.

courts rule on the basis of norms which do not emanate from such sources, the logic of the sources thesis has it that judges cannot be applying already existing law.[17] Hart himself seemed to count among those (inclusive) legal positivists who do not discount the possibility of recognized sources incorporating considerations of morality, so that a court's 'moral' decisions can amount to law-application rather than reliance on non-legal argument to answer legal questions.[18] It is notable that Ronald Dworkin, throughout his many works critiquing this (as he came to call it) 'conventionalist' legal perspective, referred to law having 'grounds' rather than 'sources'—grounds being circumstances in which legal statements can be accepted as sound or true.[19] Consistent with his theory of law as integrity, Dworkin emphasized not sources of law but 'sources of legal rights'[20]—sources enabling determinations of peoples' rights ('enforceable on demand in an adjudicative political institution such as a court')[21] in accordance with those principles that provide the best justification of legal practice as a whole.[22]

b) *Interpretivism and sources*

The concept of sources of law is bound up with the notion that legal systems have rules of recognition—rules enabling judges to distinguish primary sources from secondary ones. It might be expected that a legal theory which rejects this notion—which maintains that tests of validity which focus on pedigree cannot accommodate principles among the sources of law[23]—would be untroubled by a concept which it does not employ. Yet at the core of Dworkin's theory of law as integrity we discover two conundrums regarding sources.

---

[17] Ibid. 90.

[18] Hart, *The Concept of Law* (n 7) 72, 247 (postscript), 250; also his 'Positivism and the Separation of Law and Morals' (1958) 71 *Harv. L. Rev.* 593, 599; 'Policies, Principles, and Adjudication (*c.* 1977–82)' (2024) 69 *Am. J. Juris.* 127, 128.

[19] Ronald Dworkin, *Law's Empire* (London: Fontana, 1986), 110, 262.

[20] Ibid. 99.

[21] Ronald Dworkin, *Justice for Hedgehogs* (Cambridge, Mass.: Belknap Press, 2011), 404–405. On legal as distinct from legislative rights, see ibid. 406. The proposition that it is in the nature of a legal right that it is enforceable on demand has to contend with the fact that it is not inconceivable for a court to hold that a litigant has a right (which has been infringed) but has no remedy—as when a UK court issues a declaration of incompatibility under the Human Rights Act 1998, s. 4. Dworkin does not address this particular example, though he would presumably (see ibid. 412) have argued that the right which the court finds to have been infringed—a right which the litigant claims by virtue of the UK being a signatory to the European Convention on Human Rights—is 'best treated as [a] political but not legal' right (ibid.).

[22] See Dworkin, *Law's Empire* (n 19) 152, 351–352, 400.

[23] Ronald Dworkin, *Taking Rights Seriously* (London: Duckworth, 1977), 39–41.

The general contours of law as integrity are well known. Integrity in the interpretation (or rather, the construction)[24] of statutes means seeking to put the statute in its best light by reading the enacted text in the context of 'principles embedded in the law as a whole'.[25] Integrity in adjudication means not consistency with other judicial decisions but 'coherence with fundamental principle'—principle that best fits with and justifies past institutional action.[26] Judges who aspire to interpretive and adjudicative integrity are neither straightforwardly finding nor inventing law.[27] They may have to part ways with precedent,[28] or may have to rely on past judgments not for their precedential status but rather for some scheme of principle to be located within them.[29] Judges motivated by integrity have 'to be wide-ranging and imaginative',[30] and 'endemically constructive',[31] drawing on 'the legal record as a whole'[32] (which might mean unearthing from that record 'a principle that has never been recognized explicitly').[33] It might be necessary for them to resort to 'extralegal standards'[34] in order to discover the 'genuine rights litigants have'.[35] It might be that they must not 'insist that the legal rights of the parties are to be settled entirely by consulting the traditional sources of law'.[36]

It is one thing to maintain that a litigant's legal rights might not be wholly settled by traditional sources of law and something else again to maintain that traditional sources of law never determine people's legal rights. More often than not, they determine them so thoroughly that courts refuse leave to appeal, that litigants abandon lawsuits, that people don't become litigants in the first place.[37] Even in a hard case, one calling for judges to be especially attendant to extralegal principles, rarely if ever will the moral reasoning applied by the court to determine the parties' rights and obligations be entirely divorced from legal norms identifiable according to conventional criteria of validity. Integrity is 'at work in easy cases'—Dworkin was consistent on this point—'but since the answers to the question that it puts are ... obvious, or at least seem to be

---

[24] Dworkin, *Law's Empire* (n 19) 17–19; also Ronald Dworkin, *Justice in Robes* (Cambridge, Mass.: Belknap Press, 2006), 127.
[25] Dworkin, *Justice in Robes* (n 24) 104; see also *Law's Empire* (n 19) 52–53, 56, 67, 90, 144, 215–216.
[26] Dworkin, *Law's Empire* (n 19) 220.
[27] Ibid. 225.
[28] Ibid. 219.
[29] Ibid. 227; see also *Justice in Robes* (n 24) 70.
[30] Dworkin, *Law's Empire* (n 19) 220.
[31] Ibid. 228.
[32] Ibid. 226.
[33] Ibid. 247.
[34] Ibid. 117.
[35] Ibid. 218.
[36] Dworkin, *Justice in Robes* (n 24) 165.
[37] Brian Leiter, 'Explaining Theoretical Disagreement' (2009) 76 *Univ. Chicago L. Rev.* 1215, 1227.

so, we are not aware that any theory is at work at all'.[38] His position on whether traditional sources of law are always at work in hard cases is more difficult to pin down.

This much is evident from the disagreements that have emerged among legal philosophers over whether Dworkin's jurisprudence is accurately described as incorporating, or as denuded of, conventionalist predispositions.[39] While any '[t]wo lawyers are likely to differ about the best interpretation of . . . legislation or precedent in a particular case', he observed in *Law's Empire*,[40] they will nevertheless agree that statute and precedent are examples of 'what counts as . . . the raw data of [their] interpretive community',[41] that 'legislation and precedent are conventions . . . are, in principle, sources of law'.[42] In the year that *Law's Empire* was published, one eminent legal positivist 'venture[d] to suggest that Dworkin's theory implies the acceptance of something that is at least like the Rule of Recognition as a necessary means for the identification of legal sources.'[43] Near the end of his life, Dworkin seemed amenable to this verdict, conceding that, in early writings, he had been striving to fill gaps left by, rather than reject, the sources thesis. 'I assumed that law and morals are different systems of norms and that the crucial question is how they interact.'[44] The concession, however, was by way of lament: 'I did not fully appreciate the nature of that picture . . . until later.'[45] Dworkin was clearly exasperated when, in 2006, *Law's Empire* was depicted by another eminent legal positivist 'as a . . . back-handed defence of . . . the thesis' that the validity of norms within a legal system depends on legal officials attributing them to the system's primary sources of law.[46] The 'misreading' was possible, Dworkin retorted, only 'by ignoring everything I have written about interpretation and law since 1986'.[47] He'd moved on.

---

[38] Dworkin, *Law's Empire* (n 19) 354.

[39] Whether, that is, Dworkin was a hybrid interpretivist or a pure interpretivist. On the two camps, see Nicos Stavropoulos, 'Legal Interpretivism', in *The Stanford Encyclopedia of Philosophy*, ed. E. N. Zalta (2021 edn), at https://plato.stanford.edu/archives/spr2021/entries/law-interpretivist/ (accessed 29 January 2024), sections 3 and 4. According to Stavropoulos, '[h]ybrid interpretivism gives us no reason to abandon a sharp distinction between the pre-interpretively given corpus of institutionally valid norms . . . and the final set of norms that interpretation yields', whereas pure interpretivism 'holds that morality determines how institutional practice affects rights and obligations'.

[40] Dworkin, *Law's Empire* (n 19) 123.

[41] Ibid. 67. And compare Hart, *The Concept of Law* (n 7) 105 ('[T]he judge . . . identifying what is to count as law in his court').

[42] Dworkin, *Law's Empire* (n 19) 123.

[43] Joseph Raz, 'Dworkin: A New Link in the Chain' (1986) 74 *California L. Rev.* 1103, 1109.

[44] Dworkin, *Justice for Hedgehogs* (n 21) 402.

[45] Ibid.

[46] John Gardner, 'Law's Aims in *Law's Empire*', in *Exploring Law's Empire: The Jurisprudence of Ronald Dworkin*, ed., S. Hershovitz (Oxford: OUP, 2006), 207–223 at 222.

[47] Ronald Dworkin, 'Response', in Hershovitz (ed.), *Exploring Law's Empire* (n 46) 291–311 at 310, 309.

But—the first conundrum—how far had he moved? Much as Dworkin was disparaging of conventionalist legal philosophy, he stopped short of dismissing it.[48] His own legal philosophy, moreover, never seems completely shorn of it. His final major book, rejecting 'the dead-end two-systems model' in favour of an 'integrated, one system theory of law . . . as a branch of political morality,'[49] is very much a statement of dissatisfaction with the traditional direction of jurisprudential travel. Dworkin was exasperated by legal theory that builds from 'criterial'[50] questions about what counts as valid law instead of 'in the opposite direction'[51]—from questions such as why 'moral argument' might condemn an enactment as 'too unjust to count as valid law.'[52] The plea, crudely speaking, is for reorientation rather than exclusion. A theory of law as an aspect of political morality is one of an integrated system, Dworkin makes clear, a theory which can accommodate 'a narrower, more selective kind of positivism defended on political grounds.'[53] (One of the most adroit developments of Dworkin's legal philosophy, while inclining towards pure interpretivism, is similarly accommodating.)[54] 'It must be part of any responsible answer' to questions about the conditions under which people 'acquire genuine rights and duties . . . enforceable on demand', Dworkin observes,

---

[48] See e.g. Dworkin, 'Response' (n 47) 309 ('No doubt arguments can be made in defense of legal positivism, though . . . these arguments have yet to be made').

[49] Dworkin, *Justice for Hedgehogs* (n 21) 409–410.

[50] Ibid. 404.

[51] Ibid. 407.

[52] Ibid. 411.

[53] Ibid. 409.

[54] This is arguably true of Mark Greenberg, 'The Moral Impact Theory of Law' (2014) 123 *Yale L. J.* 1288. According to Greenberg, although 'whether we classify institutions as legal or not has no effect on what we take our genuine obligations to be . . . it is an important question what makes an institution a legal institution. For example, which institutions are legal, and therefore which obligations are legal, will have implications for which obligations a legal system should enforce' (ibid. 1323–1324 n 73). A degree of accommodation on the part of some pure interpretivists is also detected by Julie Dickson, *Content-Independence in Law* (Cambridge: CUP, 2024), 24–28. But accommodation certainly isn't the way of all pure interpretivists. Scott Hershovitz, for example, distances his own Dworkin-inspired argument from Greenberg's remark about legal institutions: see Scott Hershovitz, 'The End of Jurisprudence' (2015) 124 *Yale L. J.* 1160, 1199–1200. For Hershovitz, 'Greenberg will have to offer an account of what legal institutions are, as well as an account of the legally proper ways for those institutions to affect our moral rights and obligations' (ibid. 1200 n 83). Hershovitz avoids the same burden by treating 'legal obligations' as simply a label that we sometimes find it useful to attach to moral obligations: ibid. 1202 (emphasis in original) ('Lawyers do not consult *the law* to ascertain what legal obligations people have. Rather, they read records of their community's legal history—statute books, case reports, and the like—and then they construct arguments about what obligations people have as a result. . . . I do not object to talking about what the law requires. . . . I am happy to allow that some of our moral rights, obligations, privileges, and powers are helpfully labeled "legal." But there are many helpful ways to use that label'). See also Scott Hershovitz, *Law is a Moral Practice* (Cambridge, Mass.: Harvard UP, 2023), 183.

that historical facts about legislation and, perhaps, social convention do play a role. How great or exclusive a role these play is a matter of contest. Legal positivism argues that such historical acts or conduct is exclusively decisive in deciding what legal rights people have. Interpretivism offers a different answer, in which principles of political morality also have a part to play.[55]

We will have reason to return to this late-period espousal of integrative interpretivism—cautioning against treating positivism and interpretivism 'as rival claims'[56]—in the final section of chapter 7. Its relevance to the present analysis is that it seems broadly consistent with arguments that Dworkin advanced in the mid-1980s. '[T]he brute facts of legal history',[57] he accepted at that time, cannot be ignored just because they happen to be condemned by integrity. An integrity-motivated judge must 'interpret the legal history he finds, not . . . invent a better history'.[58] Whatever the quality of a final court precedent, it binds in the lower courts. 'If a judge is satisfied that a statute admits of only one interpretation, then, barring any constitutional impediment, he must enforce this as law even if he thinks the statute inconsistent in principle with the law more broadly seen.'[59] Were a judge to choose 'to ignore legislative supremacy and strict precedent . . . he would have violated integrity overall. For any successful general interpretation of our legal practice must recognize these institutional constraints.'[60] Law as integrity finds the concept of the rule of recognition wanting, but it doesn't render it redundant: a Dworkinian judge, seeking to know 'what sorts of material figure in the best understanding of what the law requires',[61] may still identify a rule as legally valid by virtue of its having emanated from a primary source.[62]

---

[55] Dworkin, *Justice for Hedgehogs* (n 21) 407.
[56] Ibid.
[57] Dworkin, *Law's Empire* (n 19) 255.
[58] Ronald Dworkin, *A Matter of Principle* (Oxford: Clarendon Press, 1986), 160.
[59] Dworkin, *Law's Empire* (n 19) 401.
[60] Ibid.
[61] Dworkin, *Justice in Robes* (n 24) 230.
[62] Dworkin, understandably, emphasized just how little of the rule of recognition he thought survived once the implications of integrity are accepted. See e.g. Ronald Dworkin, 'Hart's Posthumous Reply' (2017) 130 *Harv. L. Rev.* 2096, 2118: 'On my view, there is no fully shared rule of recognition at all: the supposed convention, that the American Constitution is the supreme law of the land or that Parliament is the supreme lawgiver in Britain, can only be described as conventionally accepted if we ignore the fact that what those abstract formulations mean to some lawyers, as guides to identifying true, concrete propositions of law, is very different from what they mean to others.' To support his point as it relates to parliamentary supremacy, Dworkin refers to the 'dispute among British lawyers in recent years about whether . . . a statute is invalid, under domestic British law administered by British judges, if it offends, for example, Article 10 of the European Convention' (ibid. 2119). At the time that Dworkin wrote these words (September 1994), just as now, British lawyers did not accept the proposition that the fact of a statute offending against a Convention norm could render it invalid.

c) *Source appropriateness*

The second, somewhat thornier conundrum concerns secondary sources. Just what Dworkin understands secondary sources to be, and what they count for in his jurisprudential scheme, isn't entirely clear. His idealized judge, Hercules, 'need not worry about the press of time and docket'[63]—'[h]e does what [real judges] would do if they had a career to devote to a single decision'[64]—and so has the capacity to draw upon any *obiter* observation, minority opinion, law review article, or other secondary source that he might care to use in his quest to decide according to principles which provide the best justification of legal practice as a whole. Yet Dworkin accords these sources barely any role in Hercules' enterprise.

Judges with Hercules' aspirations make decisions on grounds of principle, answering questions of political morality, in order to protect legal rights: their rulings, even in hard cases, are 'conclusions of law'.[65] Certainly these judges are (cautiously) receptive to legislative history as a statutory-interpretive aid.[66] There are instances, moreover, when they might have a *prima facie* duty to abide by convergent foreign judgments (see chapter 5).[67] But Dworkin was also of the view that—on 'the question of what sorts or sources of argument are appropriate' to 'cases in which what lawyers regard as settled law does not decide the immediate issue'[68]—there are 'constraints on what . . . judges can cite . . . in justifying the law's record as a whole'.[69] He was sure that they can rely on liberal political philosophy ('[j]udges interpreting a string of cases in tort law can appeal to Rawls's theory of justice as a ground for rejecting a utilitarian interpretation of past decisions').[70] But he insisted that they should not rely on personal religious convictions (to 'take a position about', say, 'whether . . . women have a . . . right to abortion'),[71] since integrity deems it 'wrong for them to deploy certain kinds of arguments'[72]—those arguments, that is, which 'cannot figure in an overall comprehensive justification of the legal structure of a liberal and tolerant pluralistic community'.[73]

---

[63] Dworkin, *Law's Empire* (n 19) 380.
[64] Ibid. 265.
[65] Ibid. 262.
[66] Ibid. 342–349.
[67] Ronald Dworkin, 'A New Philosophy for International Law' (2013) 41 *Philos. & Pub. Affs* 2, 19–22.
[68] Dworkin, *Justice in Robes* (n 24) 242.
[69] Ibid. 251.
[70] Ibid. 254.
[71] Ibid. 253.
[72] Ibid. 251.
[73] Ibid. 254.

Of course, secondary source materials—scholarship, *obiter dicta*, out-of-court judicial pronouncements, *amicus curiae* briefs, and the like—not only explore such arguments but sometimes advance them as well (Dworkin was himself, famously, one of six eminent American philosophers who produced a brief aimed at convincing the US Supreme Court to declare a constitutional right to physician-assisted suicide).[74] But exactly what integrity might categorize as the wrong kind of argument, and where it might ordain that a judge shouldn't cite a source which advances such an argument, would seem to be an unanswerable question. Integrity, for Dworkin, speaks against prohibitions on same-sex marriage and refusals to recognize a constitutional right to abortion.[75] One of Dworkin's former colleagues, John Finnis, is responsible for an estimable body of source material—submissions to courts as well as essays and articles—in which he argues that abortion is unconstitutional and that same-sex intercourse is morally wrong.[76] When these materials have proved persuasive in legal judgments on these topics (the best-known instance is the judgment overruling *Roe v Wade*),[77] should the court be considered to have offended against, or to have proceeded in a manner consistent with, integrity?

Integrity-minded judges are meant to rely only on sources that facilitate integrity. Principled coherence with legal practice and the structure of law does not award them a *carte blanche* to rely on whatever they like. This stricture holds good, Dworkin maintains, even when the source is a secondary source. Central to this chapter has been the question of how integrity interacts with a primary source. Since a fair amount of detail has accompanied the answer to that question, it perhaps makes sense to conclude with a terse statement of what

[74] 'Brief for Ronald Dworkin et al. as *Amici Curiae* in Support of Respondents, *Washington v Glucksberg*' (filed 10 December 1996), 117 S. Ct 2258 (1997), Nos. 95-1858, 96-110. 1996 WL 708956; repr. as Ronald Dworkin et al., 'Assisted Suicide: The Philosophers' Brief', in *New York Rev. of Books*, 27 March 1997 at 41–47.

[75] See Dworkin, *Justice for Hedgehogs* (n 21) 369 ('Prohibitions on same-sex intercourse or marriage constrain foundational choices . . .'), 378 ('It must be left to women, as their dignity demands, each to take responsibility for her own ethical convictions'); also his *Religion Without God* (Cambridge, Mass.: Harvard UP, 2013), 144.

[76] See e.g. 'Brief of *Amici Curiae* Scholars of Jurisprudence John M. Finnis and Robert P. George in Support of Petitioners' (filed 29 July 2021), 142 S. Ct 2228 (2022) No. 19-1392, 2021 WL 3374325; 'Affidavit of John Mitchell Finnis' (8 October 1993), filed in *Evans v Romer*, 63 Empl. Prac. Dec. (CCH) ¶ 42,719 (Colo. D. Ct 14 December 1993); John Finnis, 'Abortion is Unconstitutional', *First Things*, 1 April 2021, at firstthings.com/article/2021/04/abortion-is-unconstitutional (accessed 31 January 2024); 'Born and Unborn: Answering Objections to Constitutional Personhood', *First Things*, 9 April 2021, at firstthings.com/web-exclusives/2021/04/born-and-unborn-answering-objections-to-constitutional-personhood (accessed 31 January 2024); '"Shameless Acts" in Colorado: Abuse of Scholarship in Constitutional Cases' (1994) 7 *Academic Questions* 10; 'Law, Morality and "Sexual Orientation"' (1994) 69 *Notre Dame L. Rev* 1049 (repr. with additions at (1995) 9 *Notre Dame Jnl Law, Ethics & Public Policy* 11). This last article contains much of the content of the affidavits that Finnis produced relating to *Evans v Romer*.

[77] *Dobbs v Jackson Women's Health Org.*, 597 US 215, 252 n 38 (2022).

that answer actually is. Just as modern positivism distinguishes sources which do and do not enable the identification of valid law, Dworkinian interpretivism distinguishes sources which do and do not assist in the adjudicative goal of justifying decisions in accordance with whatever principles and standards provide the most coherent account of law and legal practices taken as a whole. The mid-twentieth century witnessed the emergence of a new conceptualization of primary sources, one which explained them not as origins to which laws can be traced but rather as conditions that legal officials, particularly judges, identify as having to be met if a norm can be applied as a binding legal rule. Dworkin proved to be an astute critic of the positivist methodology associated with this so-called sources thesis. But his theory of law as integrity never entirely breaks free of the thesis itself.

4

The concept of the secondary source

Dworkin's jurisprudence is troubled by questions about sources just as is the modern positivist tradition that he took to task. But it is the positivists who put the difficulties into sharp relief. The positivist tradition is met with indifference, if not resistance, by many legal theorists in continental European jurisdictions, where it is commonly accepted not only that what officials recognize to be primary sources tends to differ between legal systems, but also that, even within a legal system, there can be considerable uncertainty as to the standing of a source. The Italian comparatist, Rodolfo Sacco, drew the conventional 'distinction between those legal formants that are themselves rules of conduct and others that are developed in order to provide . . . justifications of rules and conduct'.[1] His not-so-conventional choice of 'legal formant' to describe legal source-material is meant to convey the idea that sources of law are dynamic, that the status and the range of sources within a legal system evolve (in Latin, *formare*) over time.[2]

This way of thinking about sources, common to European jurists, is predicated on a catholic conception of what qualifies as a primary source and is very much receptive to the idea that a secondary source might actually be a primary source in waiting. The terminology that some French legal theorists like to employ when articulating this way of thinking has it that there are not only primary *sources du droit* which yield binding legal rules, but also *sources de droit* which offer up information and reasoning which might assist law-makers when they create binding rules, and which might be made to stand in for—or even turned into—binding rules when the *sources du droit* exhibit a gap in the law

---

[1] Rodolfo Sacco, 'Legal Formants: A Dynamic Approach to Comparative Law' (2 parts) (1991) 39 *Am. J. Comparative Law* 1, 343 pt 1 at 34.

[2] 'In most legal systems', another comparatist elaborates, 'the conventions as to the determination of the sources of law are far from settled. . . . Domestic lawyers learn to discern the different strength of the various formants, that is, the difference in weight that is accorded to the respective sources, by years of training and experience.' Stefan Vogenauer, 'Sources of Law and Legal Method in Comparative Law', in *The Oxford Handbook of Comparative Law*, ed. M. Reimann and R. Zimmermann (Oxford: OUP, 2006), 869–898 at 885.

Law's Sources. Neil Duxbury, Oxford University Press. © Neil Duxbury 2025.
DOI: 10.1093/9780198981183.003.0004

or produce an evidently unsatisfactory legal answer.[3] In France, as in common-law legal systems, legislation and custom are routinely and unequivocally ranked as primary sources. But in France, unlike in common-law legal systems, one sometimes encounters the argument that primary source status does not attach to *jurisprudence* or judicial decisions, even though it might attach to legal scholarship (*la doctrine*).[4] Not only did legal pluralism take longer to feature in common law than it did in French legal theory—Henri Lévi-Bruhl was already arguing in the early 1950s that private organizations can be sources of law[5]—but many modern French legal analysts routinely accept standard pluralist propositions, such as that contract-formation is a primary source of law and that the same status might be accorded to some religious texts.[6] Relative amenability to pluralism, and a correspondingly unreceptive attitude to positivism, explains why, as compared with their common-law counterparts, French jurists generally subscribe to more expansive conceptions, and are likely to come up with longer lists, of primary sources.

a) *The contours of secondary sources*

By conceiving of primary sources as criteria of validity rather than as origins, modern legal positivists have an explanation for what counts as law within a legal system, and for why what counts as law can differ among systems. But is their explanation compelling? Even positivists have been reluctant to answer

---

[3] See Catherine Thibierge, 'Sources du droit, sources de droit: une cartographie', in *Libres propos sur les sources du droit: Mélanges en l'honneur de Philippe Jestaz*, ed. P. Ancel (Paris: Dalloz, 2006), 519–546 at 532–534; Stefan Goltzberg, *Les sources du droit*, 2nd edn (Paris: PUF, 2018), 70.

[4] See Goltzberg, *Les sources du droit* (n 3) 71–78; Thibierge, 'Sources du droit, sources de droit' (n 3) 541; Frédéric Zenati-Castaing, *Le savoir des lois* (Paris: Dalloz, 2021), 89; Sacco, 'Legal Formants' (n 1) pt 2, 346; Philippe Jestaz and Christophe Jamin, *La doctrine* (Paris: Dalloz, 2004), 5 ('[E]veryone implicitly considers legal scholarship as . . . part of the sources of law. . . . Indirect, informal source . . . but source all the same'); and, for a more circumspect view, cf Rémy Libchaber, *L'ordre juridique et le discours du droit: Essai sur les limites de la connaissance du droit* (Paris: LGDJ, 2013), 352 ('[I]t is not clear if the accepted meaning of the word [*sc., doctrine*] constrains us from excluding it from living sources').

[5] Henri Lévi-Bruhl, 'Esquisse d'une théorie des sources du droit' [1951] *Année Sociologique* 3. For Lévi-Bruhl, 'the rule of law is not necessarily linked to political organisation' because some syndicates and private bodies 'can . . . enact legal rules' (ibid. 7). See also Libchaber, *L'ordre juridique et le discours du droit* (n 4) 78–81.

[6] See Goltzberg, *Les sources du droit* (n 3) 81–83, 115–118; Thibierge, 'Sources du droit, sources de droit' (n 3) 525; Philippe Jestaz, *Les sources du droit*, 3rd edn (Paris: Dalloz, 2022), 29–37, 129–130, 133; Emeric Nicolas, *Penser les flux normatifs: Essai sur le droit fluide* (Paris: Mare & Martin, 2018), 84–85; also *Il Congreso di Partido* [1978] QB 500, 529 (Goff J). The idea that contract-formation is a primary source of law (as distinct from the proposition that primary sources enable determinations as to whether agreements are legally binding contracts) has not been entirely without common-law adherents: see e.g. John Salmond, *Jurisprudence,* 9th edn, ed. J. L. Parker (London: Sweet & Maxwell, 1937; 1st edn publ. 1902), 113–114, 256–260.

this question with a dogmatic affirmative. Primary sources are not always called primary sources. They are also referred to (by judges as well as by academics)[7] as binding, mandatory, material, or formal sources. But whatever name they are given, the point is the same: they are the sources of those directives which—no matter how much room for manoeuvre law-enforcing organs might have when interpreting them—must be applied as law.[8] With secondary sources, the picture is more complicated. Whereas, according to Hart, primary sources are ' "mandatory" legal or formal sources'—the type of source to which 'a court in deciding a case is bound to attend'—secondary or ' "permissive" legal sources' are ones which '[t]he legal system does not require' the court to attend to but which it is nevertheless 'perfectly proper' for judges to treat 'as "good reasons" for decisions.'[9] The Statute of Westminster, that thirteenth-century law establishing a limitation period, was being invoked as this kind of source when judges elected—they were certainly not bound—to apply it to determine if local customs had prescribed (see chapter 2, section (c)).

Hart conceded that although it is possible to draw a 'clear distinction' between primary and secondary sources, it 'may be blurred in actual practice.'[10] A secondary source will sometimes take the form of a pronouncement which yields no binding law yet carries significant weight, so that a court, when deciding a matter to which the pronouncement relates, is not bound to attend to it yet would be remiss if it did not (there are some *dicta*, Lord Atkin remarked, that are 'of so great weight that I should probably feel compelled to follow them').[11] When the court has difficulty ascertaining relevant primary sources, secondary sources might supply answers: material on what constitutes a political crime under the Geneva Convention 'does not have the force of law itself', one law lord once observed with regard to immigration and asylum judgments, but it can be an 'important source of law' in so far as it can help a court reach conclusions as to what does have the force of law.[12] Distinguishing what binds and what is supplementary in a judgment can be difficult when the

---

[7] See e.g. *Sandoz v Searle* [2018] EWCA Civ 49 at [54]; *Mohamed v Breish* [2020] EWHC 696 (Comm) at [101]; *XZ (Russia) v Secretary of State for the Home Department* [2008] EWCA Civ 180 at [4]; *National Bank Trust v Yurov* [2020] EWHC 100 (Comm) at [936], [953], [954], [986].

[8] Joseph Raz, *The Authority of Law*, 2nd edn (Oxford: OUP, 2009), 90–91.

[9] H. L. A. Hart, *The Concept of Law*, 3rd edn (Oxford: OUP, 2012), 294.

[10] Ibid. See also Raz, *The Authority of Law* (n 8) 94–95.

[11] *Gibson v Gibson* [1913] 3 KB 379, 388. See also Aleksander Peczenik, *Scientia Juris: Legal Doctrine as Knowledge of Law and as a Source of Law* (Dordrecht: Springer, 2005), 16 ('should-sources', as distinct from must-sources and may-sources); Aulis Aarnio, *Essays on the Doctrinal Study of Law* (Dordrecht: Springer, 2011), 153–158; Hélène Tyrrell, *Human Rights in the UK and the Influence of Foreign Jurisprudence* (Oxford: Hart, 2018), 210 ('a non-binding source of law . . . that would be unfairly characterised as merely "persuasive" ').

[12] *T v Secretary of State for the Home Department* [1996] AC 742, 786 (Lord Lloyd).

judgment is grounded in multiple sources.[13] A court could be confronted with a *Sorenson's case* scenario,[14] one in which the primary sources turn out to be 'an authoritative desert',[15] and so could end up drawing on secondary sources *faute de mieux*.[16]

There is another way in which the picture is more complicated. While the terms used to describe primary sources convey a single insight—that they are sources of law—two distinct connotations attach to the language associated with secondary sources. There is the idea of a secondary source in the sense that Hart meant: judges, in the course of producing a judgment, being permitted to rely on the source material, but not being required to negotiate it as would be the case were it applicable, binding authority. But there is also the idea of a source being secondary not in the sense that judges are entitled to draft it into service if they wish, but rather in the sense that it helps them interpret—and helps lawyers seeking to convince a court of the right way to interpret—the law that is applied in the course of reaching a judgment. These two conceptions of secondary source—permissive on the one hand, persuasive (or epistemic) on the other—are not entirely distinct.

The notion that there is a permissive dimension to judges and lawyers relying on secondary sources purely as sources of legal information seems, on the face of it, completely obvious. Should anyone want to use a secondary source when settling on how to interpret and apply the law, after all, there exists no effective way of prohibiting them: it is perfectly possible for lawyers and judges to rely on secondary sources without disclosing that they have done so. Yet it is not unknown for courts to abide by conventions restricting their explicit use, even when the sources would only ever be relied on as sources of legal information and argument. English judges were slow to come round to the view that it is not beyond the realms of possibility that there are benefits to be drawn from admitting legislative history into court when interpreting ambiguous statutory language.[17] There was a time, moreover, when they generally would not cite—and would not allow lawyers arguing before them to cite— juristic writings while the authors were still alive.[18]

---

[13] For judgments fitting the bill, see *Mohammed v Ministry of Defence* [2017] UKSC 1; *QD (Iraq) v Secretary of State for the Home Department* [2009] EWCA Civ 620 (refugees' and asylum-seekers' *non-refoulement* rights traceable to more than one source).

[14] Ronald Dworkin, *Justice in Robes* (Cambridge, Mass.: Belknap Press, 2006), 7–9, 143–145, 164.

[15] Tom Bingham, *The Business of Judging* (Oxford: OUP, 2000), 39.

[16] See *Swinfen v Chelmsford* (1860) 5 Hurl. & N. 890, 918 (Pollock CB).

[17] The convention against consultation was brought to an end by the House of Lords in *Pepper v Hart* [1993] AC 593. See, generally, John J. Magyar, 'The Slow Death of a Dogma? The Prohibition of Legislative History in the 20th Century' (2021) 50 *Common Law World Rev.* 120.

[18] See Alexandra Braun, 'Burying the Living? The Citation of Legal Writings in English Courts' (2010) 58 *Am. J. Comp. L.* 27.

b) *Non-legal and upgraded sources*

Little, if any, explicit support for conventions like these persists nowadays. There remain, nevertheless, at least two lingering questions about secondary sources understood as sources that lawyers and judges are permitted to use. First, what sources are courts permitted to accept and invoke as secondary sources? It is a commonplace that courts can reject sources when establishing facts, as when a source presented as character evidence is considered to fall short of an admissibility threshold.[19] But what of refusals to countenance types of source on the basis that using them as persuasive or epistemic authority is inappropriate?

Secondary source materials are usually non-binding legal pronouncements: juristic writings, foreign judgments, *obiter dicta*, statements on the legislative record, *amicus* interventions, *travaux préparatoires*, and other types of advisory document. These pronouncements will likely have some sort of legal provenance. Now and again, however, it is evident that judicial reasoning on a matter of law is influenced by a 'non-legal' source—as when judges find support for a legal position or principle in a religious text,[20] literary classics,[21] historical scholarship,[22] political theory,[23] or social science.[24] This type of source makes for an open-ended list; it may well be—law professors in the United States often argue—that courts, over time, tend to become more amenable to accepting non-legal materials as sources of legal information and reasoning.[25] And so the question of how far the concept of the secondary but non-legal source stretches cannot be definitively answered. Certainly courts will consider non-legal materials when they are introduced as evidence— newspaper and magazine articles, say, or expert witness documents—and,

---

[19] See Mike Redmayne, *Character in the Criminal Trial* (Oxford: OUP, 2015), 145–172.

[20] *Reninger v Fogossa* (1550) 1 Plowd. 1, 19.

[21] *Midland Bank v Green (No. 3)* [1979] Ch. 496, 527 (Oliver J).

[22] *Fisher v Oldham Corp.* [1930] 2 KB 364, 369 (McCardie J). (McCardie assumed the article he cited (H. B. Simpson, 'The Office of Constable' (1895) 10 *English Historical Rev.* 624–641) to be the work of a professor. Simpson was, in fact, a Home Office official.)

[23] *Interfact v Liverpool CC* [2010] EWCA Crim 1486 at [3].

[24] See John Monahan and Laurens Walker, 'Social Authority: Obtaining, Evaluating, and Establishing Social Science in Law' (1986) 134 *Univ. Pa L. Rev.* 477, 483–484 (on the US Supreme Court's willingness in the 1950s—as compared with its unwillingness in the 1900s—to treat empirical social science as epistemic authority).

[25] See Ellie Margolis, 'Authority Without Borders: The World Wide Web and the Delegalization of Law' (2011) 41 *Seton Hall L. Rev.* 909; Michael Whiteman, 'The Death of Twentieth-Century Authority' (2010) 58 *UCLA L. Rev. Discourse* 27; Robert C. Berring, 'Legal Information and the Search for Cognitive Authority' (2000) 88 *California L. Rev.* 1673; Frederick Schauer and Virginia J. Wise, 'Nonlegal Information and the Delegalization of Law' (2000) 29 *Jnl Leg. Studs* 495; Schauer, 'Law's Boundaries' (2017) 130 *Harv. L. Rev.* 2434, 2456–2460.

unless a source is privileged or reliance on it entails illegality, judges can use any such materials (no matter their provenance) in support of their own legal pronouncements.[26] But these materials are, more often than not, intrinsically unsuited to serving as epistemic legal authority, and so judges have little if any reason to rely on them. When they do rely on them, moreover, the likelihood is that they will be making a point which is of no particular, or perhaps simply of no, legal consequence—as when they draw attention to cautionary tales (*Bleak House* being a particular favourite),[27] to the state of the world as they see it or some feature of the human condition,[28] to baffling complexity or inordinate (archetypically 'Kafkaesque') bureaucracy,[29] to their own erudition (the lower court judge 'called it limbo, but theologians have recently decided that there is no such place'),[30] or to the gulf between a legal and a particular non-legal approach to an issue before the court.[31]

The second, more intriguing question about secondary sources concerns not whether, but how, courts are permitted to rely on a source as a form of authority. The function of a secondary source might alter because its status is altered, as when a court determines that a type of judicial pronouncement which, to date, has had only secondary status—judicial *dicta*, say, or the opinions of a court not within the jurisdiction—will henceforth, even if only in limited circumstances, be on a par with precedent.[32] In these instances, the content of the legal system's rule of recognition is modified so that the

---

[26] User-generated repositories and social media posts are obvious modern examples. See Neil C. Thompson et al., 'User-Generated Content Shapes Judicial Reasoning: Evidence from a Randomized Control Trial on Wikipedia' (2024) 35 *Information Systems Research* 1948–1964; *Hawaii v Trump*, 859 F.3d 741, 773 n 14 (9th Cir. 2017) (Ninth Circuit taking 'judicial notice' of the White House Press Secretary's confirmation that Donald Trump's tweets were to be considered official presidential statements); *Trump v Hawaii*, 138 S. Ct 2392, 2437 n 1 (2018) (Sotomayor and Ginsburg JJ, dissenting).

[27] See e.g. *The Ampthill Peerage* [1977] AC 547, 575; *Brook v Read* [2011] EWCA Civ 331 at [6]; *Coleman v Balkcom*, 451 US 949, 958 (1981); also (for a non-Dickensian example) *R (Abdelghani) v Home Secretary* [2010] EWHC 1227 (Admin) at [54].

[28] See e.g. *Eatery Corp. v City of New York*, 408 F.Supp.3d 424, 470 (S.D.N.Y. 2019) ('As Proust might say,...'); *Tennant v Associated Newspapers* [1979] FSR 298, 303.

[29] See e.g. *Cruz v Arizona*, 598 US 17, 29 (2023); *Zagorski v Parker*, 139 S. Ct 11, 13 (Mem) (2018); *R (Roberts) v Parole Board* [2005] UKHL 45 at [95] and [126]; *Oldendorff & Co. v Tradax* [1974] AC 479, 511; *Roth v Home Secretary* [2002] EWCA Civ 158 at [98].

[30] *R v Home Secretary* [2009] EWCA Civ 1310 at [2]. See also *Bowman v Secular Society* [1917] AC 406, 470–471; *X v Persons Unknown* [2006] EWHC 2783 (QB) at [37].

[31] See e.g. *Bank of Toronto v Lambe* (1887) 12 App. Cas. 575 (PC) 581; *Chester CC v Arriva Plc* [2007] EWHC 1373 (Ch) at [147]; also Bezalel Stern, 'Nonlegal Citations and the Failure of Law: A Case Study of the Supreme Court 2010–11 Term' (2013) 35 *Whittier L. Rev.* 79.

[32] For English law examples, see *R v Barton* [2020] EWCA Crim 575, in which the Court of Appeal determined that recent Supreme Court *dicta* had negated the test for dishonesty set out in one of the Court of Appeal's own precedents (see chapter 6, section (b)), and *Willers v Joyce* [2016] UKSC 44, in which the Supreme Court determined that, henceforth, it could direct domestic courts to treat decisions of the Judicial Committee of the Privy Council—not a court of the jurisdiction—'as representing the law of England and Wales'. Ibid. at [21].

secondary source is made not to do the work of, but rather is made into, a primary source. However, a secondary source which judges rely on as they would a primary source—which they acknowledge does not bind them even though they elect, exceptionally, to apply as if it did—does not fall within the purview of a system's rule of recognition. If legal systems yield instances of this kind, in which sources operate as primary sources but retain their secondary status, the concept of a rule of recognition would seem to come up short. The next two chapters present some evidence of common-law legal systems offering up precisely these kinds of instances. But the evidence, we will see, needs to be treated with a good deal of caution. Whether all secondary sources of law are, or even can be, enlisted to fill in for primary sources seems doubtful. Sometimes, moreover, the correct interpretation of the evidence is not that judges are making an acknowledged secondary source operate like a primary one, but rather that the source has been formally re-categorized as a primary source—that the rule of recognition's content has been altered—or that it is still being relied on only for its persuasive or epistemic value.

5

Secondary sources as sources of law

Some of the most compelling evidence on how a source may retain secondary status while performing a primary function is to be found in that vast realm of judicial utterances qualifying as *obiter dicta*. The elevation of *dicta* by common-law courts need not entail an alteration to the rule of recognition. Judges will occasionally abide by a *dictum* as if they were following precedent, making it clear that they know they don't have to treat the *dictum* in this way but rather are choosing to follow it because they feel that they should.[1] When judges do this, they sometimes make a point of recognizing that the *dictum* is not formally binding while venturing that it is presumptively or *de facto* binding—that, for all that there would be nothing technically remiss in their not following the *dictum*, they would be demonstrating obvious poor judgment if they did not.[2]

There are certainly judges who make a point of not being seduced by *dicta*. 'Views of two or three judges in an opinion on matters that are not necessarily dispositive of the case', according to one former US federal circuit judge, 'are no different from the same views expressed in a law review article; neither should be treated as a judicial act that is entitled to binding effect'.[3] *Ad hoc*, casual elevation of *dicta* is, nevertheless, a moderately popular common-law pastime. Examples of US judges choosing *dicta* over precedent might not be rife, but neither are they thin on the ground.[4] (The Supreme Court's doctrine

---

[1] See e.g. *Pew v Metropolitan Board of Works* (1865) 6 B. & S. 235, 248 (Blackburn J); *Tees Conservancy Commissioners v James* [1935] Ch. 544, 560 (Farwell J) ('. . . *dicta* which I think I ought to follow'); *Woodcock v South West Electricity Board* [1975] 1 WLR 983, 987 (Dunn J).

[2] See e.g. *Casswell v Cheshire Lines Committee* [1907] 2 KB 499, 504 (Darling J) ('[W]e cannot, I think, neglect such an expression of opinion as that'); *Slack v Leeds Industrial Co-operative Society* [1923] 1 Ch. 431, 446 (Warrington LJ); *Steadman v Steadman* [1974] QB 161, 177 (Roskill LJ) ('It is true that this expression of opinion is technically not binding on this court, but its correctness has never been challenged and for my part I am not prepared to say that the *obiter dicta* of a Court of Appeal so constituted were erroneous'); *Sayce v TNT Ltd* [2011] EWCA Civ 1583 at [24] (Moore-Bick LJ); also (Canada) *R v Prokofiew* (2010) 256 CCC (3d) 355 (Can. SC) at para. 21.

[3] *Barapind v Enomoto*, 400 F.3d 744, 759 (9th Cir. 2005) (Rymer J, concurring in part and dissenting in part).

[4] See e.g. David M. Dorsen, *Henry Friendly: Greatest Judge of His Era* (Cambridge, Mass.: Belknap Press, 2012), 217; also Judith M. Stinson, 'Why *Dicta* Becomes Holding and Why it Matters' (2010) 76 *Brooklyn L. Rev.* 219.

Law's Sources. Neil Duxbury, Oxford University Press. © Neil Duxbury 2025.
DOI: 10.1093/9780198981183.003.0005

of strict scrutiny is, famously, contained not in a case holding but in a footnote in a judgment about milk products.)[5] In recent years, Canadian and Australian lower courts have occasionally opted to follow particular final court *dicta* in preference to identified precedents.[6] Perhaps common-law judges are willing to upgrade *obiter* opinion because they recognize it to be different from other types of secondary source: because they understand their enterprise to be that of making decisions which stand as rulings of a court within a jurisdiction, and delivery of *dicta* as part of a judicial opinion is, unlike the production of other forms of persuasive authority, intrinsic to the conduct of—including their own individual contributions to—that enterprise.[7]

Even extra-jurisdictional judicial opinion can seem exalted as compared with other secondary source material. Although the doctrine of horizontal precedent does not strictly apply across the United States Courts of Appeals, the federal circuit courts, 'adher[ing] to the policy that a sister circuit's reasoned decision deserves great weight and precedential value', customarily stave off inter-circuit precedential disharmony by surveying one another's judgments on an issue before ruling on the issue for themselves.[8] In the twentieth century there were periods when, without treaties obliging them to do so, the apex courts of some former British dominions accepted House of Lords precedents as binding. In 1943, the Chief Justice of Australia's High Court ventured that 'in cases of clear conflict between a decision of the House of Lords and of the High Court, this court, and other courts in Australia, should follow a decision of the House of Lords'.[9] Two decades on and the convention had gone,[10] though in New Zealand it took root in the 1920s and persisted for half a century.[11]

---

[5] See *United States v Carolene Products*, 304 US 144, 152–153 n 4 (1938); also Abner J. Mikva, 'Goodbye to Footnotes' (1985) 56 *Univ. Colorado L. Rev.* 647, 649.

[6] See e.g. *J. K. Read Engineering Ltd v R* [2015] 2 CTC 2023 (Tax Court of Canada) at para. 29; *ACT v Queanbeyan CC* (2010) 188 FCR 541 (FCA), 586 (Perram J); also Matthew Harding and Ian Malkin, 'The High Court of Australia's *Obiter Dicta* and Decision-Making in Lower Courts' (2012) 34 *Sydney L. Rev.* 239.

[7] See *R v Bishop of Oxford* (1879) 4 QBD 525, 599–600 (Thesiger LJ). On the nature of the judicial function and non-binding judicial opinion, see also Chad Flanders, 'Toward a Theory of Persuasive Authority' (2009) 62 *Oklahoma L. Rev.* 55, 71–72.

[8] *Alden's, Inc. v Miller* 610 F.2d 538, 541 (8th Cir. 1979). Despite not binding strictly (on which, see Jeffrey C. Dobbins, 'Structure and Precedent' (2010) 108 *Michigan L. Rev.* 1453, 1486–1487), a circuit's precedents on a particular issue may carry especial weight owing to the fact that the circuit is considered to have expertise in the relevant area of law.

[9] *Piro v W. Foster & Co. Ltd* (1943) 68 CLR 313, 320 (Latham CJ). See also ibid. 325–326 (Rich J), 326–327 (Starke J), 336 (McTiernan J), and 341 (Williams J).

[10] Dixon CJ delivered the *coup de grâce* in *Parker v The Queen* (1963) 111 CLR 610, 632–633.

[11] See *Barker v Barker* [1924] NZLR 1078 (SC), 1085 (Herdman J) ('I think that it is best in New Zealand that we should endeavour to decide contests in the Divorce Court upon principles which, as far as our statute law will permit, are in unison with the principles acted upon in the English courts'); *Smith v Wellington Woollen Manufacturing Co. Ltd* [1956] NZLR 491 (CA), 500 (McGregor J) ('[I]t is the duty of this Court to follow the authoritative decision of the supreme tribunal of the British

There has also been notable judicial introspection on the question of whether, and if so how, a national court should reckon with convergent foreign precedent when the precedent shows the court to be out of step with other jurisdictions on a rights issue. No judge appears to have gone quite so far as to claim that when a jurisdiction is an outlier on a legal controversy and foreign judgments converge on how the controversy is to be settled, those judgments constitute *ius gentium*, 'binding . . . as . . . the law of the whole world'.[12] But there are certainly judges who believe that the weight and persuasiveness of convergent foreign material will sometimes place a *prima facie* duty, or at least considerable pressure, on an outlier jurisdiction to overturn relevant domestic precedent.[13] 'If . . . a decision is given in this country which offends one's basic sense of justice', one UK law lord remarked in 2002, 'and if consideration of international sources suggests that a different and more acceptable decision would be given in most other jurisdictions . . . this must prompt anxious review of the decision in question'.[14]

The remark came around the time that the US Supreme Court handed down a judgment (overturning a state anti-sodomy law)[15] which added a new layer of significance to this idea of anxious review: what if the sources of foreign information lead the Court to reinterpret the Constitution? The question raised its head again three years later, when the Court set aside a death penalty verdict for a juvenile offender.[16] In this instance the ruling was guided, Ernest Young has argued, not by the reasoning contained in the foreign judgments but rather by the simple fact that numerous jurisdictions had converged on a very different answer to the United States' answer to the particular legal controversy. According to Young, the Court's willingness to accept the foreign judgments in this way—to accept them irrespective of the reasons that foreign judges gave to justify them—is evidence that they were being treated as 'binding legal authority'.[17] The majority responsible for the decision was

---

Commonwealth'); and—the decision marking the end of the era—*Bognuda v Upton & Shearer Ltd* [1972] NZLR 741 (CA), 757 (North P), also 771 (Woodhouse J).

[12] Jeremy Waldron, *'Partly Laws Common to All Mankind': Foreign Law in American Courts* (New Haven: Yale UP, 2012), 49, and see also 43, 51, 56.

[13] Ronald Dworkin, 'A New Philosophy for International Law' (2013) 41 *Philos. & Pub. Affs* 2, 19 ('If a significant number of states, encompassing a significant population, has developed an agreed code of practice, either by treaty or by other form of coordination, then other states have at least a *prima facie* duty to subscribe to that practice as well, with the important proviso that this duty holds only if a more general practice to that effect, expanded in that way, would improve the legitimacy of the subscribing state and the international order as a whole').

[14] *Fairchild v Glenhaven* [2003] 1 AC 32, 66 (Lord Bingham). (Case decided June 2002.)

[15] *Lawrence v Texas* 539 US 558 (2002).

[16] *Roper v Simmons* 543 US 551 (2005).

[17] Ernest A. Young, 'Foreign Law and the Denominator Problem' (2005) 119 *Harv. L. Rev.* 148, 151.

of a different view: '[t]he opinion of the world community, while not controlling our outcome, does provide respected and significant confirmation for our own conclusions.'[18] This cut no ice with the principal dissentient. The reliance on these judgments was indeed a choice rather than a duty, *prima facie* or otherwise, to fall in line with other jurisdictions' courts; the judgments of those courts did not bind as precedent. But the judgments were pulling the levers, controlling by stealth: the majority's countenancing of foreign constitutional court judgments motivated its decision to reverse its own precedent,[19] and interpret the Eighth Amendment afresh. Judgments of foreign courts—so ran the argument—were being used to shape the meaning of the United States Constitution.[20]

a) *Juristic authority in the civil law tradition*

Courts, certainly common-law courts, have not been entirely averse to according technically non-binding judicial opinions *de facto* binding status. But do they ever attribute the same status to other secondary sources? There definitely are instances when they do so. But they are rather less common than some legal observers maintain. Take, first of all, the idea of legal scholarship having the force of law. Commentators sympathetic to the idea discover little, if any, support for their arguments in the common law. But this tends not to stymie their efforts, for Roman and civil law yield plenty of examples. In the Roman classical period, it seems that some juristic opinions—offered by jurists whose *responsa* on legal questions were patented by the Emperor, and which met with no dissent from jurists of comparable stature—would have carried such weight as to bind judges much as they were bound by *lex*.[21] And in the

---

[18] *Roper v Simmons* (n 16) 578 (Kennedy J)

[19] The precedent was *Stanford v Kentucky*, 492 US 361 (1989).

[20] Antonin Scalia, 'Foreign Legal Authority in the Federal Courts' (2004) 98 *Am. Soc. Int'l Law (Proceedings)* 305, 310. See also Richard Posner, 'No Thanks, We Already Have Our Own Laws', July–August 2004 *Legal Affairs* 40, 42.

[21] *Digest* 1. 2. 2. 49 (Pomponius) ('It was ... Augustus who ... first established that [juristic] opinions might be given under his authority. And from that time this began to be sought as a favour'); also Gaius, *Institutes* 1. 7 ('The answers of the learned are the decisions and opinions of those who are permitted to establish the laws. If all their opinions converge, what they hold has the force of *lex*'). There is a fair amount of dispute over the interpretation of both these passages (see Alan Watson, *Sources of Law, Legal Change and Ambiguity* (Edinburgh: Clark, 1984), 6–7), and there is a diversity of views as to the extent to which, in the classical period, judges would have considered themselves bound to treat juristic opinion as authority. For a sample from the range, see Barry Nicholas, *An Introduction to Roman Law* (Oxford: Clarendon Press, 1962), 31–32; Bruce W. Frier, *The Rise of the Roman Jurists: Studies in Cicero's 'Pro Caecina'* (Princeton: Princeton UP, 1985), 187–188; David Ibbetson, 'Sources of Law from the Republic to the Dominate', in *The Cambridge Companion to Roman Law*, ed. D. Johnston (Cambridge: CUP, 2005), 25–44 at 35–36.

sixth century, Justinian accorded statutory status to all three elements of the *Corpus iuris civilis*—to the compilation of constitutions (*Codex Justinianus*), to the *Digest* of excerpts from (mainly classical period) juristic writings, and even to the student text (the *Institutes*).[22] Roman jurists did not issue—did not conceive themselves to be in the business of issuing—legally binding opinions;[23] for all that their pronouncements could possess a rule-like quality, they were statements about and expositions of the law, responses to legal questions, explanations of legal phenomena.[24] They were, nevertheless, opinions that spurred legal development and were sometimes given legislative force; they were a source of Roman law. After the twelfth-century revival of the *Corpus iuris*, they became sources of law and legal ideas in other systems too.

> The jurists of the early twelfth century had no jurisprudence to draw upon. ... [T]hey ... had to confront the rules that ... ancient Roman jurists ... had laid down to govern very practical questions. What should the proper length of time for a prescription of a property right be? Could women testify in court? Could they hold public office? What role should ignorance of the law play in determining guilt? These questions could be simple and practical, but even the most simple had moral and ethical ramifications. The first teachers of Roman law and their students had to decide how Justinian's authoritative compilation could be used to provide guidance for constructing legal systems that were based on justice and reason ...[25]

There is, nonetheless, a risk of moving too fast when looking to Roman law for evidence of legal scholarship functioning as a primary source. The difficulty is not with the idea that Roman juristic opinion at times did function thus. The difficulty, rather, rests with the idea that it equated to legal scholarship. Some Roman jurists may have been academics—this is probably true of Gaius and Pomponius—and they certainly taught law, in so far as opportunities to teach were available. But jurists were typically upper-class statesmen with legal expertise, who contributed to public life, and influenced the day-to-day practice of the law, by providing (without remuneration) advice on the

---

[22] See Peter Stein, *Roman Law in European History* (Cambridge: CUP, 1999), 32–35; Nicholas, *An Introduction to Roman Law* (n 21) 39–42.

[23] '[I]t is never stated in the sources that such-and-such is a rule of law *because* it was so laid down by jurists'. John Crook, *Law and Life of Rome* (Ithaca: Cornell UP, 1967), 26. (Emphasis in original.)

[24] See Peter Stein, *Regulae Iuris: From Juristic Rules to Legal Maxims* (Edinburgh: Edinburgh UP, 1966), 47–48, 65–66, 90, 102–103.

[25] Kenneth Pennington, 'The "Big Bang": Roman Law in the Early Twelfth-Century' (2007) 18 *Rivista international di diritto commune* 43, 44–45.

drafting of legal documents, the formulation of edicts, and on the application of customary or statutory law (and likely remedies) in individual cases.[26] No doubt the figure of the Roman jurisconsult does, as is commonly maintained, epitomize the centrality of the legal scholar to the civil law tradition.[27] It is nevertheless worth bearing in mind that his modes of legal engagement were very much of his time.

The civil law tradition itself is, of course, a different proposition. Those jurists—glossators—who emerged from the twelfth century onwards, and who set about systematizing and interpreting re-discovered Roman legal texts, were university professors; '[g]losses were clearly a by-product of teaching.'[28] Medieval European law was fragmented—within the same state, the law on a matter could vary from one region to the next—and often unwritten. Judges, when deciding disputes, might find more than one possible answer, or maybe no answer, in local statutes and customs. Majority-supported juristic interpretations of Roman law, *communis opinio*, provided solutions and filled gaps: judges relied on juristic opinion to settle legal disputes when applicable law was impossible to determine, or absent.[29] Glossators associated with *communis opinio* were icons.[30] Late-medieval lore had it that legal arguments out of step with Azo's early thirteenth-century *Summa Codicis* would never be entertained by, let alone make an impression on, a tribunal; if you don't have Azo, the legal proverb ran, you don't go to the *palazzo*.[31] Azo's pupil, Accursius, produced a work, the *Glossa Ordinaria*, which acquired similar status and a comparable tag line: what the gloss—Accursius's *Glossa*—does not recognize, the court does not recognize.[32] By the fourteenth century, works exemplifying the glossatorial tradition 'enjoyed . . . a prestige comparable only with that of

---

[26] See Fritz Schulz, *History of Roman Legal Science* (Oxford: Clarendon Press, 1953 [1946]), 1–2; James Gordley, *The Jurists: A Critical History* (Oxford: OUP, 2013), 5–6; Nicholas, *An Introduction to Roman Law* (n 21) 28–29; Crook, *Law and Life of Rome* (n 23) 89–90; Stein, *Regulae Iuris* (n 24) 27, 83.

[27] See e.g. John Henry Merryman, *The Civil Law Tradition*, 2nd edn (Stanford: Stanford UP, 1985), 57.

[28] Franz Wieacker, *A History of Private Law in Europe: With Particular Reference to Germany*, trans. T. Weir (Oxford: Clarendon Press, 1995), 44.

[29] When litigants lost because a judge overlooked applicable law, moreover, personal judicial liability for delivering an incorrect verdict could be escaped if the judge's mistake was attributable to his having relied on *communis opinio*. Nicolaus Everardus, *Centum modi argumentandi topicorum* (Lyon: de Millis, 1545), 358–360.

[30] See Donald R. Kelley, 'Jurisconsultus Perfectus: The Lawyer as Renaissance Man' (1988) 51 *Jnl Warburg & Courtauld Inst.* 84, 87–88.

[31] *Chi non ha Azzo, non vada a palazzo.* See H. F. Jolowicz, 'Revivals of Roman Law' (1952) 15 *Jnl Warburg & Courtauld Inst.* 88, 96.

[32] *Quidquid non agnoscit glossa nec agnoscit forum.* See Peter Stein, 'Judge and Jurist in the Civil Law: A Historical Interpretation' (1985) 46 *Louisiana L. Rev.* 241, 244–245; C. C. Turpin, 'The Antecedents of Roman-Dutch Law' [1963] *Acta Juridica* 1, 42.

decisions of supreme courts today, save that their authority lasted longer and extended over the whole of [continental] Europe.[33]

Yet works of this stature still only had what medieval logicians (usually drawing on Aristotle) called 'probable' as distinct from 'necessary' authority.[34] As statements of law, opinions set forth in these works were strongly presumed, but not guaranteed, to have binding force.[35] When courts unequivocally treated *communis opinio* as a primary source of law—as happened in Portugal from the 1440s onwards[36]—it was because statutes conferred this status on the works of selected jurists.[37] Medieval and early modern European judges were not averse to following juristic opinion, even in preference to local customs, and they would often only be willing to derogate from it in exceptional circumstances. But, apart from when opinion was made binding by statute, it overstates matters to describe it as law that judges had to apply.

It is nevertheless understandable that modern European academics should regularly observe of civil law scholarship that, even if it is not a primary source of law, it carries, in European legal systems, greater authority than other types of secondary source.[38] Civilian jurists shaped the law, filled legal gaps, advised advocates and judges, explained enacted rules and judicial rulings,[39] and were known to produce text—the incorporation verbatim of passages from Domat and Pothier into the French *Code Civil* illustrates the point[40]—which was converted into law. This willingness to elevate the authority of juristic opinion is not confined to pure civil law systems. When no primary source of law enables South African judges to resolve a matter before them—South Africa has a

---

[33] Wieacker, *A History of Private Law in Europe* (n 28) 58–59.

[34] See e.g. John Buridan (*c.* 1295–1361), *Summulae de dialectica*, trans. G. Klima (New Haven: Yale UP, 2001), 480–481; also Aristotle, *Topica* I. 1. 100^{a}25–100^{b}24.

[35] See Stefan Vogenauer, 'An Empire of Light? Learning and Lawmaking in the History of German Law' (2005) 64 *CLJ* 481, 487.

[36] Legislation enacted at this time (and which remained in force until the eighteenth century) enabled Portuguese courts to resort to Baldus's writings to break judicial deadlocks: Mário Júlio de Almeida Costa, 'Romanisme et Bartolisme dans le droit portugais', in *Bartolo de Sassoferato: Studi e documenti per il VI Centenario*, 2 vols, ed. D. Segoloni (Milan: Giuffrè, 1962), I, 314–345.

[37] See Julius Kirshner, '*Consilia* as Authority in Late Medieval Italy: The Case of Florence', in *Legal Consulting in the Civil Law Tradition*, ed. M. Ascheri et al. (Berkeley: Robbins Collection, 1999), 107–140 at 128 n 71.

[38] See e.g. Franziska Brachthäuser, 'Standardkommentare zwischen Hegemonietheorie und Pragmatismus' (2017) 50 *Kritische Justiz* 448, 450 ('[C]ommentary stands out from other legal sources'); David Kästle-Lamparter, 'Kommentarkulturen? Einführung und historische Einordnung', in *Juristische Kommentare: Ein internationaler Vergleich*, ed. D. Kästle-Lamparter et al. (Tübingen: Mohr Siebeck, 2020), 1–60 at 4–5; Frédéric Zénati, 'L'évolution des sources de droit dans le pays de droit civil' [2002] *Recueil Dalloz* 15, 16–18; Edouart Vieujean, 'Place de la doctrine dans le droit belge actuel' [1997] *Annales de droit de Louvain* 21, 24–25; René David and John E. C. Brierley, *Major Legal Systems in the World Today*, 2nd edn (London: Stevens, 1978), 134–135.

[39] See Stein, 'Judge and Jurist in the Civil Law' (n 32) 249–250.

[40] See R. C. van Caenegem, *Judges, Legislators and Professors: Chapters in European Legal History* (Cambridge: CUP, 1987), 70.

hybrid (civil law–common law) system—the convention is that the court may, rather in the fashion of the International Court of Justice, consult writings by 'authoritative publicists of the law' to see if they might be put to use as binding authority.[41] South Africa's Constitutional Court has, in recent years, even gone so far as to describe 'academic law that is used for teaching purposes' as a form of indigenous law.[42] In the civilian (including the quasi-civilian) legal context, the case for treating juristic writings as not only influencing the application and the creation of law, but also supplying material from which laws are created—which might even serve as law—is not especially difficult to make.

b) *The common law*

The common law tradition poses a bigger challenge. We know that common-law courts are not entirely averse to upgrading the authority of non-binding judicial opinions. But do they ever proceed in a similar fashion when negotiating legal scholarship? Fábio Shecaira offers an insightful and intricately formulated answer in the affirmative.

Shecaira observes that '[s]tandard legal scholarship'—prescriptive scholarship, produced with legal officials and practitioners as well as with other academics in mind—is routinely accorded secondary source status.[43] But what of the notion that it might serve as a 'source of valid (or binding) law'[44] for judges when they make legal judgments? While 'it seems wise ... to ... avoid treating interpretive materials as sources of law',[45] it is also a mistake, Shecaira claims, not to concede that legal scholarship—no less than 'the standard sources'[46]—is sometimes a source of norms which courts have to apply. As with '[l]egislation, precedent, and custom',[47] legal scholarship is, to use the relevant jurisprudential language, a source from which courts can derive norms providing *content-independent* reasons for decisions. Courts which proceed in this way treat norms derived from scholarship as providing sufficient reasons for deciding

---

[41] See Ellison Kahn, 'The Role of Doctrine and Judicial Decisions in South African Law', in *The Role of Judicial Decisions and Doctrine in Civil Law and Mixed Jurisdictions*, ed. J. Dainow (Baton Rouge: Louisiana State UP, 1974), 224–271 at 247–253; also Statute of the International Court of Justice, Art. 38(1)(d) ('The Court ... shall apply ... teachings of the most highly qualified publicists ... as subsidiary means for the determination of rules of law').

[42] *Bhe v Magistrate, Khayelitsha & Ors* 2005 (1) SA 580 (Const. Ct) at para. 152; also *Alexkor Ltd v Richtersveld Community* 2003 (12) BCLR 1301 (Const. Ct) at para. 52.

[43] Fábio Perin Shecaira, *Legal Scholarship as a Source of Law*, 2nd edn (Cham: Springer, 2024), 37–46.

[44] Ibid. 17.

[45] Ibid. 14.

[46] Ibid. 30.

[47] Ibid. 17.

as they do notwithstanding that those reasons may differ from, and require decisions which differ from, whatever reasons the judges responsible for the decisions would come up with were they to reason purely according to their own lights.[48]

Shecaira seems to equivocate over this claim. The essence of content-independence, in the context of judicial decision-making, is that judges must recognize the binding status of (which doesn't mean they can never distinguish or domesticate) an authority even if its content—the stipulations set down in the statute, the *ratio* of the precedent, the burden imposed by a prescribed custom—is not as they would like it to be. The nature of the authority is such that it requires judges to treat it as a reason for decision irrespective of the merits or demerits of doing so; they cannot opt to reject the authority as a reason for decision just because they take exception to its content. It is a mark of authorities of this kind that they are attributable to primary sources. Norms derived from the standard primary sources, according to Shecaira, 'ordinarily defeat conflicting reasons that bear on the wisdom or soundness' of ruling in accordance with the source.[49] But norms derived from secondary sources—the 'role that scholarship often plays'— 'are not authoritative in a strict sense';[50] 'the content-independent reasons for action provided by scholars', indeed, 'are not normally as strong as the content-independent reasons provided by statutes and precedents'.[51]

When is the content-independent reasoning offered up by scholarship ever on a par with that provided by statutes and precedents? '[I]t is conceptually possible for scholarship to be treated as a genuine source of content-independent reasons',[52] because it is 'perfectly conceivable'[53] that a piece, or a body, of legal scholarship could be made into a 'genuine source of law' through an alteration to the content of a legal system's rule of recognition.[54] Indeed, this 'sometimes' does happen.[55] And so to maintain that 'legal scholarship does not *ever* issue such authoritative reasons',[56] that it 'can only play the role of a permissive source of law . . . is false'.[57] It is 'not implausible',[58] in essence, that

---

[48] See ibid. 7–8, 31–35, 53, 85; also—for an overview of content-independence as it bears upon questions concerning the creation, identification, and application of law—Julie Dickson, *Content-Independence in Law* (Cambridge: CUP, 2024).

[49] Shecaira, *Legal Scholarship as a Source of Law*, 2nd edn (n 43) 30.

[50] Ibid., also 32 ('not genuinely authoritative').

[51] Ibid. 116.

[52] Ibid.

[53] Ibid. 53.

[54] Ibid. 21, also 64–65, 147.

[55] Ibid. 53. Art. 38(1)(d) of the Statute of the International Court of Justice (n 41) is a prime example. Other examples are provided in the final paragraph of the previous chapter.

[56] Shecaira, *Legal Scholarship as a Source of Law*, 2nd edn (n 43) 48.

[57] Ibid. 54.

[58] Ibid. 60.

scholarship be enlisted as 'a formal source of law, ... issuing norms that judges regard themselves as being bound (or having reason) to apply.'[59]

But what if there has not been an alteration to the rule of recognition? We have considered already how the weight of some secondary source material might be such that a court deciding a case to which the material relates concludes that, though it is not technically required to treat the material as authority, it would risk being considered certainly eccentric if not outright irresponsible were it not to treat it thus. But choosing, even being under pressure, to treat as binding is not the same as being bound (as *having no choice but to* treat as binding). When a source is a formal source, any reason judges have for applying the norm that it yields must be content-independent. In the absence of an alteration to a system's rule of recognition, when does legal scholarship yield norms comparable to those which law-applying officials derive from orthodox formal sources?

For Shecaira, 'legal scholarship can—and indeed often does—function ... as a source of law. ... [T]hat is, ... it is treated by judges and other legal actors as providing content-independent reasons of varying weight for deciding cases one way or another.'[60] All sources of law carry weight, he maintains, and the difference in weight between legal scholarship and standard issue primary-sources 'is a difference of degree.'[61] In a common law context, however, legal scholarship, even on Shecaira's own account, is a different kind of source than, say, statute or precedent because its status as authority binding on a court depends on its being deployed in conjunction with conventional primary source authority. If judges choose to 'treat a piece of scholarship as providing reasons for action'[62]—and even if, short of being bound, they think they really ought to rely on the scholarship as a source yielding a reason for their decision[63]— the scholarship 'is never by itself a reason for action.'[64] The 'meaning and relevance' of scholarship 'to adjudication depends upon its connection with other sources. It is not ... the kind of source of law that is thought capable of appearing alone in judicial argument.'[65] Even when Shecaira finds a case in which the court relies on scholarship and appears to him to be treating 'just the authors' word' as authority (for the proposition that the civil standard of

---

[59] Ibid. 47.

[60] Ibid. 151; see also 38 ('(more or less weighty) content-independent reasons for deciding cases in a particular way') and 163.

[61] Ibid. 116.

[62] Ibid. 49.

[63] See ibid. 33, also 87.

[64] Ibid. 48, also 53.

[65] Ibid. 165.

proof admits of different degrees of probability depending on the nature of the case),[66] an examination of the relevant judgment tells a different story.[67]

Legal scholarship 'could serve' as a primary source, Shecaira believes, but he concedes that he 'would need ... to show' that the scholarship is '*in fact* ... being used as a source of content-independent reasons for action'.[68] Yet it is difficult to see how legal scholarship can provide genuinely content-independent reasons for reaching particular decisions if it only ever supplies 'reasons that can be *added to* the reasons given by other law-making agents'.[69] If legal scholarship never operates as a stand-alone primary source, reasons offered up by scholarship but not by any recognized primary source are not reasons which judges must negotiate as reasons for deciding particular cases in particular ways irrespective of whether those reasons meet with their approval. Modern judges—like their medieval counterparts—may find juristic writings, particularly a 'consensus of respected writers', difficult to ignore.[70] But there is a difference between establishing that judges consider themselves actually 'enjoined ... to use'[71] secondary sources and establishing that judges understand themselves to be under a burden not to presume that these sources 'can only serve a persuasive function'.[72]

When judges do detect a burden to take account of particular secondary sources, Shecaira acknowledges, the likelihood is that they feel obliged to use them either as interpretive aids or as 'supplements'[73] to applicable law, as additional material which serves 'to bolster their decisions'.[74] He also concedes, however, that 'one would be hard-pressed to find clear examples of scholarly writings being used as mandatory sources of law in modern municipal

---

[66] Ibid. 123.

[67] *R v Oakes* [1986] 1 SCR 133 at para. 67, citing John Sopinka and Sidney N. Lederman, *The Law of Evidence in Civil Cases* (Toronto: Butterworths, 1974), 385 but also *Bater v Bater* [1950] 2 All ER 458 (CA), 459 (Lord Denning) ('The case may be proved by a preponderance of probability, but there may be degrees of probability within that standard. The degree depends on the subject-matter. A civil court ... require[s] a degree of probability which is commensurate with the occasion'). At the page in Sopinka and Lederman referred to by the court, the authors cite as authority for the proposition Ritchie J's observation (in *McGregor v Ryan* [1965] SCR 757, 766) that '[t]he extent of the proof required is proportionate to the gravity of the suspicion and the degree of suspicion varies with the circumstances of each case'.

[68] Shecaira, *Legal Scholarship as a Source of Law*, 2nd edn (n 43) 52 n 13. (Emphasis in original.) In the doctorate on which the first edition of the book is based, his position was that the relevant scholarship 'can serve as genuine (probably permissive) sources of law' in cases 'where law is not clearly settled'. Fábio P. Shecaira, *Legal Scholarship as a Source of Law* (Ph.D. dissertation, McMaster University (Department of Philosophy), 2011), 84 n 34.

[69] Shecaira, *Legal Scholarship as a Source of Law*, 2nd edn (n 43) 163–164. (Emphasis in original.)

[70] Ibid. 55.

[71] Ibid. 58

[72] Ibid. 65.

[73] Ibid. 56, also 46.

[74] Ibid. 52.

systems'.[75] An eminent English legal academic, Peter Birks, once seemed to suggest that the modern common law offers up many examples of legal scholarship serving as a primary source. '[T]he self-image of the common law as judge-made is', he maintained, 'incomplete. It is judge-and-jurist-made. The common law is to be found in its library, and the law library is nowadays not written only by its judges but also by its jurists'.[76] Yet all the examples adduced by Birks are of the types that we will encounter in chapter 8 (and which are central to Shecaira's argument),[77] examples which show jurists not to be making law but rather to be influencing or assisting law-makers—which show them to be contributing to the 'interpretative development of the law'[78] by supplying sources of reasoning and information on which legislatures and courts might draw when determining whether or how to create new or fashion existing law.

Judicial *dicta* and foreign judgments are, we know, types of secondary source material that are amenable to being made to perform as primary source material. It is tempting to speculate (I once did speculate)[79] that the reason legal scholarship is not equally amenable is that judges who produce non-binding—foreign, *obiter*, concurring, dissenting, extra-curial—opinion are in the business of delivering binding judgments as well, whereas the delivery of judicial rulings is not in an academic lawyer's job-description. Courts might be receptive to upgrading the non-binding utterances of legal actors who also deliver binding opinions, but wary of doing the same with non-binding opinions issued by legal actors whose opinions never bind.

The speculation meets with at least two objections. First, non-binding opinions do not gain special authority just because the people who deliver them are in the business of making law. That a law review article is the work of a judge moonlighting as an academic doesn't invest it with the binding force denied to regular law review articles. And while judges accept statutes as law, they withhold that status from the opinions that lawmakers advance when debating the texts that the legislature enacts. Secondly, perhaps more importantly, we move far too quickly if we conclude that legal scholarship *tout court* is, unlike *obiter* judicial opinion, never accorded *de facto* binding status by common-law

---

[75] Ibid. 57.

[76] Peter Birks, 'The Academic and the Practitioner' (1998) 18 *Legal Studies* 397, 399.

[77] 'When a judge uses a scholar's work as a source of guidance on how to resolve a case that could not be resolved simply by applying prescriptions contained within other sources of law, the scholar ... actively contributes to the shaping of the law.' Shecaira, *Legal Scholarship as a Source of* Law, 2nd edn (n 43) 148.

[78] Birks, 'The Academic and the Practitioner' (n 76) 413.

[79] Neil Duxbury, 'The Law of the Land' (2015) 78 *MLR* 26, 53–54.

courts. Being hard-pressed to find clear examples is not the same as drawing a blank.

Those who caution against drawing a blank tend to cite a specific form of legal scholarship to make their case: treatise writing. Recently, the capacity of the treatise to serve as legal authority has been analysed with particular care by a private law scholar, Andy Summers, who considers the impact of Harvey McGregor's treatise on the law of damages on English mitigation doctrine. 'McGregor on Damages', according to Summers, 'stands above all others for its influence on the conventional understanding of mitigation. . . . In several cases, whole passages from McGregor . . . have been cited by courts verbatim, sometimes directly as authority instead of citing judicial precedents.'[80] He backs up this observation with pinpoint references to passages in judicial opinions where McGregor is quoted extensively and often referred to repeatedly. In one opinion, two legal propositions are mentioned together, and the treatise is invoked as authority for one of them while final court precedent is cited as authority for the other.[81] Most of the cases noted by Summers attest, nevertheless, to the distinction implicit in his observation: judges sometimes forgo citing precedents and cite McGregor instead because it accurately and economically captures law offered up more obtusely or circuitously by the actual precedents.[82] In none of the cases that Summers cites—even in the one where the treatise and the precedent are accorded the same authoritative weight—is McGregor being treated as law applicable to the facts of the dispute. Common-law courts are no more likely to 'apply' legal treatises, indeed, than they are to distinguish them, overrule them, hold them to be per incuriam, adjudicate on their compatibility with fundamental rights, or rely on judicially recognized interpretive principles and presumptions when problems arise with the meaning of the text.

In the United States, there are treatises, some of them iconic, which almost always feature in decisions on particular points of law: reference to them is 'virtually mandatory'.[83] Legal theorists who make this observation are also

---

[80] Andy Summers, Mitigation in the Law of Damages (Oxford: OUP, 2025), 17–18.

[81] Borealis AB v Geogas Trading SA [2010] EWHC 2789 (Comm) at [50] (Gross J).

[82] From among the cases that Summers cites, see e.g. Lagden v O'Connor [2003] UKHL 64 at [78] (Lord Scott) (McGregor as an authoritative statement of 'well established law'); Sayce v TNT (UK) Ltd [2011] EWCA Civ 1583 at [29] (Moore-Bick LJ) ('[T]he principle . . . to be derived from the leading cases and summarised in McGregor on Damages'); Linklaters Business Services v Sir Robert McAlpine Ltd [2010] EWHC 2931 (TCC) at [159] (Akenhead J) (McGregor as an authoritative statement of the 'rule' pronounced by Haldane LC in British Westinghouse v Underground Electric Railways Co. [1912] AC 673).

[83] Amy J. Griffin, 'Dethroning the Hierarchy of Authority' (2018) 97 Oregon L. Rev. 51, 75; also Frederick Schauer, 'Authority and Authorities' (2008) 94 Va L. Rev. 1931, 1958.

wont to argue that it is incoherent to describe a non-mandatory authority as a 'persuasive authority'—there is no need for an authority to be persuasive[84]— and that the more accurate term is 'optional authority'.[85] If courts treat reference to a treatise as *de facto* mandatory in certain types of case, describing the treatise as optional authority is hardly accurate. Treatises, however, highlight how legal source content might not be optional authority but also not attributable to a primary source of law. If a court were to determine that it had no option but to resort to a particular treatise on a point of law, the treatise would not become 'mandatory authority' in the way that this term describes primary source material, unless judges thereby became compelled to treat treatise content as dispositive (as distinct from providing an authoritative interpretation or summary) of that point of law—unless, that is, they were to recognize the treatise as yielding content-independent reasons for the court's decision on a legal matter.

It is quite common, in the United States, for legal analysts to argue that courts are sometimes compelled not only to resort to a treatise, but also to resort to it as a source of law rather than as a source of legal information. There was, according to Melvin Eisenberg, a period in the twentieth century when 'certain . . . treatises were frequently cited by courts in the same way as binding precedents'.[86] He stops short of putting these treatises on a par with binding precedents. They are cited, he maintains, as 'authoritative although not legally binding rules'.[87]

The evidence he presents in fact supports a different conclusion: that treatises can yield authoritative, but not legally binding, representations or synopses of legal rules. In *Contemporary Mission, Inc. v Famous Music Corp.* (1977), the Second Circuit appeared—Eisenberg certainly considers it—to be treating § 411 of *Williston on Contracts* as authority for the proposition that one cannot assign contractual liabilities without the consent of the party to whom one is liable. The court provided a quotation containing this proposition and a justification for it, followed by a reference to § 411.[88] But the court also made it clear that its reference to § 411 omitted a footnote. Look to the footnote and one finds that, while the justification for the proposition endorsed by the court

---

[84] J. D. Heydon, 'Threats to Judicial Independence: The Enemy Within' (2013) 129 *LQR* 205, 210 ('Authorities are followed because they are authorities, not because their reasoning is admired'); see also Schauer, 'Authority and Authorities' (n 83) 1943.

[85] See Griffin, 'Dethroning the Hierarchy of Authority' (n 83) 65–66; Schauer, 'Authority and Authorities' (n 83) 1946.

[86] Melvin A. Eisenberg, *Legal Reasoning* (Cambridge: CUP, 2022), 39.

[87] Ibid.

[88] *Contemporary Mission, Inc. v Famous Music Corp.*, 557 F.2d 918, 924 (2nd Cir. 1977).

is indeed from *Williston*, the quotation of the actual proposition in the text of the opinion is taken from a late-nineteenth-century judgment of the Maryland Court of Appeals.[89]

What seems more clear-cut in *Contemporary Mission* is the court's citation of § 418 of *Williston* as authority for the proposition that '[t]he assignment of a bilateral contract includes both an assignment of rights and a delegation of duties'.[90] In this instance, the court summarizes rather than quotes from *Williston*. But it is summarizing a summary: § 418 refers to a number of cases as authority for the proposition that 'when a bilateral contract still executory on both sides is spoken of as assignable it can mean no more than that performance of the duties can be delegated and that the rights can be assigned'.[91] In *Contemporary Mission*, *Williston* is used not in the same way as a binding precedent would be used, but rather to provide a statement or conspectus of precedential authority (just as another contracts treatise referenced in the case, *Calamari & Perillo*, is used to explain the distinction between assignment and delegation).[92] *Williston* is used, in short, much as English courts use *McGregor on Damages* when deciding cases concerning mitigation doctrine.

Precisely how *Williston* was being used in *Contemporary Mission* would likely not have been lost on Samuel Williston himself. When William Draper Lewis, the founding President of the American Law Institute (ALI), was asked to state the law of agency as it existed in the United States in 1925, he confessed his 'habit, when it comes to saying what the law is all over the United States, of leaning on my friend Williston',[93] who happened to be sitting alongside him and whose five-volume treatise had been published in its first edition over the previous four years.[94] According to Lewis, Williston endorsed 'a number of *dicta* in favor of the law as ... expressed' in a proposed Restatement provision. But the endorsement was authoritative, Lewis was careful to add, only in the sense that it confirmed, as regards the common-law principles of agency, that 'you cannot say what the law of the United States is with positiveness'.[95] Lewis's basic contention—Williston did not demur!—was that a treatise writer might

---

[89] *Eastern Advertising Co. v McGaw*, 42 A. 923, 925 (Md 1899), where McSherry CJ formulates the proposition—for which he cites precedent—in the course of considering British contracts treatises.

[90] *Contemporary Mission* (n 88) 924, quoting Samuel Williston, *A Treatise on the Law of Contracts*, 3rd edn, ed. W. H. E. Jaeger (New York: Baker, Voorhis & Co., 1960), § 418.

[91] *Williston* (n 90) § 418, citing, *inter alia, Anderson v De Urioste*, 96 Cal. 404 (Cal. 1892).

[92] *Contemporary Mission* (n 88) 924, quoting John D. Calamari and Joseph M. Perillo, *The Law of Contracts* (St Paul: West Publishing Co., 1970), § 254.

[93] 'Minutes of the Third Annual [ALI] Meeting Held in Washington, DC—May 1 and 2, 1925' (1925) 3 *ALI Proceedings* 82, 199.

[94] Samuel Williston, *The Law of Contracts*, 5 vols (New York: Baker, Voorhis & Co., 1920–1924).

[95] 'Minutes of the Third Annual [ALI] Meeting' (n 93) 199.

be trusted to capture the intricacies of, but was not to be considered a creator of, the rules that judges apply when they decide cases.

The following decade, Williston served as the reporter for the ALI's First Restatement of Contracts. From the outset, the ALI intended the Restatements to be a weightier form of authority than legal treatises; while Williston the Restatement contributor was not a lawmaker, his product ranked higher in the secondary source pecking order than did that of Williston the treatise writer. Then, as now, the quasi-juristic output of the ALI was considered to be, first and foremost, a category of non-binding source material. But the Restatements were to take on a life of their own—arguments that Restatement provisions can acquire genuine primary source status would become more prevalent and, indeed, more convincing. It is easy to exaggerate the idea, and American lawyers do sometimes exaggerate the idea, that Restatements are legally binding in their own right. But, as will become clear in the next chapter, the notion has some truth to it.

6

Code source

The argument that legal scholarship can acquire *de facto* binding status becomes more convincing if the category is taken to include those works—typically produced by, or with contributions from, academic lawyers—which fit under the general heading of 'non-legislative codifications'; works which, in the United States, are devised by the ALI and are called 'Restatements of the Law'.[1] Nils Jansen argues that even though works of this type are not the product of law-making institutions, they sometimes yield propositions which are 'regarded as effectively binding in legal discourse',[2] 'ultimate authority without requiring further justification',[3] assertions 'which may assume similar or even greater authority than legislation in actual legal practice'.[4]

The authority which these propositions assume Jansen terms 'textual authority'.[5] If a legal text has authority, he argues, 'the legal profession' has made a determination that it is to be accepted 'as an ultimate source of the law, without requiring further legal reasons to do so';[6] 'the idea of textual authority . . . denotes the . . . content-independent force . . . of textual sources of the law, such as legislation, judicial decisions, or textbooks and commentaries'.[7] If statements contained in a legal text are authoritative not because they 'can be taken as

---

[1] Few English law texts are devised as restatements. But it is not a non-existent genre: see *A Restatement of the English Law of Contract*, 2nd edn (Oxford: OUP, 2020); *A Restatement of the English Law of Unjust Enrichment* (Oxford: OUP, 2012). Moreover, some iconic English legal texts not only have restatement-like content but are accorded restatement-like status by the legal profession and the courts: besides *McGregor on Damages* (chapter 5, section (b)), see e.g. *Dicey, Morris & Collins on the Conflict of Laws*, 16th edn (London: Sweet & Maxwell, 2023); *Goff & Jones: The Law of Unjust Enrichment*, 10th edn (London: Sweet & Maxwell, 2022);and, for illustrative treatments, see e.g. *Skatteforvaltningen v Solo Capital Partners* [2023] UKSC 40; *H.& P. Advisory v Barrick Gold* [2025] EWHC 562 (Ch).

[2] Nils Jansen, *The Making of Legal Authority: Non-legislative Codifications in Historical and Comparative Perspective* (Oxford: OUP, 2010), 5.

[3] Ibid. 8.

[4] Ibid. 84, also 138. (Jansen observes of 'doctrinal treatises and commentaries' that 'they have often influenced and changed the law'. Ibid. 90. It is perhaps more accurate to claim that they have often prompted or inspired changes to, rather than they have changed, the law.)

[5] Ibid. 41.

[6] Ibid. 43, see also 96. On the legal profession determining textual authority, see ibid. 45, also 49 and 89.

[7] Ibid. 41–42.

Law's Sources. Neil Duxbury, Oxford University Press. © Neil Duxbury 2025.
DOI: 10.1093/9780198981183.003.0006

binding commands', but because they 'may be understood as arguments that must be taken into consideration',[8] then they are not content-independent reasons for judicial decisions. Jansen contends that non-legislative codifications can have content-independent force—that, notwithstanding the distinction to be drawn 'between the law and its scholarly description',[9] they are sometimes 'used as immediately applicable law'.[10]

The principal difficulty with this contention is that a codification of this kind is, as Jansen himself explains, a 'largely declaratory'[11] distillation or explanation of existing legal authority: an exercise in 'stating the law'.[12] Even his more sinuous version of the argument—that 'non-legislative codifications can only gain legal authority if they can be understood as a conveniently applicable expression of the law'[13]—runs into the objection that courts apply law rather than statements of the law, that it is not the statements but the laws they state which have binding force. Two of his other modern examples of non-legislative codifications (aside from the Restatements) serve to illustrate the difficulty. The Principles of European Contract Law have been 'recognized by . . . scholars, as a "source of law" in a broad sense, and they have even been treated as authoritative reference texts by European courts'.[14] But though they might 'very much look like an official piece of legislation',[15] they cannot by themselves be immediately applicable law but rather must be transformed into such by a replicating enactment or 'a judicial change of the law'.[16] Similarly the Principles of International Commercial Contracts (PICC), published under the auspices of the International Institute for the Unification of Private Law (known as UNIDROIT): 'arbitrators are increasingly inclined to apply' the PICC,[17] yet it is used not as immediately applicable law but 'in a formal sense . . . as . . . *obiter dictum*'[18] or a 'non-legislative reference text. . . . It is therefore applied subsidiarily'—priority being given to national legislative solutions for choice-of-law disputes—'and it informs the interpretation of a particular law'.[19]

---

[8] Ibid. 42.
[9] Ibid. 119 (though cf 124–125, where Jansen queries this distinction as applied to one form of German legal commentary).
[10] Ibid. 81.
[11] Ibid. 86.
[12] Ibid. 90.
[13] Ibid. 110.
[14] Ibid. 62.
[15] Ibid. 64.
[16] Ibid., and, on replicating enactment, see 63.
[17] Ibid. 72.
[18] Ibid. 73.
[19] Ibid. 74, and see also 77.

a) *The US Restatements*

Are non-legislative codifications ever exercises 'in *making* legal authority'[20] rather than merely 'authoritative statements of the law'?[21] The ALI's Restatements are different from other codification initiatives, Jansen believes, because lawyers and legal officials sometimes accord them the status of 'proposal[s] of . . . new rules'[22]—rules with 'legal authority for which no further support is necessary'.[23] Even the ALI's founders were insistent that a Restatement would be more than a 'mere academic restatement of the law': '[t]o fulfill its objects', it was proposed, 'the restatement must have authority greater than that . . . accorded to any legal treatise, an authority more nearly on a par with that accorded the decisions of the courts'.[24] From the time of the ALI's inception onwards, orthodoxy has had it that, even though the Restatements are not a primary source of law, it is somehow inaccurate to categorize them as just another type of secondary source.[25]

But what of the stronger claim—Jansen is not alone in making it[26]—that a Restatement will in some cases serve as, might even be unusually effective as, a primary source? American law lends weight to this claim in three distinct ways. First, a US federal court might rely on a Restatement provision when 'declaring' federal common law.[27] Instances in which courts make such declarations do, occasionally, show judges purporting to identify as applicable law the position set out in a Restatement.[28] It is more common, however, for

---

[20] Ibid. 76. (Emphasis in original.)

[21] Ibid. 133, and see also 137.

[22] Ibid. 134, and see also 89 ('the status which is assigned to them by participants to the legal discourse').

[23] Ibid. 54–55, and see also 93, 132 ('establishing legal authority').

[24] *Report of the Committee on the Establishment of a Permanent Organization for the Improvement of the Law Proposing the Establishment of an American Law Institute*, at (1923) 1 *Proceedings of the American Law Institute* 1, 29.

[25] See e.g. Herbert F. Goodrich, 'The Story of the American Law Institute' [1951] *Washington Univ. L. Q.* 283, 290–292; John P. Frank, 'The American Law Institute, 1923–1998' (1998) 26 *Hofstra L. Rev.* 615, 621; Shyamkrishna Balganesh, 'Relying on Restatements' (2022) 122 *Columb. L. Rev.* 2119, 2129 ('Restatements quite deliberately straddle the divide between primary and secondary authority').

[26] In a similar vein, see e.g. David V. Snyder, 'Private Lawmaking' (2003) 64 *Ohio State L. J.* 371, 384 ('[T]he ALI . . . make[s] law, at least in a practical sense'); Amy J. Griffin, 'Dethroning the Hierarchy of Authority' (2018) 97 *Oregon L. Rev.* 51, 103; Melvin A. Eisenberg, *Legal Reasoning* (Cambridge: CUP, 2022), 37–38; Frederick Schauer, 'The Restatements as Law', in *The American Law Institute: A Centennial History*, ed. A. S. Gold and R. W. Gordon (Oxford: OUP, 2023), 425–440.

[27] Richard L. Revesz, 'Restatements and the Federal Common Law', *ALI Quarterly Newsletter*, 27 September 2016 at 3.

[28] See e.g. *Schoenberg v Exportadora de Sal*, 930 F.2d 777, 782 (9th Cir. 1991) ('Federal common law follows the approach of the Restatement (Second) of Conflict of Laws'); *Harris v Polskie Linie Lotnicze*, 820 F.2d 1000, 1003 (9th Cir. 1987) ('The Restatement (Second) of Conflict of Laws (1969) . . . is a source of general choice-of-law principles and an appropriate starting point for applying federal common law in this area'); *United States v Hercules, Inc.*, 247 F.3d 706, 717 (8th Cir. 2001) ('The

judges to acknowledge—if only tacitly—that the law being declared is not the Restatement but the law that the Restatement restates: '[f]ederal common law tracks the consensus of states', the Seventh Circuit observed in 1995, and so '[w]e ... turn to the *Restatement of Restitution* (1937), which summarizes the dominant themes of state common law'.[29] Secondly, it is not unknown for jurisdiction-specific rules of recognition to confer on Restatements the status of binding authority: two US territorial legislatures have—rather as medieval European assemblies occasionally accorded primary source status to *communis opinio* (see chapter 5, section (a))—statutorily incorporated the Restatements as *de facto* common law rules, to be followed by the territory's courts in the absence of applicable local laws.[30]

Most forms of modern juristic writing—certainly academic monographs and articles—resist recognition as binding authority, whether or not there exists the will to accord them this status, because they yield neither the canonical form of words that a statute has nor the holding, or *ratio decidendi*, that a precedent has; they contain nothing resembling an enforceable rule. The point was slightly overstated but captured nevertheless by the renowned twentieth-century international-court judge, Gerald Fitzmaurice, when he observed that a primary source-authority typically 'has an actuality and a concrete character that causes it to impinge directly on the matters at issue, in a way that an abstract [juristic] opinion, however good, can never do'.[31] Restatements are atypical as

---

universal starting point for divisibility of harm analyses in CERCLA cases is the Restatement (Second) of Torts').

[29] *Central States SE & SW Areas Health & Welfare Fund v Pathology Labs of Arkansas*, 71 F.3d 1251, 1254 (7th Cir. 1995). For observations in the same vein, see *Long Island Savings Bank v United States*, 503 F.3d 1234, 1245 (Fed. Cir. 2007); *United States v Monsanto Co.*, 858 F.2d 160, 172 (4th Cir. 1988).

[30] The code of the Northern Mariana Islands contains, and the code of the Virgin Islands used to contain, an operative provision to the effect that common law rules as expressed in the ALI's Restatements 'shall be the rules of decision' in the territory's courts in the absence of local laws to the contrary: see *US Virgin Islands Code* title 1, § 4; *Northern Mariana Islands Commonwealth Code* title 7, § 3401; *Commonwealth Ports Authority v Leo E. Daly Co.*, No. 1:12–CV–0005, 2013 WL 12244456 1, 4 (Dist. Ct Northern Mariana Islands, 20 February 2013) ('[T]he right to indemnity is embodied in the Restatement (Third) of Torts'); also Kristen David Adams, 'The Folly of Uniformity? Lessons from the Restatement Movement' (2004) 33 *Hofstra L. Rev.* 423; Richard L. Revesz, 'Restatements as Legislative Enactments', *ALI Quarterly Newsletter*, 7 August 2018 at 1–3. The Virgin Islands provision was impliedly repealed in 2004, and the territory's Supreme Court, since acquiring appellate jurisdiction in 2007, has viewed Restatements as 'merely ... persuasive authority, just like law review commentaries and decisions rendered by courts outside of the Virgin Islands' (*Government of Virgin Islands v Connor*, 60 VI 597, 602 (SC VI 2014)). There are instances, nevertheless, in which the Court still elects to adopt (or continue to follow) Restatement provisions as representative of the territory's law: see e.g. *Banks v International Rental & Leasing Corp.*, 55 VI 967, 982–983 (SC VI 2011); also Kristen David Adams, 'Living With *Banks*: Trends and Lessons from the First Five Years' (2017) 46 *Stetson L. Rev.* 391.

[31] Gerald Fitzmaurice, 'Some Problems Regarding the Formal Sources of International Law', in *Symbolae Verzijl: Présentées au professeur J. H. W. Verzijl à l'occasion de son LXXX-ième anniversaire* (The Hague: Nijhoff, 1958), 153–176 at 172.

secondary sources, because they contain rule-like elements. The primary or 'black-letter' text contained in a Restatement is—perhaps so that courts might engage with it much as they would with the enacted law—deliberately drafted like statutory text.[32] Since the formulation of Restatement provisions makes them amenable to being co-opted as legal rules, it is perhaps not surprising— here we come to the third, and the most intriguing, illustration of the American Law Institute's output being accorded primary source status—that state courts should sometimes choose to adopt Restatement provisions as 'authoritative' rather than advisory,[33] as statute-like expressions of the jurisdiction's common law as it applies in particular cases.

Some academic lawyers argue that Restatement provisions are legal rules in their own right because 'it is reasonable to predict that most courts will follow them'[34]—because they provide 'a good indicator of what the court will do'.[35] The basic flaw in this position is that it neglects what medieval civilians framed as a distinction (see, again, chapter 5, section (a)) between necessary and probable authority: it presumes a statement about the law on a matter to have validity as a legal rule simply by virtue of the fact that judicial decisions on the matter will most likely align with the statement. The more pressing question concerns judicial adoptions of Restatement provisions: do they modify the content of a jurisdiction's rule of recognition, so that Restatements become primary sources of law?

Courts regularly adopt Restatement provisions as authoritative explanations of legal principles, representations of applicable rules, definitions of terms and concepts, formulations of legal tests, and the like. 'The Restatement (Second) Conflict of Laws . . . summarizes the rules which we think are applicable to this case . . . [and] which we adopt.'[36] '[W]e adopt and apply the principles

[32] See ALI, *Capturing the Voice of the American Law Institute: A Handbook for ALI Reporters and Those Who Review Their Work*, rev. edn (Philadelphia: American Law Institute, 2015), 5, and see also 37 ('[T]he black-letter provisions are intended to constitute a model statute, they should be drafted in the form of a codification of the subject in question'); Balganesh, 'Relying on Restatements' (n 25) 2123 ('Restatements . . . embody very distinct structural similarities to statutes . . . in the unstated hope that courts will engage them just as they do ordinary statutes'). Although juristic writings generally lack these structural similarities, Restatements sometimes derive content from them: see *Neurotron v Medical Service Association of Pennsylvania, Inc.*, 254 F.3d 444, 451 n 4 (3rd Cir. 2001).

[33] See e.g. *Coward v Wellmont Health System*, 812 S.E.2d 766, 771 (Va 2018); *Ackerman v Sobol Family Partnership*, 4 A.3d 288, 300 (Conn. 2010) ('[T]he applicable Restatements of the Law . . . have served as authoritative support for many of our holdings'); *SmithKline Beecham v Doe*, 903 S.W.2d 347, 351 (Tex. 1995); *Reitmeyer v Sprecher*, 243 A.2d 395, 398 (Pa 1968); also *Alfaro-Huitron v Cervantes Agribusiness*, 982 F.3d 1242, 1250–1251 (10th Cir. 2020).

[34] Gregory E. Maggs, 'Ipse Dixit: The Restatement (Second) of Contracts and the Modern Development of Contract Law' (1998) 66 *Geo. Wash. L. Rev.* 508, 513.

[35] Snyder, 'Private Lawmaking' (n 26) 382.

[36] *Mitchell v Craft*, 211 So.2d 509, 515–516 (Miss. 1968).

enunciated in the Restatement of Torts, Second, 400 and 402A.[37] State court jurisprudence offers up an abundance of pronouncements like these.[38] But courts can also be seen adopting or affirming Restatement provisions as 'the law' of the relevant jurisdiction: 'Restatement (Second) of Torts, § 460 is the law in Colorado';[39] '[w]e adopt Restatement [(Third) of Restitution & Unjust Enrichment] § 30 as the governing law for this case'.[40] Granted, judges are more likely to observe that Restatements are not law.[41] Granted, too, that judicial assertions to the effect that a Restatement provision is being adopted as law will, in some instances, be but shorthand for a more prosaic manoeuvre: adoption of the provision 'as an appropriate statement of the law'.[42] When, for example, the Supreme Court of Arizona observed in 1985 that, '[i]n the absence of contrary authority Arizona courts follow the Restatement of the Law', it supported the observation with Arizona case law in which Restatement provisions were being relied on not as applicable legal rules but as authoritative synopses of the applicable rules.[43]

Nevertheless, the notion that a provision might be adopted as actual binding law is not entirely fanciful. There are certainly cases in which adoption has been deemed necessary to plug a legal gap.[44] When adoption serves this function, the Restatement provision acquires, at the very least, what civil lawyers call 'relative force'—it binds parties in the case before the court.[45] The greater

---

[37] *Soileau v Nicklos Drilling Co.*, 302 F.Supp. 119, 127 (WD La 1969).

[38] See e.g. *Scott v Kay*, 227 A.2d 572, 574 (Del. 1967); *Distad v Cubin*, 633 P.2d 167, 175 n 7 (Wyo. 1981) ('The Restatement, Torts 2d contains and we adopt . . . the following definitions pertinent not only to this rule but as may otherwise be used in this opinion'); *Leithead v American Colloid Co.*, 721 P.2d 1059, 1065–1067 (Wyo. 1986); *A. W. v Lancaster County School District*, 784 N.W.2d 907, 918 (Neb. 2010) ('[W]e find the clarification of the duty analysis contained in the Restatement (Third) of Torts, § 7, to be compelling, and we adopt it'); *Ludman v Davenport Assumption High School*, 895 N.W.2d 902, 910 (Iowa 2017).

[39] *Smartt v Lamar Oil Co.*, 623 P.2d 73, 75 (Colo. App. 1980).

[40] *Birchwood Land Co. v Krizan*, 115 A.3d 1009, 1015 (Vt 2015). In a similar vein, see *Phillips v General Motors Corp.*, 995 P.2d 1002, 1015 (Mont. 2000) ('[W]e adopt the Restatement (Second) of Conflict of Laws for tort actions'); *N. Country Villas Homeowners' Association v Kokenge*, 163 P.3d 1247, 1250 (Kan. App. Ct 2007); *Rivera v Philip Morris, Inc.*, 209 P.3d 271, 276 (Nev. 2009).

[41] See e.g. *Helmerich & Payne Int'l Drilling Co. v Petróleos de Venezuela*, No. 11-CV-1735 (CRC), 2024 WL 4253142 1, 16 (DC Dist. Ct, 20 September 2024); *Cobb v Washington Metro. Area Transit Authority*, No. 20-CV-3522 (BAH), 2021 WL 2935891 1, 7 n 4 (DC Dist. Ct, 13 July 2021) ('Restatements are statements of general legal principles, not binding law'); *McCants v NCAA*, 201 F.Supp.3d 732, 742–743 (MD NC 2016).

[42] *Paull v Park County*, 218 P.3d 1198, 1205 (Mont. 2009).

[43] *Bank of America v J. & S. Auto Repairs*, 694 P.2d 246, 248 (Ariz. 1985).

[44] See e.g. *Hornung v Richardson-Merrill, Inc.*, 317 F.Supp. 183, 184 (Mont. 1970) ('In the absence of a controlling decision of the Supreme Court of the State of Montana, the federal courts in Montana sitting in diversity cases have looked to and adopted as the applicable rule of law in Montana the Restatement of the Law of Torts, Second, and the strict liability rule announced therein. The strict liability rule will be applied in this case').

[45] See Balganesh, 'Relying on Restatements' (n 25) 2160 ('[The court's] ability to formulate the law is tied to its common law decision-making, which is in theory limited to its formal holding and disposition. Consequently, despite such adoption into the law—and not just into its own rule of decision—any

likelihood, however, is that the court espies no gap but rather is overruling its own precedent in favour of the Restatement, so that the relevant provision is binding on a point of law not only in the immediate case but in future ones as well.[46] 'We adopt today the Second Restatement's imposition of strict liability for abnormally dangerous activities', the Supreme Judicial Court of Maine pronounced in 2009, and '[i]n doing so, we overrule our prior opinions requiring proof of negligence in blasting cases'.[47] Likewise the Supreme Court of Pennsylvania sixty years earlier: '[t]o the extent that past cases are in conflict with the view of section 339 of the Restatement of the Law of Torts, which we have adopted, they are no longer authority'.[48] State court judges, one of the ALI's advisers has observed, might 'rely on an individual Restatement-rule to justify a decision and thus create a precedent for future cases'.[49] The discussion has moved some distance from the question posed in the previous chapter—whether any type of secondary source apart from non-binding judicial opinion is ever upgraded so that it performs as a primary source—but now we have an answer to it: there are certainly instances in which the Restatements, primarily through adoption, are to be found, perhaps uniquely among secondary sources without judicial origin, functioning as primary sources of law.

When, by virtue of judicial adoption, Restatements acquire primary source status, of what sort of law are they a source? Although they synthesize and explicate general common law, they do so through formulations resembling statute law.[50] Courts, perhaps not surprisingly, occasionally resort to

---

formal legal authority that such adoption invests in the Restatement provision is closely tied to the court's own application of it in the case being decided'). On relative force, see *Code Civil* Art. 1355 ('L'autorité de la chose jugée n'a lieu qu'à l'égard de ce qui a fait l'objet du jugement [The authority of res judicata applies only with regard to what was made the object of judgment]'); *Codice Civile* Art. 2909; *Zivilprozessordnung* § 325(1); also Sebastian Lewis, *Justifying Precedent in Law* (D.Phil. dissertation, Oxford University (Faculty of Law), 2022), 48–49.

[46] See Balganesh, 'Relying on Restatements' (n 25) 2160–2161.

[47] *Dyer v Maine Drilling & Blasting, Inc.*, 984 A.2d 210, 215 (Maine 2009).

[48] *Bartleson v Glen Alden Coal Co.*, 64 A.2d 846, 851 (Pa 1949); also *Street v Calvert*, 541 S.W.2d 576, 583 (Tenn. 1976) ('It is our opinion that the rules governing all aspects of the last clear chance doctrine are best stated in the Restatement of the Law, Torts, 2d, ss 479, 480. We adopt said sections as the law in Tennessee governing last clear chance and overrule all the cases in conflict with the principles contained therein'). In *Bartleson*, the conflict between past cases and section 339 was not especially pronounced: see Henry A. Gladstone, 'The Supreme Court of Pennsylvania and Section 339 of the Restatement of Torts: A Case Study of Opinion-Writing' (1965) 113 *Univ. Pa L. Rev.* 563.

[49] Joachim Zekoll, 'Das American Law Institute—ein Vorbild für Europa?', in *Globalisierung und Entstaatlichung des Rechts. Teil. 2: Nichtstaatliches Privatrecht—Geltung und Genese*, ed. R. Zimmermann et al. (Tübingen: Mohr Siebeck, 2008), 101–127 at 115.

[50] '[T]he Restatements of Contracts', according to Richard Brooks, 'have achieved the status of a canon . . . a body of texts through and around which knowledge of the common law of promissory exchange is acquired, debated, and refined'. Richard R. W. Brooks, 'Canon and Fireworks: Reliance in the Restatements on Contracts and Reliance on Them', in Gold and Gordon (eds), *The American Law*

basic principles of statutory interpretation when ascertaining the meaning of a Restatement's black-letter content. It is evident '[f]rom a literal reading of the language of the Restatement' (Second) of Torts § 402A, an Alabama district court ventured in 1993, 'that the doctrine of strict liability is limited to users and consumers of the defective product'.[51] But Restatements are not—since the ALI has no legislative mandate from the electorate, they cannot be—enacted law. 'Even where this Court has "adopted" a section of the Restatement as the law of Pennsylvania', the Supreme Court of Pennsylvania cautioned in 1991, 'the language is not to be considered controlling in the manner of a statute.... Were it otherwise, our recognition of the work of the American Law Institute would approach an improper conferral of legislative authority'.[52] The Court elaborated on the point in 2014:

> the adoption of a restatement formulation intended to advance the law cannot be so unmoored from existing common law ... that it amounts in actuality or public perception ... to ... the ... suggestion that ... [legislative] authority is reposed in the Judiciary or in the American Law Institute.... [T]he language of a provision of the restatement ... has not been vetted through the crucible of the legislative process.[53]

Note how the Court was mindful of public perception. If a Restatement provision is adopted as if it were a newly implemented common-law rule, binding in the case before the court and all subsequent cases concerning materially identical facts, the party who loses could object that the imposition of the provision 'is essentially retrospective', that its application to the facts of the case could not 'be determined in advance'.[54] It is difficult to imagine the objection carrying much, if any, weight. Courts, after all, apply retroactive law whenever they devise new common-law rule formulations to decide cases. Parties who lose cases can hardly grumble about defeat by *ex post facto* law if the reason for

---

Institute (n 26) 101–131 at 102. He notes, nevertheless, that reliance on these Restatements is not akin to deference to a statutory text (ibid. 104 n 17).

[51] *Rivers v Great Dane Trailers*, 816 F.Supp. 1525, 1530 (MD Ala 1993). In a similar vein, see *St James Village, Inc. v Cunningham*, 210 P.3d 190, 193 (Nev. 2009); ('In adopting the Restatement rule, we determine that the plain meaning of the rule's introductory language prohibits [its] application'); *Manisalco v Brother International (USA)*, 709 F.3d 202, 208 (3rd Cir. 2003) ('We find this approach contradictory to the plain language of the Restatement'); though cf *In re Hanford Nuclear Reservation Litigation*, 497 F.3d 1005, 1024 (9th Cir. 2007) ('[W]e generally do not parse the language of a restatement as meticulously as that of a statute').

[52] *Coyle v Richardson-Merrell, Inc.*, 584 A.2d 1383, 1385 (Pa 1991).

[53] *Tincher v Omega Flex, Inc.*, 104 A.3d 328, 354 (Pa 2014).

[54] Jansen, *The Making of Legal Authority* (n 2) 89.

the litigation, perhaps the reason they themselves litigated, was that nobody could ascertain how the common law applied to the cause of action at the time that the impugned action was taken.[55] But the Supreme Court of Pennsylvania was concerned with what Jansen would term the 'constitutional assumptions'[56] underpinning the proposition that judges might adopt Restatement provisions as *de facto* enacted law—in particular, with the assumption that courts might determine that Restatement provisions have the binding force of statutory provisions even though members of the American Law Institute, unlike members of a legislature, are not subject to election and removal by public vote.

b) *The sliding scale of authority*

Whereas the Supreme Court of Pennsylvania drew attention to the possibility of a Restatement being the source of rules which bind regular citizens, academic lawyers tend to be more concerned with how—by virtue of courts electing to treat it as authoritative—the content of a Restatement, and of other secondary sources, can bind judges when they make legal decisions. In each instance, the object of focus is the same: 'the norms by which courts are bound to evaluate behaviour ... are the very same norms which are legally binding on the individual whose behaviour is evaluated.'[57] But the reason an individual is bound by a norm derived from a secondary source—a source which has not been transformed into a primary source through modification of the rule of recognition—might be that a court has chosen to treat the norm as the one which the court itself must apply when determining how the law governs the individual's behaviour.

This scenario, in which a dispute is settled through the application of a norm selected by rather than forced upon decision-makers, perhaps goes some way to explaining the obtuseness inherent in refrains such as that there can come from secondary sources norms which have 'the effect of law',[58] 'textual authority',[59] are 'invoked ... as claims of law',[60] offer up 'legal rule[s] even if ... not binding'.[61] The idea—we have encountered it more than once already in

---

[55] See Joseph Raz, *The Authority of Law*, 2nd edn (Oxford: OUP, 2009), 198.

[56] Jansen, *The Making of Legal Authority* (n 2) 83.

[57] Raz, *The Authority of Law* (n 55) 113.

[58] Snyder, 'Private Lawmaking' (n 26) 421.

[59] Jansen, *The Making of Legal Authority* (n 2) 137.

[60] Melvin A. Eisenberg, 'The Concept of National Law and the Rule of Recognition' (2002) 29 *Florida State Univ. L. Rev.* 1229, 1256. (Emphasis removed.)

[61] Ibid. 1257. In legal theory, this idea—that rules can be laws without being binding rules—is often captured by the term, 'soft law'. Actual laws can be soft in the sense that a binding rule could have 'soft' content (for example, an enacted law requiring drivers to drive at a reasonable speed). The

this study—is that only an errant court would choose not to regard the norm as one which it is bound to apply, even though technically it is not bound to apply it. Hart, we saw, acknowledged that the distinction between sources of binding norms and sources of quasi-binding norms is blurred in practice. Close to a decade before Hart made this observation, John Henry Merryman had argued that there is no real distinction to be drawn:

> a court may feel more strongly persuaded by some authority than by some other. . . . But the subjective and accidental factors involved in the choice of possibly applicable decisions . . . leave so much room to avoid being 'bound' that it is not very realistic to speak of authority in terms of absolutes. . . . In practice it is quite possible for a secondary authority to be *more* persuasive than primary authorities. . .[62]

The argument, stripped bare, appears to be that if it is accepted that legal directives never bind as fetters bind, the question whether secondary sources might ever function as primary sources becomes irrelevant, because all legal authorities are essentially of a piece. 'Little if any law is perfectly authoritative.'[63] A secondary source might not yield a binding legal norm, but then nor does a primary source. Considered from this perspective, 'common law rules'—which some courts have the 'power to overturn' and which, '[u]sing an even more common process, a court can . . . change . . . through the process of distinguishing'—'are not binding in any rigorous sense.'[64] '[T]he Restatements', viewed from the same perspective, 'are no more the law than most of the other more familiar legal items and legal sources. But nor are they any less.'[65] To adopt this perspective is to displace the distinction which Hart never quite jettisons in favour of a 'holistic' conception of legal authority which 'allows for a continuum of weight rather than a binary view.'[66]

concept of 'soft law', however, is typically used to refer not to actual law but rather to advisory pronouncements with law-like normative weight (for example, a regulatory body's guidance on responsible lending practices). The core argument for treating pronouncements of this kind as a type of law seems be that their implementation is meant to have legal effects even though they are not implemented as valid legal norms. See Anne Ruth Mackor, 'What Is Legal Validity and Is It Important? Some Critical Remarks About the Legal Status of Soft Law', in *Legal Validity and Soft Law*, ed. P. Westerman et al. (Cham: Springer, 2018), 125–144.

[62] John Henry Merryman, 'The Authority of Authority: What the California Supreme Court Cited in 1950' (1954) 6 *Stanford L. Rev.* 613, 620–621.

[63] Snyder, 'Private Lawmaking' (n 26) 382.

[64] Eisenberg, 'The Concept of National Law' (n 60) 1257–1258.

[65] Schauer, 'The Restatements as Law' (n 26) 440.

[66] Griffin, 'Dethroning the Hierarchy of Authority' (n 26) 88–89; see also her 'Problems with Authority' (2023) 97 *St John's L. Rev.* 113, 126. We have seen already—chapter 5, section(b)—how this

The reception and treatment of the Restatements in the US courts is evidence alone that the holistic outlook has much to commend it. Yet there is a genuine distinction to be drawn between primary-source and secondary-source authorities. A primary-source authority binds, unless or until it is dis-applied or abrogated. A secondary-source authority does not bind, though a court might be able to follow or adopt it as if it were binding. It might also be possible for a court—as it is for a legislature—to alter the content of a legal system's rule of recognition so that a non-binding pronouncement is transformed into a binding one. Primary-source authorities are binding-until-made-not-to-bind, whereas secondary-source authorities are not-binding-until-made-to-bind. A primary-source authority does not lose its status as a binding authority because a court subjects it to an interpretation which renders it inapplicable to particular instances, or because its content is modified (as when a statute is amended), or even because a court determines in a particular case that a party has forsaken the opportunity to rely on it (see chapter 7, section (c)). The distinguishing of a precedent does not render the precedent's *ratio* or holding non-binding, moreover, but rather identifies facts to which the binding force of the *ratio* might have been presumed to, but to which it does not, extend.

To defend the primary-secondary distinction in this way is to rely on the rule of recognition: primary-source authorities are, in essence, ones which qualify as law in a courtroom. Legal scholars of a holistic bent object not so much to the drawing of this distinction as to the idea that the distinction is somehow settled: normative material situated in the secondary column—this is their standard refrain—is quite often moved over to the primary column. Since there is much that can make its way into the courtroom that will remain in, may well be consigned to, the secondary column, it makes perfect sense that a capaciously-minded analyst of legal sources should—as is the case with Jansen—reject Hart's idea of the rule of recognition as 'inappropriately simple'[67] while also constructing an argument which introduces the same basic idea of legal systems embodying tests of validity ('the distinction between law and non-law', Jansen acknowledges, 'is usually constructed by formal criteria').[68] The capacious approach seems to invoke not a rule of recognition but—assertions to this effect are abundant—a rule of treatment: what counts as law is what law-applying officials choose to treat as law. '[I]f the rule

holistic conception of legal authority underpins Shecaira's case for treating legal scholarship as something like (if not quite) a primary source of law.

[67] Jansen, *The Making of Legal Authority* (n 2) 139, and see also 2–3.
[68] Ibid. 111.

of recognition is taken as a postulate, . . . then we must follow the views of the profession wherever they lead us'.[69] '[T]he legal decision-maker is constrained to justify decisions by reference to what is currently treated as authoritative within the legal community'.[70] 'The jurisprudential lesson from Hart and others is that whatever courts treat as authoritative is the law', and if statements taken from secondary sources are 'treated . . . as the law . . . then they *are* the law'.[71] The approach appears to be not so much a recalibration of modern legal positivism as evocative of a lesson taught by crude legal realism. If the law governing the facts of a dispute is simply whatever is treated as relevant authority, an appeal against a judgment on the basis that the court had made an error as to applicable law would really only amount to an objection that the court had made a bad choice rather than a wrong choice. The appellant would have no way of establishing a misapplication of the law, because the law to be applied would be a matter of subjective judgment—of what a court (or 'the profession', or 'the legal community') chooses to treat as law—rather than norms conforming to established criteria of legal validity and pertaining to the facts of the particular dispute.

Yet we do know that some secondary source materials—certainly particular *dicta* and Restatement provisions—are followed, or adopted, as if they were binding authority, even though there has been no alteration to a rule of recognition's content so as to accord them this status. In instances of this kind, might the rule of recognition have been modified implicitly? There was an explicit change to the rule of recognition in English law in 2020 when the Court of Appeal announced that henceforth, when the UK 'Supreme Court . . . directs that an otherwise binding decision of the Court of Appeal should no longer be followed and proposes an alternative test that it says must be adopted, the Court of Appeal is bound to follow what amounts to a direction from the UK Supreme Court even though it is strictly *obiter*'.[72] The more common way with super-*dicta*, however, is that they are elevated (often by judges in the court from which they hail) not with an announcement but *sotto voce*. In *Gardner Steel v Sheffield Brothers* (1978), a two-judge Court of Appeal followed *dictum* from three years earlier (delivered in the same Court by Denning MR) which, both judges acknowledged, contradicted an eligibility-for-appeal rule contained in a statutory instrument.[73] Three years later, a judge bound by Court of Appeal

---

[69] Eisenberg, 'The Concept of National Law' (n 60) 1260.
[70] John Bell, 'Sources of Law' (2018) 77 *CLJ* 40, 51.
[71] Schauer, 'The Restatements as Law' (n 26) 438–439. (Emphasis in original.)
[72] *R v Barton* [2020] EWCA Crim 575 at [104].
[73] *Gardner Steel v Sheffield Brothers (Profiles) Ltd* [1978] 1 WLR 916 at 918 (Stephenson LJ) and 920 (Ormrod LJ).

precedent applied *Gardner* to settle an appeal application, conceding all the while that *Gardner* was founded on *obiter dictum*.[74] Had some tiny element of the rule of recognition been tacitly altered? Was the relevant rule on eligibility for appeal now to be identified not in codified but in judge-made law?

Easily the strongest answer is that nothing had changed. The ruling in *Gardner* did not—could not—nullify the procedural rule (which remained in force until the end of the twentieth century, when the implementation of a new civil procedure code impliedly repealed it).[75] The judge who applied *Gardner*, moreover, considered the Court of Appeal not to have been displacing the procedural rule but rather relying on *dictum* so as to avoid interpreting it narrowly.[76]

Yet it would have been understandable, in the wake of this judge's ruling, if lawyers—advising clients dissatisfied with summary judgments on their prospects of being granted appeal—were to conclude that something *had* changed. Denning issued a plea not for broad judicial interpretation, but rather for displacement, of the procedural rule: the Court of Appeal, he ventured, ought to countenance appeals from parties who have received a summary judgment in a lower court even though the statutory instrument confined the right of appeal to parties whose cases had undergone a full trial.[77] This was the *obiter dictum* endorsed in *Gardner*, and on which the judge who applied *Gardner* was, indirectly, basing his decision when he held that ' "tried" ... simply means "determined" ... irrespective of how the judgment is arrived at'.[78] The judge, by no means unconvincingly, explained the decision as a matter of statutory interpretation. Denning, nevertheless, in issuing the *dictum* to which the decision could be traced, was urging not that the procedural rule be interpreted in a particular way but—something of a Denning trait[79]—that this was an instance

---

[74] See *Alex Lawrie Factors Ltd v Modern Injection Moulds Ltd* [1981] 3 All ER 658, 622–623 (Drake J).

[75] The Civil Procedure Rules 1998 (SI 1998/3132), which came into force on 26 April 1999.

[76] See *Alex Lawrie Factors v Modern Injection Moulds* (n 74) 663.

[77] *Wallersteiner v Moir* [1975] QB 373, 387.

[78] *Alex Lawrie Factors v Modern Injection Moulds* (n 74) 663; and see also *Gardner Steel v Sheffield Bros* (n 73) 920 (Ormrod LJ) ('I respectfully ... agree with the observations made by Lord Denning MR in the *Wallersteiner* case.... "Tried" must mean "determined" ...').

[79] See *Seaford Court Estates Ltd v Asher* [1949] 2 KB 481 (CA), 499; *Magor & St. Mellons RDC v Newport Corporation* [1950] 2 All ER 1226 (CA), 1236. In the year that *Wallersteiner v Moir* was decided, Denning observed *obiter* in another case that a court might be entitled to decline to apply a statutory provision where its application would violate a fundamental right (such as the right not to be detained unlawfully): *Birdi v Secretary of State for Home Affairs* (1975) 119 Sol. Jo. 322. Lord Simonds famously admonished Denning for approaching inconvenient statutes with the mentality of '[w]hat the legislature has not written, the court must write'—which, for Simonds, amounted to 'a naked usurpation of the legislative function under the thin disguise of interpretation'. *Magor & St. Mellons RDC v Newport Corporation* [1952] AC 189 (HL), 191.

in which a codified legal norm might be supplanted in favour of a judicially formulated one.

The case of Denning's *dictum* is indicative of how the elevation of source material, its journey from secondary to primary status, can be subtle and incremental. Denning made a pronouncement which two judges opted to follow as they would were it a binding rule. Another judge then had to apply their judgment as binding precedent. When judges treat secondary-source authority as *de facto* binding—when their negotiation of it as akin to primary-source authority is ascribable to feelings that have them act as they would were they under an actual duty—there arises the thorny question of whether, and if so at what point, the authority becomes law. It is certainly treated as law enforceable *inter partes* on the facts of a particular case. Litigants who lose as a consequence of it being treated thus might complain that they had no way of knowing—at the time that they engaged in what the court has now ruled is liability-incurring action—that they would be judged according to propositions which were, on anyone's assessment at the time that the action took place, nothing other than pronouncements with the status of secondary-source material. But once this judgment had been made, and assuming no further judicial or legislative interventions, future litigants might reasonably expect that, should their case concern materially identical facts, a court will presume the secondary authority affirmed (followed, adopted) in the earlier judgment to be binding on the basis that like cases should be treated alike.[80] If a court chooses to rely on secondary source material as if it has primary source status, in short, judges deciding later cases—perhaps particularly judges in lower courts—might be constrained from backtracking on that choice. This is the type of borderline instance—the absorption of permissive authority into the legal system's repertoire of legal rules without any obvious change to the rule of recognition—which Hart thought blurred the boundary between permissive and mandatory authority, and which some legal theorists cite as evidence that it makes more sense to think of primary-secondary as a spectrum rather than as a distinction.

---

[80] See Raz, *The Authority of Law* (n 55) 90–91 n 8 ('In . . . cases [where a court applies a rule that it has no duty to apply] the court transforms the rule into a law of the system if and only if as a result of its recognition by the court in this case there arises a duty to apply it in other cases: that is, if the system has some rule of precedent').

7

Source identification: some difficulties

The capacious perspective considered in the previous chapter emphasizes not just that secondary source materials sometimes operate as would binding law, but also that the very idea of binding law—of legal rules providing content-independent reasons for action—warrants serious scrutiny. Binding legal authorities do not bind as fetters bind. So, just how do they bind? What is the binding nature of binding authority?

Addressees might be aware that an authority technically binds them, yet they might act without regard for it, perhaps in deliberate contravention of it, because they are confident that it will not or cannot be effectively enforced. The actual binding capacity—as distinct from the formal binding status—of a primary-source authority is relative to an addressee's or recipient's ability to limit or circumvent it. Justinian might have been trying to curb the authority-eroding potential of one category of addressee when he determined that the *Digest* not only had legislative force but that, since no interpretation of the text could improve on its clarity, jurists were barred from producing commentary on it.[1] The principal addressee, the one most obviously on the receiving end of legal authority, is the ordinary citizen. Oliver Wendell Holmes famously set out this citizen's perspective at the start of his iconic 1897 lecture: '[p]eople want to know under what circumstances and how far they will run the risk of coming against what is so much stronger than themselves, and hence . . . [t]he object of our study . . . is . . . the prediction of the incidence of the public force through the instrumentality of the courts.'[2]

---

[1] *De confirmatione Digestorum (Tanta)* § 21 ('[N]o one, of those who are skilled in the law at the present day or shall be hereafter, may dare to compose any commentary on these laws, except in so far as he may wish to translate them into the Greek language in the same order and sequence as those in which the Roman words are written (known to the Greeks as κατά πόδα [word for word]), or to annotate titles to explain any fine points, or to compose what are called παράτιτλα [explanatory notes]. We do not permit them [*sc.*, jurists] to put forward other interpretations, or rather perversions, of the laws, lest their verbosity may cause such confusion in our legislation as to bring discredit upon it'). See H. J. Scheltema, 'Das Kommentarverbot Justinians' (1977) 45 *Tijdschrift voor Rechtsgeschiedenis* 307; Fritz Pringsheim, 'Justinian's Prohibition of Commentaries to the *Digest*' (1950) 5 *Revue internationale des droits de l'antiquité* 383.

[2] O. W. Holmes, Jr, 'The Path of the Law' (1897) 10 *Harv. L. Rev.* 457, 457. Note Holmes's implicit acknowledgment that courts are addressees too: citizens want to be able to predict how courts will

Law's Sources. Neil Duxbury, Oxford University Press. © Neil Duxbury 2025.
DOI: 10.1093/9780198981183.003.0007

We have observed already in this study how, in the twentieth century, legal theorists became more inclined to frame source-of-law enquiries from the perspective of courts rather than citizens: not, 'what could parties have ascertained to be the law governing their impugned actions when those actions were taken?' but rather, 'what can a court identify as the law applicable to the parties' actions when it delivers its ruling?' We have observed, too, how litigants have an obvious rule-of-law based grievance if a court decides against them on the basis that their liability-incurring action is governed by a norm attributable to a source which, at the point when the action was taken, was identifiable not as a source of law but as a source of legal argument or information. Although modern analyses of sources of law have not been inattentive to how judicial decisions supported only by secondary source materials could prompt this kind of grievance, they have tended to focus more on the fanciness of a court's footwork when it decides according to what was, possibly still is, thought to be non-binding authority. The court's decision, we know, might entail a modification to the content of the legal system's rule of recognition. Or it might be that the court is negotiating secondary source material as if it were binding authority but without altering its secondary status.

As we saw in the previous chapter, the argument that secondary-source authority can equate to, without becoming, primary-source authority sometimes involves the claim that all sources lie on a continuum, and that no source is perfectly binding. We have also seen how Hart maintained that the primary-secondary distinction is meaningful, even if it is difficult to detect anything other than a continuum in practice. One of the well-known passages in *The Concept of Law* concerns the 'disappointed absolutist' who fails to appreciate that the fact that an authority excepts instances from its regulatory realm has no bearing on the binding force of that authority over the realm to which it does apply. This absolutist's mistake, according to Hart, is to presume that, because determinations as to which exceptions to accommodate are within a decision-maker's discretion, rules accommodating exceptions cannot bind.[3] A rule that binds on particular facts '"unless . . ." is still a rule'.[4] To invoke the continuum is to detect no line distinguishing authorities which are mandatory subject to exceptions, and authorities which are permissive but which, exceptionally, judges treat as if they were mandatory. Hart's point is that there is,

decide, and how courts decide will depend on how judges understand legal authorities to bear upon their decision-making.

[3] H. L. A. Hart, *The Concept of Law*, 3rd edn (Oxford: OUP, 2012), 139.
[4] Ibid.

however opaque it might seem, an analytical distinction to be drawn: courts are bound to apply mandatory authorities to those instances that do not classify as exceptions, but are making a choice—which is not to deny that they may be under considerable pressure to make the choice—when they enlist a permissive authority to perform as would a binding one.

a) *Hazards of identification*

It is understandable that legal theorists should have been preoccupied with the idea of secondary source material functioning as law while eluding identification as such according to a system's tests of legal validity. Somewhat less examined is the primary source side of the equation. It is not unusual for common-law judges explicitly to identify (occasionally, to confess their inability to identify) the sources giving rise to the laws governing decisions that they make.[5] Once in a while, they impress upon lawyers arguing before the court that source-identification is a two-way street—that judges are entitled to expect litigants and their representatives, just as litigants and their representatives have reason to expect judges, to state what they consider to be the source-material governing the case at hand.[6] In English law, barristers are now and again reprimanded by judges for thinking too narrowly or unimaginatively about source-material relevant to a decision.[7] Occasionally, a judge will apologize to a barrister for referring to primary-source authorities which neither party's legal team included in their arguments before court.[8] (We will see,

---

[5] For examples from a vast range, see *Montejo v Louisiana*, 556 US 778, 794 (2009); *Harisiades v Shaughnessy*, 342 US 580, 585 (1952); *Cook v Moffat*, 46 US 295, 300 (1847); *R (Jackson) v Attorney General* [2005] UKHL 56 at [168] (Lord Carswell); *Rizeq v Western Australia* (2017) 262 CLR 1 at para. 57 (Bell, Gageler, Keane, Nettle, and Gordon JJ); *Proulx v Québec* [2001] SCC 66 at paras 72–79. For examples of cases in which the court drew a blank, see *Jean v Collins*, 155 F.3d 701, 712 (4th Cir. 1998); *Peters v City of Shreveport*, 818 F.2d 1148, 1159–1160 (5th Cir. 1987). Sometimes, a court will stipulate that the onus of identifying a source was on a particular party, and that the court's ruling against that party is attributable to the party having adduced 'no source of law'. See e.g. *In re al-Tamir*, 993 F.3d 906, 917 (DC Cir. 2021); *Roth v King*, 449 F.3d 1272, 1285 (DC Cir. 2006); *Morin v Canada* [2019] FC 638 at para. 28.

[6] See e.g. *Ruffin v Nicely*, 183 Fed. Appx. 505, 510–511 (6th Cir. 2006); *FS Cairo (Nile Plaza) v Brownlie* [2020] EWCA Civ 996 at [116]–[117] (Arnold LJ); *BE (Iran) v Secretary of State for the Home Department* [2008] EWCA Civ 540 at [21].

[7] See e.g. *Allford v Allford* [1965] P. 117, 122–123 (Sir Jocelyn Simon P) ('It was suggested in argument that no such duty is to be found in the pre-existing law. But this is taking altogether too narrow a view of the sources of law. *Cursus curiae [est] lex curiae* [The practice of the court is the law of the court]'); also *Boake Allen Ltd v Revenue and Customs Commissioners* [2006] EWCA Civ 25 at [101] (Sedley LJ) ('The growing specialisation of sectors of the legal profession, particularly the Bar, is constricting and in some instances fragmenting the sources of law which are deployed in argument').

[8] See e.g. *R (Schmidt) v Secretary of State for the Home Department* [1994] 2 All ER 784 (QBD), 803 (Sedley J) ('[W]ith apologies to counsel for citing sources of law not canvassed in argument...').

before this chapter is out, that common-law judges are sometimes not simply referring to these authorities but are making decisions that depend on them.) It is certainly quite common for judges, when deciding cases, to observe that the court's judgment identifies and is supported by not one source but rather multiple sources of law.[9] In public international law, the stark closure rule known as the *Lotus* principle posits that the law must be presumed to permit whatever it doesn't forbid, and that the action of a sovereign state therefore cannot be prohibited if no source of law can be identified to support a ruling that it is.[10]

Source-identification becomes a more interesting endeavour once one starts to conceive of it as bound up with a system's conventions and rules on how authorities bind courts. The nuances of *stare decisis* are illustrative in this regard. Although, within a legal system, a particular court's judgments might be binding in lower courts—and might even bind the court itself[11]—the purpose of appeal would be defeated if they also bound in higher ones. When judges do acknowledge precedent as a primary source of law, their acknowledgement might be but prefatory to the court's pronouncement that the facts of the prior judicial decision, or decisions, on which a litigant's claim is based are materially different from the facts in the litigant's case. The precedents relied upon by counsel for one of the defendants 'are binding on this court ... unless they can be distinguished', Lord Woolf MR observed in *Kent v Griffiths* (2001).[12] He then concluded that they could be distinguished.[13] When an appeal court anticipates that its judgment on a matter will prove especially contentious, the judges responsible for that judgment (and probably also the lawyers for the party who wanted them to reach it) might pay close attention to precedent not

[9] See e.g. *TMJ Implants, Inc. v Aetna, Inc.* 498 F.3d 1175, 1181–1182 (10th Cir. 2007); *Strathclyde Regional Council v Wallace* [1998] ICR 205, 212 (Lord Browne-Wilkinson); *Galerie d'art du Petit Champlain v Théberge* [2002] SCC 34 at para. 116. For a cautionary perspective, cf *R (Al-Saadoon) v Secretary of State for Defence* [2009] EWCA Civ 7 at [62] (Laws LJ) ('Some of these materials are not sources of law...').

[10] *The Case of the SS 'Lotus'* (PCIJ, 7 September 1927), ser. A, no. 10, *Publications of the Permanent Court of International Justice* 1, 18 ('International law governs relations between independent States. The rules of law binding upon States therefore emanate from their own free will as expressed in conventions or by usages generally accepted as expressing principles of law and established in order to regulate the relations between these co-existing independent communities or with a view to the achievement of common aims. Restrictions upon the independence of States cannot therefore be presumed').

[11] As regards England's Court of Appeal, see *Young v Bristol Aeroplane Co.* [1944] KB 718.

[12] *Kent v Griffiths (No. 3)* [2001] QB 36 (CA), 43.

[13] 'Before you can apply one case by analogy to another you need to be clear as to the facts to which you are applying it. Otherwise there is a risk that a principle can be applied to a situation where it produces a result which should offend your sense of justice. This ... would be the consequence here of accepting [defence counsel]'s argument.' Ibid. 50–51. See also *Starmark Enterprises v CPL Distribution* [2001] EWCA Civ 1252 at [97] (Peter Gibson LJ) ('Where the *ratio* of an earlier decision of this court is directly applicable to the circumstances of a case before this court but that decision has been wrongly distinguished in a later decision of this court, in principle it must be open to this court to apply the *ratio* of the earlier decision and to decline to follow the later decision').

because it provides direct authority for the judgment—the contentiousness of the case might be down to the fact that there is no such authority—but because it can plausibly be read as leaving the door open, clearing the path, perhaps even providing cover for (but not actually requiring) the court to move the law in a particular direction.[14] A judge might observe of a judgment that it would have been overruled had it been necessary for the court to engage with it. The observation might basically signal that, come the time that the court does have to engage with this judgment, its days as a precedent are numbered. But since the court did not engage with the judgment—since the judge's observation was *obiter*—its binding status remains unaltered. Although 'the [United States] Supreme Court ... has somewhat cryptically cast doubt on its holding in' *Supreme Court of Virginia v Consumers Union of the United States* (1980),[15] the Second Circuit observed in 2007, the case is 'squarely-applicable precedent' and 'we are unwilling to ignore' it 'simply because of broadly-stated *dicta*'.[16]

When a court identifies enacted legislation as the primary source material relevant to the case to be decided, it might determine that applying a statutory provision depends on the negation of precedent, as when a judgment is overturned because the court or agency responsible for it (the scenario is common to administrative law) sought to apply a binding statutory rule but interpreted the rule in a way which the statute does not permit.[17] A court might be simultaneously bound to apply a statute while also bound to try to find a way of interpreting it so that it bears on a case differently from how it does on the face of the text.[18] It is even possible that a system's constitutional setup binds a court to the application of a particular rule to the facts of a case while also requiring the court to disapprove of the rule that it has applied. The Human Rights Act 1998 requires the United Kingdom's higher courts to declare a national statute incompatible with the European Convention on Human Rights (ratified by the UK in 1951) when it proves impossible to interpret the statute in such a way as

---

[14] See Julius Yam, 'Judging Under Authoritarianism' (2024) 87 *MLR* 894, 915–917; Richard M. Re, 'Precedent as Permission' (2021) 99 *Texas L. Rev.* 907, 925–929; also Patricia M. Wald, 'The Rhetoric of Results and the Results of Rhetoric: Judicial Writings' (1995) 62 *Univ. Chicago L. Rev.* 1371, 1401 ('[P]recedents ... discussed in terms of what they did not say rather than what they did say').

[15] *State Employees Bargaining Agent Coalition v Rowland*, 494 F.3d 71, 84 (2nd Cir. 2007) (citing *Supreme Court of Virginia v Consumers Union of the United States*, 446 US 719 (1980)).

[16] *State Employees Bargaining Agent Coalition v Rowland* (n 15) 86–87. In a similar vein, see *Garrus v Secretary of Pennsylvania Dept of Corrections*, 694 F.3d 394, 422 (3rd Cir. 2012) (Greenaway J, dissenting); *Pegasus Management Holdings v Ernst & Young* [2010] EWCA Civ 181 at [74] (Rimer LJ).

[17] For an American illustration, drawing on the (now overruled) decision in *Chevron USA v Natural Resources Defense Council*, 467 US 837 (1984), see Caleb Nelson, 'Stare Decisis and Demonstrably Erroneous Precedents' (2001) 87 *Va L. Rev.* 1, 6–7.

[18] Courts conventionally presume against absurdity when interpreting statutes. The statutorily imposed interpretive duty, however, typically concerns not preventing absurd rulings but rather ensuring constitution- or treaty-compliant ones.

to make it Convention-compliant. But the declaration 'does not affect the validity, continuing operation or enforcement of [a statutory] provision in respect of which it is given . . . and . . . is not binding on the parties to the proceedings in which it is made'.[19] The court that issues the declaration is still bound to apply the impugned national law.

b) *The void* ab initio *conundrum*

One of the most intriguing ways in which a court might have reason to pause over the status of a norm attributable to a primary source is to be found in the broad field of constitutional legality. If a norm is voided, was it ever a law? The era of the Puritan rebellion offers up a stark illustration of the conundrum. Laws created during the Interregnum didn't receive royal assent (before 1649, they were called parliamentary ordinances rather than acts). On the restoration of the Stuart monarchy, all ordinances and acts from 1642 to 1660 were rendered null and void—some were even committed to public destruction.[20] What are we to make of norms that suffer this kind of erasure? Is a norm made unconstitutional a valid legal norm—binding law—up to the point that its unconstitutionality is declared? Or was it never binding law in the first place?

Consider how Hans Kelsen wrestled with the conundrum in his writings on constitutional adjudication. There is little if any reward in challenging the constitutionality of a statute, Kelsen observed, if invalidating judgments issued by constitutional courts do not apply to the facts that prompt the rulings. So constitutional judgments should apply retroactively, though their retroactive effect should be limited to the case before the court.[21]

---

[19] Human Rights Act 1998, s 4(6). There are Australian and Irish statutes which use much the same form of words: Victoria Charter of Human Rights and Responsibilities Act 2006, s 36(5); Human Rights Act 2004 (Australian Capital Territory), s 32(3); European Convention on Human Rights Act 2003 (Ireland), s 5(2).

[20] See C. H. Firth, 'Introduction', in *Acts and Ordinances of the Interregnum, 1642–1660*, 3 vols, ed. C. H. Firth and R. S. Rait (London: HMSO, 1911), III, iii–xxxviii at xxxiii–xxxvi. Interregnum acts and ordinances are often said to have been 'declared' null and void—see e.g. Jean Mather, 'The Moral Code of the English Civil War and Interregnum' (1982) 44 *The Historian* 207, 225 ('By July of 1661, Charles II was back on the throne, the Maypoles were back on the village greens, all legislation of the Interregnum had been declared null and void')—but nullification was, in every instance, implied or indirect; the Convention parliament that was formed with the restoration of Charles II never expressly negated any Interregnum enactment (Firth, 'Introduction', xxxiii). Parliament affirmed, moreover, that the validity of court rulings delivered, and marriage ceremonies conducted, between 1642 and 1660 was never in question (ibid. xxxii).

[21] Hans Kelsen, 'Wesen und Entwicklung der Staatsgerichtsbarkeit' (1929), in *Wer soll der Hüter der Verfassung sein? Abhandlungen zur Theorie der Verfassungsgerichtsbarkeit in der pluralistischen, parlamentarischen Demokratie*, ed. R. C. van Ooyen (Tübingen: Mohr Siebeck, 2019), 1–57 at 44, and see also 19, 48. On Kelsen's recommendation, Austria's constitution was amended in 1929 so that the

Treating such judgments as binding with complete retroactive effect struck him as more troublesome. Constitutional adjudication cannot invalidate a norm if it was never valid in the first place.[22] On 'very rare'[23] occasions a court will, Kelsen maintained, declare that a directive is an *a priori* nullity, emanating from a source that is not a source of law. (His curious but memorable example of this kind of source is Wilhelm Voigt, 'The Captain of Köpenick', a German criminal and cause célèbre who, in 1906, assumed the guise of a military officer and, with the help of unsuspecting soldiers, successfully ordered the arrest of Köpenick's mayor and council secretary and divested the municipal treasury of all its available cash.)[24] A judicial declaration that a directive is *a priori* null amounts not to invalidation, but rather to the 'dissolution of the . . . *appearance* of a valid legal norm'.[25] The standard judicial review scenario, by contrast, has a constitutional court testing a norm derived from a primary source of law: typically, a statute attributable to a legislative organ that had the authority to enact it. For Kelsen, any such statute is a valid legal norm, albeit unconstitutional law, unless or until it is abrogated.[26] An unconstitutional law binds until a court determines that it no longer binds because it is unconstitutional.

The principal difficulty, Kelsen came to realize, is that it is not beyond the bounds of constitutional courts to determine that an impugned norm is both attributable to a source with the authority to issue it as a legal norm *and* to be treated *a priori* null. What American lawyers often refer to as the 'void *ab*

---

retroactive effect of a constitutional judgment was limited to the case that gave rise to it: *Österreichische Bundesverfassung*, arts 139(6) and 140(7).

[22] See Hans Kelsen, *Pure Theory of Law*, 2nd edn trans. M. Knight (Berkeley: University of California Press, 1967 [1960]), 271.

[23] Hans Kelsen, *Peace Through Law* (Chapel Hill: University of North Carolina Press, 1944), 106.

[24] See e.g. Hans Kelsen, *Introduction to the Problems of Legal Theory*, trans. B. L. and S. L. Paulson (Oxford: Clarendon Press, 1992 [1934]), 9. Voigt was sentenced to four years in prison for the heist. The episode made him something of a celebrity and, after serving his time, he profited considerably from it: Christopher Clark, *Iron Kingdom: The Rise and Downfall of Prussia 1600–1947* (London: Penguin, 2007), 596–599.

[25] Kelsen, *Introduction to the Problems of Legal Theory* (n 24) 74–75. (Emphasis added.) Kelsen struggled with the idea of courts dissolving nullities. The Pure Theory of Law, he liked to assert, is a general theory which identifies legal norms, and only legal norms, as the object of legal science. See e.g. Kelsen, *Pure Theory of Law* (n 22) 4, 68, 70, 75. A nullity in the guise of a norm emanating from a source incapable of conferring legal validity surely has no place in its realm. Kelsen's answer to this conundrum was characteristically idiosyncratic. Law, he maintained, has its own version of the Midas touch: everything it touches is turned into legal phenomena (if not quite into law). So, from the standpoint of legal science, the court which confirms that a norm was never valid accords that norm the same 'legal character' that it accords a norm which was valid till it was found to be unconstitutional. Kelsen, *Pure Theory of Law* (n 22) 278; also Hans Kelsen, *General Theory of Law and State*, trans. A. Wedberg (Cambridge, Mass.: Harvard UP, 1945), 161.

[26] Kelsen, *Introduction to the Problems of Legal Theory* (n 24) 72.

initio' theory exemplifies the difficulty.[27] The colonial legislatures had exercised delegated rather than sovereign law-making powers, and it was not unknown for the Privy Council to pronounce colonial laws that contradicted English law to be null and void.[28] Two decades after the colonies declared their independence, and very soon after the federal Constitution took effect, a US circuit court concluded that a statute ruled unconstitutional 'was invalid from the beginning, . . . as if it had not been made'.[29] The reasoning is to be found in *Marbury v Madison* eight years later: if the Constitution is not 'on a level with ordinary legislative acts' but rather 'is . . . a superior, paramount law', Marshall CJ observed, 'then a legislative act contrary to the Constitution is not law'.[30] The best-known formulation of the void *ab initio* doctrine came in 1886 when Field J, speaking for the Supreme Court, pronounced that:

> . . . an unconstitutional act is not a law; it confers no rights; it imposes no duties; it affords no protection; it creates no office; it is, in legal contemplation, as inoperative as though it had never been passed.[31]

Kelsen was aware that, even when Field made this pronouncement, there existed superior court rulings to the effect that a statute found to be unconstitutional might be presumed valid until publication of the judgment, and even then might be deemed invalid only as regards its application to the parties in the particular case.[32] Granted, the 'theory that an unconstitutional statute is void *ab initio* is the traditional doctrine of the American courts as to the effect of an unconstitutional statute', an eminent constitutional lawyer wrote at the time that Kelsen moved to the United States, but 'it is no longer the sole rule on the effect of an invalid statute'.[33] If, having found a statute to be unconstitutional, we subsequently overrule ourselves, the Supreme Court of Indiana held in 1874, our overruling decision does not reinstate the statute's validity, for the statute was never invalidated; the statute 'must be regarded as having all the

---

[27] Hans Kelsen, 'Judicial Review of Legislation: A Comparative Study of the Austrian and the American Constitution' (1942) 4 *Jnl of Politics* 183, 189.

[28] As when it pronounced a Connecticut intestacy statute which contradicted the common law rule of succession by primogeniture to be 'null and void and of no force or effect whatever'. *Winthrop v Lechmere* (1727), in *Acts of the Privy Council of England (Colonial ser.): Vol V,* ed. J. Munro and A. W. Fitzroy (London: HMSO, 1912), 88.

[29] *Van Horne's Lessee v Dorrance*, 2 Dall. 304, 320 (C.C.D. Pa 1795).

[30] *Marbury v Madison*, 5 US (1 Cranch) 137, 177 (1803).

[31] *Norton v Shelby County*, 118 US 425, 442 (1886).

[32] Kelsen, 'Judicial Review of Legislation' (n 27) 199; see also J. A. C. Grant, 'The Legal Effect of a Ruling that a Statute is Unconstitutional' [1978] *Detroit College of Law Rev.* 201, 232.

[33] Oliver P. Field, *The Effect of an Unconstitutional Statute* (Minneapolis: University of Minnesota Press, 1935), 2. Kelsen moved to the United States in 1934.

time been the law of the State. This court has no power to repeal or "abolish" statutes.'[34] If this court 'finds [a statute] in conflict with the Constitution', the Supreme Court of West Virginia held in 1887, 'it does not strike the statute from the statute-book. . . . The parties to that suit are concluded by the judgment, but no one else is bound'.[35]

Rulings such as these were far more congenial to Kelsen's own constitutional mindset than were those that affirmed the void *ab initio* doctrine. To pronounce a properly enacted but unconstitutional statute void *ab initio* is 'not at all satisfactory', Kelsen argued, because it is, in effect, to rule that whatever law it was supposed to replace never was replaced, and so (assuming no other legal act has resulted in its abrogation) is still in force.[36] In the time between when the statute eventually adjudged null was brought into existence and when its status as a nullity is pronounced, people who choose not to obey it act on the risk of a court ruling that it is in fact constitutional, and that their conduct is therefore unlawful. But if the statute is ruled void *ab initio*, anyone who has acted in accordance with it may have contravened whatever law was never replaced.[37] Should a court rule that a statute is void *ab initio* and that ruling is then overruled by another court, moreover, there arises the question of what liabilities, if any, attach to actions taken in contravention of the statute between the time of its enactment and the issuing of the overruling decision.[38] However one acts in response to the statute, 'it is . . . impossible to know the law at the moment when the act is performed'.[39] Kelsen—who died within three weeks of

---

[34] *Pierce v Pierce*, 46 Ind. 86, 95 (1874). The court in fact erred because the statute at issue in the case that was overruled was a different one from the statute addressed in the overruling case: Oliver P. Field, 'Effect of an Unconstitutional Statute' (1926) 1 *Indiana L. J.* 1, 13–14.

[35] *Shepherd v City of Wheeling*, 4 S.E. 635, 637 (W. Va 1887).

[36] Kelsen, 'Judicial Review of Legislation' (n 27) 199; also 'Wesen und Entwicklung der Staatsgerichtsbarkeit' (n 21) 17.

[37] See e.g. *Dennison Manufacturing Co. v Wright*, 120 S.E. 120, 123 (Ga 1923) (holding that a ruling of the Supreme Court of Georgia from 1893 made a tax collector liable to repay taxes because a 1919 statute purportedly superseding the ruling, and from which the collector thought he derived tax-collecting authority, was unconstitutional and therefore 'in reality no law . . . wholly void . . . inoperative as if it had never been passed').

[38] In *Jawish v Morlet*, 86 A.2d 96 (DC Cir. 1952), it was held that the minimum wage law passed by Congress in 1918 and held unconstitutional in *Adkins v Children's Hospital*, 261 US 525 (1923) never was unconstitutional given that *Adkins* was overruled in *West Coast Hotel Co. v Parrish*, 300 US 379 (1937). In the time between *Adkins* and *West Coast Hotel*, the statute had been 'dormant but not dead'; once *Adkins* was overruled, it became 'valid from its first effective date' (*Jawish* at 97). In criminal cases, US courts can sometimes be seen to adopt a different approach, ruling that a statute is not automatically revived *ab initio* as a consequence of the overruling decision but rather must be re-enacted by the legislature so that it takes effect prospectively. For an example concerning a penal statute the retrospective validation of which would have led to the resentencing of thousands of defendants whose sentences had been ascertained on the basis of the statute having been ruled unconstitutional, see *State v Hodge*, 941 N.E.2d 768 (Ohio 2010).

[39] Kelsen, *General Theory of Law and State* (n 25) 44.

the US Supreme Court calling time on the void *ab initio* doctrine[40]—had his preferred solution to the dilemma. But he was in no doubt that the dilemma was genuine. For if a court can pronounce on the constitutionality of a norm—if it can rule that a legislated norm was never law—the fact that the norm is attributable to a primary source need not settle its status as binding authority.

c) *The* sua sponte *reliance conundrum*

Another, rather different primary source conundrum concerns cases in which a source offers up authority which settles (or contributes to the settlement of) the parties' rights and obligations, but the court has reason to resist, or at least hesitate over, applying it.

One of the classic specimens of American realist literature is an essay by a Texan circuit judge, Joseph Hutcheson, in which he presents judges as atomistic adjudicators, unburdened by legal rules when their instincts send them on 'a roving commission to find the just solution'.[41] Considered alongside Hutcheson's later (rather more stolid) extra-curial output, the essay comes across like a rush of blood to the head.[42] While his early apostasy went down a storm with Karl Llewellyn and Jerome Frank,[43] Llewellyn ultimately seemed unconvinced that Hutcheson had genuinely Rabelaisian convictions.[44] But then Llewellyn wasn't consistently of the view that atomistic adjudication deserves to be lauded. Judges who decide cases purely according to their own instincts, he would observe near the end of his life, might leave an attorney wondering whether artful advocacy ever counts for anything—'whether . . .

---

[40] *Lemon v Kurtzman*, 411 US 192, 198–199 (1973). That it brought the doctrine to an end seems questionable. See e.g. *Perkins v Eskridge*, 278 Md 619, 637 n 7 (Md 1976) ('We do not mean to imply . . . that we totally reject the . . . void *ab initio* rule. In some cases it may be appropriate to apply the rationale').

[41] Joseph C. Hutcheson, Jr, 'The Judgment Intuitive: The Function of the "Hunch" in Judicial Decision' (1929) 14 *Cornell L. Rev.* 274, 278.

[42] Cf e.g. Joseph C. Hutcheson, Jr, 'The Common Law of the Constitution' (1937) 15 *Texas L. Rev.* 317, 336–337 ('[T]he final tribunal . . . cannot, any more than the legislature can, add to or take away . . . from the . . . Constitution. If it makes a wrong decision, this does not change the Constitution. It merely . . . settles that case by applying to the dispute before it . . . what it conceives to be the fundamental, the controlling law'); 'Judging as Administration, Administration as Judging' (1942) 21 *Texas L. Rev.* 1, 8 ('[J]udging . . . must stand or fall as the administration of justice under law').

[43] See Karl N. Llewellyn, 'Some Realism about Realism: Responding to Dean Pound' (1931) 44 *Harv. L. Rev.* 1222, 1243 n 48; Jerome Frank, *Law and the Modern Mind* (Gloucester, Mass.: Peter Smith, 1970 [1930]), 111 ('such an honest report of the judicial process').

[44] Karl N. Llewellyn, 'On Reading and Using the New Jurisprudence' (1940) 26 *Am. Bar Assoc. Jnl* 418, 421.

there is any effective craftsmanship for him to bring to bear to serve his client and justify his being'.[45]

Many legal philosophers are inclined to write about judges as if they are on something akin to Hutcheson's roving commission—striking out on their own in one way or another.[46] Yet the reality (*pace* Llewellyn) is that judicial decisions are often shaped by artful advocacy.[47] In an adversary system, the course of a case depends not only on judicial endeavour but also on what the parties, more likely their legal representatives, bring to the table—the points they plead, the authorities they invoke, the arguments they make, their dexterity and persuasiveness (or, for that matter, their ineptitude) when making those arguments. Gaining the upper hand in the courtroom, Quintilian observed, can also depend on knowing what to omit or concede.[48] Some legal outcomes, indeed areas of law, are shaped not so much by what is contained in submissions to court as by what—deliberately or because of laxness—is left out.[49]

---

[45] Karl N. Llewellyn, *The Common Law Tradition: Deciding Appeals* (Boston: Little, Brown & Co, 1960), 3–4. Though Llewellyn quickly progressed from this observation to lamenting 'the frequency with which the relevant briefs miss or obscure telling points' (ibid. 30).

[46] Ronald Dworkin's legal philosophy epitomizes the style. He adopted it with complete self-awareness: see *Law's Empire* (London: Fontana, 1986), 12 ('My project is narrow. . . . It centers on . . . judges in black robes, but these are not the only or even the most important actors in the legal drama. A more complete study of legal practice would attend to . . . a great variety of other officials').

[47] In English law, the classic illustration is criminal attempts, which was famously left in confusion by *Anderton v Ryan* [1985] AC 560. The House of Lords held in *Anderton* that one is not guilty of attempting to receive as stolen goods an item which is not stolen even though one has attempted to do something forbidden by the criminal law. One of the law lords subscribed to this position while also indicating that he would have found the defendant guilty had she been attempting to kill somebody who was already dead: see ibid. 577–578 (Lord Roskill); also Alan R. White, *Misleading Cases* (Oxford: Clarendon Press, 1991), 12. Another in the majority wrote the lead opinion for a unanimous House of Lords when it overruled *Anderton* the following year: *R v Shivpuri* [1987] AC 1 (decided 16 May 1986). The *Anderton* debacle transpired because the defendant's lead counsel, Ben Hytner (father of the theatre director, Nicholas Hytner), successfully steered the majority into concluding that a criminal attempt, the act of attempting to do what is forbidden, is not an *actus reus* in its own right. See Glanville Williams, 'The Lords and Impossible Attempts, Or *Quis Custodiet Ipsos Custodes?*' (1986) 45 *CLJ* 33, 66–70, also 73 n 55. Hytner had accomplished much the same when the House concluded similarly a decade earlier: *Haughton v Smith* [1975] AC 476. That he was able to do so again in *Anderton* is especially remarkable given that separating the two judgments was legislation stipulating that a defendant may be guilty of attempting to commit an offence which it turns out to be impossible to commit: Criminal Attempts Act 1981, s 1(2).

[48] Quintilian, *Institutio Oratoria* 7. 1. 18–19: '. . . quasdam quaestiones executi donare solemus et concedere. . . . Quod ipsum ita fieri oportet non ut damnasse eas videamur, sed omisisse quia possimus etiam sine eis vincere' ('. . . we are inclined to grant or concede some questions to the adversary. . . . This must be done in such a way that we seem not to have discarded them, but to have omitted them because we can win even without them').

[49] As when the House of Lords invoked section 4 of the Human Rights Act 1998—and held that a statutory provision authorizing detention pending removal of suspected terrorists was incompatible with Article 5(1)(f) of the European Convention on Human Rights—without first trying, under section 3, to interpret and give effect to the impugned provision in a way that rendered it Convention-compatible. In *A v Secretary of State for the Home Department* [2004] UKHL 56 the Attorney General, rather than directing the law lords to the interpretive obligation that section 3 imposed on them, opted to concede that the provision was contrary to Article 5, a concession which enabled counsel for the detainees to represent the provision as discriminatory (authorizing the indefinite detention of foreigners

Common-law judges are fond of the mantra that if lawyers do omit to plead a point and to invoke relevant authority, they shouldn't expect a helping hand from the bench.[50] 'If counsel does not present an argument, a court may well take the view that there is nothing in it and make a judgment accordingly.'[51] But—the conundrum—what if a judge knows, perhaps is all too aware,[52] that a proper examination of the relevant sources yields authority which counsel for neither side has referred to (what Stephen Sedley once termed 'uncanvassed' authority)[53] and which is directly applicable, as binding law, to the case to be decided? What is this judge meant to do?

If judges, when making decisions, ignore authority of this kind, they do not demote it to the status of secondary source material. They still recognize the authority to have binding force in cases where it is canvassed by one or both of the parties. Yet they are, in the case at hand, electing not to apply an applicable law. Just how often, indeed whether it is ever the case, that judges do this is anyone's guess. It is hardly a good judicial look, after all, to admit both to being aware of authority bearing dispositively on the case at hand and to having opted to ignore it. Close inspection of cases where judges appear to be refusing to countenance uncanvassed authority tend to attest to a more subtle manoeuvre: that the court refused to entertain not the authority, but rather a point of law addressed by the authority but not raised by either party in arguments to the court or below.[54] Common-law judges quite often observe that

---

while not authorizing the detention of terrorist suspects who are UK nationals) and therefore incompatible with the European Convention's liberty and non-discrimination norms: see John Finnis, 'Nationality, Alienage and Constitutional Principle' (2007) 123 *LQR* 417, 434–435.

[50] Owen Dixon, 'Professional Conduct' (1953), in his *Jesting Pilate and Other Papers and Addresses*, ed. C. Z. J. Woinarski (Sydney: Law Book Company, 1965), 129–134 at 134. In a similar vein, see *Rondel v Worsley* [1969] 1 AC 191, 227 (Lord Reid); Richard Du Cann, *The Art of the Advocate*, rev. edn (Harmondsworth: Penguin, 1993), 43 ('[C]ounsel . . . must . . . keep steadily before him the necessity of justly gaining and retaining the confidence of the court. That means that he should feel that the court knows that it can rely upon him without misgiving as one who will competently ascertain and present for judicial examination his client's real or strongest case and will do so intelligibly, definitely and with candour'); and David Pannick, *Advocacy* (Cambridge: CUP, 2023), 98.

[51] *R v Legal Aid Board, ex p Megarry (No 2)* [1994] PIQR 476, 489 (Popplewell J). See also *Countryliner Ltd v Surrey CC* [2011] EWCA Civ 373 at [11], [16] (Longmore LJ).

[52] See e.g. *R (Elmes) v Essex CC* [2019] 1 WLR 1686, 1732 (where the authority was not cited but the judge, knowing the authority well and recognizing its centrality to the case, considered it impossible not to have the authority in mind when delivering the judgment).

[53] *Clark v Clark Construction Initiatives Ltd* [2008] EWCA Civ 1446 at [11].

[54] See e.g. *Connecticut Fire Insurance Co. v Kavanagh* [1892] AC 473 (PC), 480 (Lord Watson); *London CC v Woolwich Union Assessment Committee* [1893] 1 QB 210, 222–223 (Esher MR); *ZT (Kosovo) v Secretary of State for the Home Dept* [2009] UKHL 6 at [38] (Lord Hope); *LM v KD* [2018] EWHC 3057 (Fam) at [71] (Baker LJ); *Okolo v Mortgages 4 Ltd* [2004] EWHC 3019 (Ch) at [20] (Lawrence Collins J); *Hartmann v Prudential Insurance Co. of America*, 9 F.3d 1207, 1214–1215 (7th Cir. 1993) (Posner J) (counsel having argued on incorrect grounds); and, more generally on US caselaw, Barry A. Miller, '*Sua Sponte* Appellate Rulings: When Courts Deprive Litigants of an Opportunity to be Heard' (2002) 39 *San Diego L. Rev.* 1253, 1269–1271. A court could, of course, decide to deal with

if counsel is remiss in failing to plead a point (and thereby invoke attendant authority), it is reasonable for the court to assume that the point has been conceded, and consideration of it impliedly waived.[55]

Judges would likely be thought to have acquitted themselves poorly if they made it known that they had refused to consider uncanvassed but materially relevant authority. Yet the verdict on their performance can also be harsh when they do the opposite—when a court identifies authority not canvassed by either party and, of its own accord (the preferred legal Latin is *sua sponte*),[56] delivers a judgment that is wholly or partly dependent on it. The New South Wales Court of Appeal made 'a grave error', a unanimous High Court of Australia ruled in *Farah Constructions v Say-Dee* (2007),[57] when it based part of its decision (which the High Court overruled) on a ground which was never pleaded or argued, and on 'authorities and writings' which neither side had canvassed.[58] The High Court considered both sides to have been disadvantaged by what the Court of Appeal had done. But the party more perplexed and aggrieved in a case of this kind will invariably be the one who bears the brunt of the judgment.[59] The judiciary, this party will likely complain, basically gate-crashed

---

a point of law that wasn't canvassed: see *R (McDonald) v Kensington & Chelsea RLBC* [2011] UKSC 33 at [61] (Lady Hale) ('[T]here is ample precedent for this court addressing itself to an important point which has not been argued by the parties').

[55] See *FS Cairo (Nile Plaza) v Brownlie* [2020] EWCA Civ 996 at [116]–[117] (Arnold LJ); *LINC Finance Corp. v Onwuteaka*, 129 F.3d 917, 921 (7th Cir. 1994) ('[T]he failure to cite authorities in support of a particular argument constitutes a waiver of the issue'); *Ruffin v Nicely*, 183 Fed. Appx. 505, 510–511 (6th Cir. 2006).

[56] There are lesser-deployed alternatives: *sponte sua* (see e.g. *Nelson v Hill*, 46 US 127, 132 (1847)), *nostra sponte* (see e.g. *Clearing House Assoc. v Cuomo*, 510 F.3d 105, 122 (2nd Cir. 2007)), *suo motu* (see e.g. *Duncan v McCall*, 139 US 449, 458 (1891)), *suo moto* (see e.g. *Ball v Hershey Foods*, 842 F.Supp. 44, 45 (D. Conn. 1993)) and *motu proprio* (see e.g. *Figueroa-Rodriguez v Aquino*, 863 F.2d 1037, 1050 (1st Cir. 1988)). Superior courts in India and Pakistan are constitutionally empowered to initiate certain types of legal proceedings *suo motu* (i.e., on their own motion rather than at the behest of parties): see *Sunil Batra v Delhi Administration* 1980 AIR 1579 (SC India); *Darshan Masih v The State* PLD 1990 SC 513 (SC Pakistan).

[57] *Farah Constructions Pty Ltd v Say-Dee Pty Ltd* [2007] HCA 22 at para. 131 (Gleeson CJ and Gummow, Callinan, Heydon, and Crennan JJ).

[58] Ibid. at paras 132–133.

[59] For the argument that a judge might be demonstrating good judgment by opting not to 'work solely with what the parties have presented' when there is 'an obvious imbalance' between them, see Chad M. Oldfather, *Judges, Judging, and Judgment: Character, Wisdom, and Humility in a Polarized World* (Cambridge: CUP, 2024), 25–26. Whether Oldfather's broader position supports this argument seems debatable. The standard model of judging, he maintains, values impartiality ('lack of extralegal preference for individual parties' (ibid. 91)) and presumes a court to be 'an institutional neutral . . . staffed . . . with decision-makers who are neutral by design' (ibid. 13). Though he considers the model 'an appealing ideal' (ibid. 174), he thinks that it 'does not always translate well into practice' (ibid. 202). Yet one imagines that losing parties would expect judges to aspire to the ideal, much as Oldfather (a former US public defender) appears to expect courts to forgo delivering opinions which don't address the arguments that counsel present on behalf of their clients (see ibid. 26 n 40).

the adversarial process by bringing into play some authority which proved a godsend to the other side. Why, they might ask, would a court ever do this?

Positivist legal philosophy, we know, supplies the court with an answer. Authority attributable to a primary source provides judges with a reason to decide a case in a particular way, irrespective of the merits or demerits of deciding thus. A judge might well be of the view that the case before the court should not be decided by reliance on uncanvassed authority. But this view has no bearing on the decision if the authority is binding on the facts of the case and its applicability is not conditional on a party or intervener having raised it.[60] That law relevant to the resolution of a dispute wasn't raised in arguments to court doesn't detract from the judicial duty to apply it.

In section (b) of chapter 3, the case was made that while Ronald Dworkin was disparaging of positivist legal philosophy, he never entirely escaped the implications of the sources thesis. From an interpretivist perspective, the determination of legal rights and duties still depends—albeit not in the way that legal positivists maintain—on the identification of true (or sound) legal propositions. Even in Dworkin's final major jurisprudential work, we saw, the idea of law as a dimension of political morality is presented in a manner that is not completely hostile to positivist legal thought.

Instances in which judges rely on uncanvassed authorities seem to lend some credence to this late-Dworkinian one-system theory. No doubt these judges, were they so minded, could justify reliance with a stock positivist answer (the same one they might give to that losing party): if uncanvassed authorities are nonetheless binding authorities, courts must accept them as issuing content-independent reasons for reaching particular decisions. That judges are inclined to resort to this answer isn't at all evident, however, from an examination of judgments across common-law jurisdictions. When judges do rely on authorities *sua sponte*, they typically justify their actions by emphasizing not the authority's binding status irrespective of the parties not having raised it, but rather one or another aspect of adjudicative integrity.

In cases involving *sua sponte* reliance, the aspect of integrity perhaps most frequently referred to by judges is natural justice. Judges invoke natural justice not as a reason for relying on uncanvassed authority, but to explain why their willingness to do so is conditional on parties being allowed to present new submissions to court.[61] The grave error identified in *Farah v Say-Dee* was not the

---

[60] On content-independent reasons and context-sensitive enforcement, see Joseph Raz, 'Two Views of the Nature of the Theory of Law: A Partial Comparison' (1998) 4 *Legal Theory* 249, 274–275; also Julie Dickson, *Content-Independence in Law* (Cambridge: CUP, 2024), 19.

[61] See e.g. *W401 v Minister for Immigration and Multicultural Affairs* [2001] FCA 1738 (Fed. Ct Aus.) at para. 27 ('. . . as a matter of procedural fairness'); *A & N Enns Trucking Ltd v Elkew* [2017] FC

overruled court's application of authority *sua sponte*. It was, rather, its failure to take the course typically preferred by Australian courts and restore the case for fresh argument.[62] Australian judges are hardly unique in being attracted to this course.[63] Employment tribunals in England, for example, abide by a specific judge-made convention—some would say rule[64]—concerning 'authority ... which [a tribunal] has not invited the parties to address'.[65] If the authority is 'central to the decision' (or will at least 'play an influential part in shaping the judgment'),[66] parties must be afforded the opportunity to comment on the authority in fresh submissions so as to avert the risk of 'substantial prejudice to the party claiming to be aggrieved'.[67] Failure to provide this opportunity 'may amount to a breach of natural justice and of the right to a fair hearing'.[68]

If you are a litigant, and the court's reliance on uncanvassed authority causes you to lose, you will probably be unimpressed by the claim that the court respected natural justice. You might object that opposing counsel should have

---

917 (Fed. Ct Can.) at paras 11–15; *Saskatchewan Joint Board v Canadian Linen & Uniform Service Co.* [2006] WWR 492 (Sask. QB) at para. 21; *Pacific Recreation Pte Ltd v S Y Technology, Inc.* [2008] 2 SLR(R) 491 (Sing. Ct App.) at [32]; *Principal Mutual Life v Charter Barclay Hospital*, 81 F.3d 53, 56 (7th Cir. 1996) (Posner J) ('Yet it would not be quite cricket ...'); Miller, '*Sua Sponte* Appellate Rulings' (n 54) 1288–1289, 1294–1297, 1305.

[62] See e.g. *Lower v Norton* (1972) 4 SASR 162, 175 (Walters J) ('... the desirable course ... is to restore the case to the list for further argument'); *Jones v Pennuto* [2020] WASC 416 at para. 36; *Stephenson v Human Rights and Equal Opportunity Commission* [1995] FCA 1757 at para. 75; also *APN Funds Management Ltd v Australian Property Investment Strategic Pty Ltd* [2012] VSC 365 at para. 4 ('The court is generally under no obligation to invite further submissions or consider further submissions in relation to a case referred to in the court's reasons for judgment and not cited by any of the parties. The position may be different if the entire case depended on the application of principles derived from binding authority and the parties did not have an opportunity to deal with the case'). Re-listing usually is not preferred where the authority only adds weight or might assist litigants in later cases: see e.g. *PharmX Pty Ltd v Fred IT* [2019] VSC 748 at para. 191 (Lyons J); *Day v The Ocean Beach Hotel Shellharbour Pty Ltd* [2013] NSWCA 250 at para. 33 (Leeming JA).

[63] The dominant judicial attitude in New Zealand is roughly similar: see Susan Glazebrook, 'Academics and the Supreme Court' (2017) 47 *Victoria Univ. of Wellington L. Rev.* 237, 246–247 ('The [New Zealand] courts are not of course necessarily limited to the legal arguments put forward by counsel and will sometimes go outside them, subject to issues of natural justice'); *Hotchin v New Zealand Guardian Trust Co. Ltd* [2016] NZSC 24 at paras 30–31 and 379 (in this instance, the court contemplated deciding on the basis of uncanvassed authorities but eventually opted not to do so); though cf *Premier Group Ltd v Lidgard* [1970] NZLR 280, 283 (Henry J interpreting an element of the law of mortgages by reference to two cases not cited by the parties, and apparently without inviting fresh submissions).

[64] Martin Kwan, 'Can Judges Conduct Independent Legal Research? The US *vs* the Common Law Approaches' (2022) 13 *Houston L. Rev. Online* 30, 34–35.

[65] *Stanley Cole v Sheridan* [2003] EWCA Civ 1046 at [21].

[66] Ibid. at [31]. Uncanvassed authorities won't always be ruled to be of this nature: see *Clark v Clark Construction Initiatives Ltd* [2008] EWCA Civ 1446 at [12]-[13] (Sedley LJ) ('The citation ... of authorities which had not ... been canvassed ... was ... uncalled for and distracting. ... But none of this ... warrants the heavy strictures placed upon the entire determination [by counsel for the appellant] ... which ... is an overreaction to a relatively venial fault in the composition of the decision').

[67] *Stanley Cole v Sheridan* (n 65) at [34].

[68] *Albion Hotel v Silva* [2002] IRLR 200 at [35].

raised the authority—or not have conceded or refused to plead the point of law to which it relates—and that courts shouldn't take measures which, in effect, compensate for deficiencies in your adversary's preparation. Even though the court allowed you to speak to what it introduced, you might add, the cards were still stacked against you. For your task was to convince the court to discount the relevance, or revise its assessment, of an authority which—given that the court raised it of its own accord—the judge, or judges, deciding the case may be presumed to have considered if not dispositive then certainly persuasive. Making accommodations to satisfy natural justice, besides vexing you, may provoke judicial disquiet as well. Reconvening to entertain fresh submissions tends to be disruptive and costly, Richard Posner once observed from the bench, as it usually means that 'we . . . take time away from our consideration and decision of other cases'.[69]

The principle of natural justice is, in any event, of limited interest for our purposes, as it only provides judges with a justification for deciding according to uncanvassed authority under procedurally fair conditions. The more interesting question is whether the demands of integrity can ever be satisfied without the parties being given the opportunity to address authority which they did not canvass but which wholly or partly underpins the court's decision. When judges answer, as they often do, that these demands may indeed be satisfied thus, they have another dimension of justice in mind.

'A judge', according to Learned Hand, 'is affirmatively charged with securing a fair trial, and he must intervene *sua sponte* to that end, when necessary'.[70] When the judge is overseeing a criminal trial, this obligation to intervene derives also from the fact that the court seeks a safe verdict. Judges might well warn criminal law barristers that they can't expect charity if they turn up to court poorly prepared.[71] But they know too that a prosecution is unsafe if there is authority supporting an acquittal and the authority is ignored by the court for no reason other than that defence counsel omitted to rely on it. Judges in criminal cases can quite often be found observing that if uncanvassed

---

[69] *Luddington v Indiana Bell Telephone Co.,* 966 F.2d 225, 230 (7th Cir. 1992) (Posner J).

[70] *Brown v Walter,* 62 F.2d 798, 799 (2nd Cir. 1933); see also *International Finance Trust Co. Ltd v NSW Crime Commission* [2009] HCA 49 at para. 146 (Heydon J); *Carlisle v United States,* 517 US 416, 437–443 (1996) (Stevens J, dissenting).

[71] See e.g. *R v Highton* [2005] EWCA Crim 1985 at [23] (Lord Woolf) ('[E]xclusion of evidence under the [statutory] provisions . . . depends on there being an application by [counsel for] the defendant. If no such application is made, no criticism can be made of the judge for failing to act of his own motion . . .'); *R v McPherson* [2010] EWCA Crim 2906 at [18]; *R v Lee* (1987) 2 WCB (2d) 271 (Brit. Columb. SC) at para. 19 ('The Crown is as much entitled to make full answer to an allegation of infringement of rights as the accused is to the offence charged. It cannot do so if the accused can pop up at the end of the Crown's case and assert, for the first time, a failure to prove a lawful arrest').

authority strengthens or secures the case for the defendant, the principle of leniency must be applied and the authority taken into account.[72] Taking the authority into account might mean re-listing the trial for a fresh hearing. But it doesn't have to mean this. The court may take the view that it matters not if the case is remitted or if fresh submissions are invited, because its process is governed first and foremost by considerations pertaining to the vulnerability of the verdict.

In cases of this kind, the fact that the uncanvassed authority is attributable to a primary source doesn't completely explain why the court applies it. Political morality is also part of the explanation: the best justification of a jurisdiction's legal practice entails applying the authority, since the delivery of unsafe verdicts cannot be integral to the moral point and purpose of that practice. While appeal court judges seek to deliver safe verdicts no less than do other judges, integrity bears upon them in an additional way: they typically aspire to ensure that the content and detail of their judgments meets with what is expected of a senior court. Some judges are '[g]reat judges', Walter Bagehot maintained, because, as 'judges for the parties', they 'are acute discerners of fact, accurate weighers of testimony, just discriminators of argument'.[73] But some judges are yet greater, he added, because they are 'judges for the lawyers', producers of judgments which are not only directed to 'the particular dispute in court' but also formulated 'in the nature of essays' that might 'fix[] the law on the matter in hand' by providing 'an ample exposition of principles applicable to other disputes'.[74] Bagehot's perspective is very much evident in Lord Denning's first ever speech to the House of Lords, delivered in 1958, in which he admitted that he had 'considered some questions and authorities which were not mentioned by counsel'.[75] The House didn't invite the parties to present fresh arguments addressing these questions and authorities, and Denning was basically reprimanded by the other four law lords for having raised them.[76]

Two decades later, Denning reflected on the speech, and on how he was unrepentant about what he had done. In delivering it, he explained, his principal

---

[72] See e.g. *Cohen v Sellar* [1926] 1 KB 536, 545–548; *R v Witty* (1994) 25 WCB (2d) 105 (Brit. Columb. SC) at para. 32; *R v Savard* [1996] BCWLD 1211 (Yukon Terr. Ct App.) at para. 24.

[73] Walter Bagehot, 'Lord Brougham' (1857), in *Bagehot's Historical Essays*, ed. Norman St John-Stevas (London: Dennis Dobson, 1971), 109–146 at 133.

[74] Ibid.

[75] *Rahimtoola v Nizan* [1958] AC 379, 423.

[76] Ibid. 380 ('We must not be taken as assenting to the views of Lord Denning upon a number of questions and authorities in regard to which the House has not had the benefit of the arguments of counsel or of the judgments of the courts below'), also 398 (Viscount Simonds). See also *P & M Kaye Ltd v Hosier & Dickinson Ltd* [1972] 1 WLR 146, 148–149 (Lord Reid); *R (Lumba) v Secretary of State for the Home Department* [2011] UKSC 12 at [25] (Lord Dyson) ('[I]n my view it is not appropriate to depart from a decision . . . unless it is obviously wrong . . . without the benefit of adversarial argument').

aspiration had been to repair the broken legal terrain—to be what Bagehot called a judge for the lawyers—rather than to address the grievances of the parties.[77] Even though it would be wrong to claim that his view had, by this point, been wholeheartedly embraced by the final court, it would also be incorrect to claim that the law lords remained steadfast in considering it heresy. 'Judges are more than mere selectors between rival views', Lord Wilberforce admitted; 'they are entitled to and do think for themselves'.[78] Some of Wilberforce's contemporaries on the Appellate Committee spoke up for *sua sponte* reliance more directly.[79] Their reasoning—Denning's reasoning—is easy to summarize: when a final court applies uncanvassed authority (which may or may not mean hearing fresh arguments first), its justification is not, or certainly not only, that the authority is ascribable to a primary source of law, but, more pertinently, that one of the core obligations of its judges is the delivery of judgments which are meant to clarify, finesse, or settle matters of general legal principle—improve upon existing renditions of the law—rather than just resolve contests between litigants.

---

[77] Lord Denning, *The Discipline of Law* (Oxford: OUP, 1979), 287–289. See also *Miliangos v George Frank (Textiles) Ltd* [1975] QB 487 (CA), 503 (Denning MR) ('The court does its own researches itself and consults authorities; and these may never receive mention in the judgments').

[78] *Saif Ali v Sydney Mitchell & Co.* [1980] AC 198, 212 (Lord Wilberforce); though cf Lord Wilberforce, 'La chambre des lords' (1978) 30 *Revue internationale de droit comparé* 85, 95 ('We hesitate, generally, to consider arguments which have not been discussed at the hearing').

[79] See e.g. *Cassell v Broome (No 1)* [1972] AC 1027, 1131 (Lord Diplock) ('[T]his House was fully entitled to come to a conclusion . . . different from that which any individual counsel had propounded'); also *Alexander Ward & Co. Ltd v Samyang Navigation Co. Ltd* [1971] 1 WLR 673, 684 (Lord Kilbrandon).

8

Scholarship as a secondary source

It is hardly surprising that legal analysts should have had a good deal to say about secondary sources functioning as primary ones. Secondary sources understood as sources of epistemic, persuasive, non-binding pronouncements—understood as secondary sources—make for a more conventional, one might think less complicated, line of enquiry. With some secondary sources, this is very much the case. For example, even though the reliance by courts on legislative history can prove contentious—statements on the record are not expressions of the legislature's intent,[1] are likely to yield ambiguities of their own,[2] might have been strategically introduced into a debate with an eye to influencing how the enacted text is construed,[3] and so on—the reason judges resort to this particular source is almost always the same: they hope the history will help them interpret the statute. But judges' motives for resorting to secondary sources are sometimes less straightforward, and in the case of one type of secondary source—scholarship with a bearing on law—the nature of, and the reasons explaining, judicial reliance are remarkably varied and intricate.

Whereas academics occasionally maintain that scholarship can function as a primary source, judges are rarely if ever attracted to this argument, and sometimes reject it point blank.[4] There are judges who would confess to having absolutely no interest in academic-legal work, just as there are academic lawyers

---

[1] See Johan Steyn, 'The Intractable Problem of the Interpretation of Legal Texts' (2003) 25 *Sydney L. Rev.* 5, 14; J. H. Baker, 'Statutory Interpretation and Parliamentary Intention' (1993) 52 *CLJ* 353, 354–355; Heidi M. Hurd, 'Sovereignty in Silence' (1990) 99 *Yale L. J.* 945, 971–973.

[2] See e.g. *A-G for England & Wales v Counsel General for Wales* [2014] UKSC 43 at [35] ('The Attorney General referred us to a statement made by the Parliamentary Under-Secretary of State for Wales . . . in a debate on the Bill. . . . In that statement the Minister stated that the purpose of the Bill was not to "broaden devolution" but to "deepen" it. . . . We do not think that the use by the Minister of such a general and ambiguous phrase can properly be of any assistance . . .'); *Citizens to Preserve Overton Park, Inc. v Volpe*, 401 US 402, 413 n 29 (1971) ('The legislative history . . . is ambiguous. . . . Because of this ambiguity it is clear that we must look primarily to the statutes themselves to find the legislative intent').

[3] See *Chartbrook Ltd v Persimmon Homes Ltd* [2009] UKHL 38 at [38] (Lord Hoffmann) ('[The willingness of UK courts to countenance legislative history] has . . . encouraged ministers and others to make statements [on the legislative record] in the hope of influencing the construction which the courts will give to a statute').

[4] See e.g. Jack Beatson, 'Legal Academics: Forgotten Players or Interlopers?', in *Judge and Jurist: Essays in Memory of Lord Rodger of Earlsferry*, ed. A. Burrows, D. Johnston, and R. Zimmermann (Oxford: OUP, 2013), 523–541 at 529–530.

Law's Sources. Neil Duxbury, Oxford University Press. © Neil Duxbury 2025.
DOI: 10.1093/9780198981183.003.0008

who pay little or no attention to judicial decision-making. When judges do show an interest in scholarship, they tend to focus on how scholarship influences the development of the law, particularly in the courts. Academics and judges inclined to reflect on how scholarship influences the business of judging broadly agree that it makes for a complicated topic. Judges, when engaged in judging, might acknowledge but not be influenced by scholarship. In the United States, there are judges who have written candidly of how references to law review articles in judicial opinions not only might have been inserted by law clerks rather than by the judges under whose names those opinions appear, but also of how those judges will often not have read the articles.[5] Conversely, judges might be influenced by scholarship but not acknowledge it. In *Miller v Miller* (2006), for example, the House of Lords' reformulation of asset-distribution principles applicable on divorce was, according to one of the deciding judges, directly influenced by an academic article relied on in arguments presented to court by one of the barristers, though the article is mentioned nowhere in the judgment.[6] Jurists might urge the courts to move some aspect of the law in a particular direction when an opportunity arises, and the courts might well do so—and might even reference the relevant juristic sources when they do. But the judges who make the move might have been ready to make it without any encouragement, and their references to jurists could be incidental or platitudinous.[7]

Legal scholarship which influences judicial reasoning as often as not bears the influence of judicial reasoning (judges, after all, inspire the academics who inspire judges).[8] It is also important to bear in mind that legal practitioners and judges, as well as academics, produce influential scholarship. Not only

---

[5] See Diane P. Wood, 'Legal Scholarship for Judges' (2015) 124 *Yale L. J.* 2592, 2595; also Patricia M. Wald, 'How I Write' (1993) 4 *Scribes Jnl of Legal Writing* 55, 59.

[6] *Miller v Miller* [2006] UKHL 24. The unacknowledged article is by Joanna Miles, 'Principle or Pragmatism in Ancillary Relief: The Virtues of Flirting with Academic Theories and Other Jurisdictions' (2005) 19 *Int'l Jnl of Law, Policy and the Family* 242. On its impact on the judgment, see Brenda Hale, 'The Influence of Academia on Family Law: From the Battlefield to Mount Olympus', in *Family Matters: Essays in Honour of John Eekelaar*, ed. J. M. Scherpe and S. Gilmore (Cambridge: Intersentia, 2022), 27–40 at 39–40.

[7] See John Smith, *Judge, Jurist and Parliament* (London: Judicial Studies Board, 2002), 3; Lord Rodger, 'Judges and Academics in the United Kingdom' (2010) 29 *Univ. Queensland L. J.* 29, 30–31.

[8] Consider e.g. Felipe Jiménez, 'On Legal Expertise' (2024) 69 *Am. J. Juris.* 141, 150, who argues that '[i]n [US] contract law, . . . the distinction between the expectation, reliance, and restitution interests and the notion of "efficient breach" are ideas that come from legal scholarship yet are, in an important sense, part of our law'. That these ideas *come from* legal scholarship seems debatable. Legal scholars began theorizing about efficient breach in the 1970s, for example, but, by this point, the expectation-based remedy that the theory supports (requiring defendants in breach of contract to pay damages to the amount that puts plaintiffs in the economic position they would have been in if the breach hadn't occurred) had long been recognized in the US courts: see e.g. *Bush v Canfield*, 2 Conn. 485 (SC Errors Conn. 1818).

might the juristic writing that features in a judge's reasoning be the work of a judge, but it might even be that judge's own work. Judicial modifications of legal principles and concepts (in English law, Lord Millett's recalibration of the *Quistclose* trust is illustrative)[9] are, occasionally, traceable to arguments that the judges who made the modifications set forth in law review articles. Richard Posner, ever the contrarian, once introduced into one of his judicial opinions a version of an argument advanced in one of his own articles (not cited in the opinion), only to dismiss it as unsupported by legal authority.[10]

a) *Judges on scholarship*

Jurists, when they consider scholarship as a secondary source, tend to enquire after the ways in which academic work impacts positively on what judges do. But while judges often follow the same path, they can also occasionally be found alighting on a more downbeat narrative. The mild version of this narrative is that influence will not necessarily be good influence. Lord Goff, a judge renowned for his willingness to countenance academic commentary in court, was not averse to warning that there are instances when following juristic opinion will guarantee a judicial wrong-turn.[11] In *Fairchild v Glenhaven* (2002), the ambition of the judgment—that material contribution to risk was sufficient to establish the causation component required to demonstrate an employer's liability to a claimant who developed mesothelioma after exposure to asbestos dust at work—reflected the tenor of the cited academic commentary (which mainly concerned the feasibility of departing from an orthodox, balance-of-probabilities application of the 'but for' causation test).[12] Just how much of a bearing the commentary had on

---

[9] *Twinsectra v Yardley* [2002] UKHL 12, where Millett rejects the explanation of the *Quistclose* trust that had been provided by Lord Wilberforce in *Barclays Bank v Quistclose Investments Ltd* [1970] AC 567 in favour of an explanation which he had already sketched out in P. J. Millett, 'The *Quistclose* Trust: Who Can Enforce It?' (1985) 101 *LQR* 269.

[10] In the article, Posner argues that there are strong economic reasons for renewing copyright indefinitely when the consequence of putting a work into the public domain is that it is likely to be 'overgrazed' and so suffer significant deterioration in commercial value: William M. Landes and Richard A. Posner, 'Indefinitely Renewable Copyright' (2003) 70 *Univ. Chicago L. Rev.* 471, 484–485. (The language of indefinite renewal bypassed, Landes and Posner thought, the constitutional prohibition on granting perpetual copyrights (ibid. 473–474).) In *Klinger v Conan Doyle Estate Ltd*, 755 F.3d 496 (7th Cir. 2014), Posner, writing for the court, concluded that the case for 'copyright protection of literary characters to . . . extraordinary lengths'—Doyle's estate sought a 135-year extension on the Sherlock Holmes character—'has no legal grounds' and, in the particular instance, 'borders on the quixotic'. Ibid. 503. See also Tim Wu, 'On Posner on Copyright' (2019) 86 *Univ. Chicago L. Rev.* 1217, 1230–1232.

[11] See e.g. *Henderson v Merrett Syndicates Ltd* [1995] 2 AC 145, 192–193.

[12] *Fairchild v Glenhaven* [2002] UKHL 22.

the judgment is impossible to ascertain—the House of Lords drew on other sources along with the commentary—though the law lord who delivered the leading judgment was clearly very receptive to it.[13] It is certainly evident, nevertheless, that some judges have come to bemoan *Fairchild* as an example of judicial overreach.[14]

In the United States, there have been some uncompromising judicial interventions—Richard Posner's *Divergent Paths* being the prime modern exhibit—conveying a somewhat harsher message: that the story of academic influence on judicial opinion writing is basically one of disappointment and failure.[15] The pared-down version of the story has it that there 'was a time when legal scholarship was understood to be doctrinal scholarship, and the more technical and intricate the doctrine, the better',[16] but that this time is no more: that 'now'—the words of a DC Circuit judge in 1992—'many of our law reviews are dominated by rather exotic offerings of increasingly out-of-touch faculty members'.[17]

In 2008, one Supreme Court Justice lamented that 'there is evidence that law review articles have left terra firma to soar into outer space'.[18] Three years later, in an off-the-cuff (and memorably parodied)[19] response to an interviewer's question, one of his colleagues echoed the sentiment:

[p]ick up a copy of any law review that you see and the first article is likely to be, you know, the influence of Immanuel Kant on evidentiary approaches

---

[13] See ibid. at [23]–[27], [32] (Lord Bingham).

[14] See e.g. *Zurich Insurance v International Insurance Group* [2015] UKSC 33 at [111] (Lord Hodge, concurring) ('[T]he courts should develop the common law in a principled way. . . . [T]he protection of the employee-victim's entitlement to recover damages is a matter for Parliament. . . . [H]aving dug a hole, the courts should not keep digging') and [211] (Lords Neuberger and Reed, dissenting) ('[I]f *Fairchild* had been decided the other way, in accordance with normal common law principles, Parliament would have intervened very promptly. That may very well have been a better solution, but it can fairly be said that that observation is made with the wisdom of hindsight').

[15] Richard A. Posner, *Divergent Paths: The Academy and the Judiciary* (Cambridge, Mass.: Harvard UP, 2016). See also Harry T. Edwards, 'The Growing Disjunction Between Legal Education and the Legal Profession' (1992) 91 *Michigan L. Rev.* 34. For cases in which supreme and federal court judges can be found expressing disappointment with either law schools or with universities more generally, see e.g. *Students for Fair Admissions, Inc. v President and Fellows of Harvard College*, 600 US 181, 256 (2023) (Thomas J, concurring) ('Universities' self-proclaimed righteousness . . .'); *Grutter v Bollinger*, 539 US 306, 346–347 (2003) (Scalia and Thomas JJ, concurring in part and dissenting in part) ('[T]he . . . Law School's mystical . . . justification for its discrimination by race challenges even the most gullible mind'); also *Speech First, Inc. v Sands*, 69 F.4th 184, 207 (4th Cir. 2023) (Wilkinson J, dissenting).

[16] Richard A. Posner, *The Problematics of Moral and Legal Theory* (Cambridge, Mass.: Belknap Press, 1999), 296.

[17] *United States v $639,558*, 955 F.2d 712, 722 (DC Cir. 1992) (Silberman J, concurring).

[18] Stephen G. Breyer, 'Response of Justice Stephen G. Breyer' (2008) 64 *NYU Ann. Surv. Am. L.* 33, 33.

[19] Orin S. Kerr 'The Influence of Immanuel Kant on Evidentiary Approaches in Eighteenth Century Bulgaria' (2015) 18 *Green Bag 2d* 251.

in eighteenth-century Bulgaria or something—which I'm sure was of great interest to the academic that wrote it, but isn't of much help to the bar.[20]

The version of the story normally told by judges minded to endorse this sentiment is slightly more nuanced: the problem has to do with picking up a copy of not 'any law review', but rather almost any student-edited law review— especially the main student-edited law review—emanating from a major law school. The law reviews perhaps provide evidence, according to one judge, not of a 'decline in doctrinal scholarship' but of 'a shift in the production of doctrinal scholarship toward scholars at law schools of the second and third tier'.[21] According to another, it is specifically 'the elite law reviews' that 'publish a disproportionate number of pieces whose substance and style are not useful or appealing to the practicing community'.[22]

Even this more finessed assessment seems open to question. Those Justices quoted a moment ago, bemoaning an abundance of recondite or ethereal law review fare, have both issued numerous opinions drawing on doctrinal legal scholarship, much of it published in the journals of elite law schools.[23] A study identifying (from the contents of 170 law reviews published between 1989 and 1991) articles most frequently cited in the US courts as of 1995 found that of the top five pieces—all of which were either doctrinal or empirical studies— three of them were published in student-edited journals connected to first-tier law schools and two of the three were authored by professors at those schools.[24] Soon after this study appeared, another study—opening with the observation that US judges 'increasingly feel that there is a lack of legal scholarship that

---

[20] 'A Conversation with Chief Justice Roberts', Fourth Circuit Court of Appeals: 77th Annual Conference (Harvie-Wilkinson J, interviewer), White Sulphur Springs, West Virginia, 25 June 2011 (www.c-span.org/video/?300203-1/conversation-chief-justice-roberts) at 30:39–32:14 (accessed 20 July 2023) esp. at 30:47–31:10. See also 'Chief Justice John G. Roberts, Jr' (interviewed by Bryan A. Garner) (2010) 13 *Scribes Jnl of Legal Writing* 5, 37.

[21] Richard A. Posner, *Overcoming Law* (Cambridge, Mass.: Harvard UP, 1995), 94. See also—an obituary containing what might be his most nuanced reflections on this topic—Richard A. Posner, 'In Memoriam: Bernard D. Meltzer (1917–2007)' (2007) 74 *Univ. Chicago L. Rev.* 435.

[22] Harry T. Edwards, 'Another Look at Professor Rodell's *Goodbye to Law Reviews*' (2014) 100 *Va L. Rev.* 1483, 1499.

[23] See e.g. *PennEast Pipeline Co. v New Jersey*, 141 S. Ct 2244, 2255 (2021); *Gill v Whitford*, 138 S. Ct 1916, 1932–1933 (2018); *United States v Booker*, 543 US 220, 334 (2005); *Zivotovsky v Clinton*, 566 US 189, 213 (2012) (Breyer J, dissenting); *Lilly v Virginia*, 527 US 116, 140 (1999) (Breyer J, concurring); also Richard M. Re, 'The Chief Justice Reads Law Reviews', *PrawfsBlawg*, 16 March 2015 https://prawfsblawg.blogs.com/prawfsblawg/2015/03/the-chief-justice-reads-law-reviews.html (accessed 2 February 2024).

[24] Deborah J. Merritt and Melanie Putnam, 'Judges and Scholars: Do Courts and Scholarly Journals Cite the Same Law Review Articles?' (1991) 71 *Chicago-Kent L. Rev.* 871.

they can use when they face their daily case loads'[25]—offered evidence of 'a substantial drop in the citation of law review articles by courts'.[26] Yet the evidence also showed (as had earlier research) that when judicial opinions did contain citations to law review articles—which they quite often still did—the citations were predominantly to articles published in top-tier law school journals.[27] Subsequent studies, focusing specifically on the Supreme Court, suggest that nothing has changed.[28] Though surveys of this kind have to be handled with care—not least because there can be citations in an opinion that are window-dressing, that might not even have been inserted by a judge—they do all point to the same conclusion: predominantly downbeat judicial estimations of US law reviews as secondary sources would seem to be at least a little bit off the mark.

Now and again, judges—and jurists[29]—from other common law jurisdictions offer the same harsh assessment, though they tend to formulate it in a less forthright fashion. In the United Kingdom, final court judges have occasionally deviated from the standard narrative. Academic legal analysis has 'little to do with the work of the courts',[30] one of them once observed, querying 'whether it is altogether satisfactory for academic writers to go direct to the more theoretical aspects of a subject without ever really engaging with the nitty-gritty of how it actually operates in practice'.[31] '[L]egal academia', another has written recently, 'appears to be intent on ... giving the impression that what goes on in the courts, as a matter of legal reasoning and argument, is rather too dull and straightforward for high academic minds'.[32] The standard narrative—the one favoured by most (including many American) common-law judges who offer an opinion, as well as by most academics lawyers who do the same—is somewhat less striking. Nobody could delve into the subject of juristic influence on judicial reasoning without quickly running into a motif: jurists and judges

---

[25] Michael D. McClintock, 'The Declining Use of Legal Scholarship by Courts: An Empirical Study' (1998) 51 *Oklahoma L. Rev.* 659, 659. For the earlier research, see Louis J. Sirico and Jeffrey B. Margulies, 'Citing of Law Reviews by the Supreme Court: An Empirical Study' (1986) 34 *UCLA L. Rev.* 131.

[26] McClintock, 'The Declining Use of Legal Scholarship' (n 25) 687.

[27] Ibid. 689.

[28] Mark Cooney, 'What Judges Cite: A Study of Three Appellate Courts' (2020) 50 *Stetson L. Rev.* 1, 37–39; Louis J. Sirico, Jr., 'The Citing of Law Reviews by the Supreme Court: 1971–1999' (2000) 75 *Indiana L. J.* 1009, 1010–1011.

[29] See e.g. Jane Stapleton, *Three Essays on Torts* (Oxford: OUP, 2021), 17–34.

[30] Rodger, 'Judges and Academics' (n 7) 34.

[31] Ibid. 36, and see also 41 ('The judges would not be human ... if ... they did not sometimes wish that the academics had taken a day off from jurisprudence or sociological analysis to provide some guidance through the tangle'); Alan Rodger, 'Savigny in the Strand' (1993–1995) n.s. 28–30 *Irish Jurist* 1, 9.

[32] Lord Burrows, 'Judges and Academics, and the Endless Road to Unattainable Perfection' (2022) 55 *Israel L. Rev.* 50, 56.

are 'laborers in the same vineyard'[33] toiling over 'different though . . . comple-
mentary'[34] quests, beneficiaries of 'a long and happy marriage',[35] 'a symbiotic
co-existence',[36] 'a constructive partnership'[37] marked by 'a healthy respect for
the work of the other'.[38] Even if claims like these are motivated at least in part
by diplomacy, with both sides sending out the sorts of signals they think the
other side wants to receive, they attest to an incontrovertible fact: just as judicial opinion bears an influence on legal scholarship, there is—as judges regularly acknowledge[39]—plenty of legal scholarship that has influenced judicial
opinion.

Yet there is no doubt too that this standard narrative can be easily exagger-
ated. When delivering judgments, even appeal court judgments, common-law
judges usually—and usually for good reasons—do not so much as disclose if
they are aware of, let alone acknowledge they are influenced by, legal scholarship pertaining to the legal issue at hand. As compared with academic lawyers,
judges are less enticed by ratiocination over legal concepts and principles,[40]

---

[33] Learned Hand, 'Have the Bench and Bar Anything to Contribute to the Teaching of Law?' (1926)
24 *Michigan L. Rev.* 466, 466.

[34] Robert Goff, 'The Search for Principle' (1983) 69 *Proc. Brit. Acad.* 169, 171; also Susan Glazebrook,
'Academics and the Supreme Court' (2017) 47 *Victoria Univ. of Wellington L. Rev.* 237, 249.

[35] Frank K. Richardson, 'Law Reviews and the Courts' (1983) 5 *Whittier L. Rev.* 385, 392; also Dennis
Archer, 'The Importance of Law Reviews to the Judiciary and the Bar' [1991] *Detroit College of Law Rev.*
229, 236.

[36] Lord Dyson, 'Academics and Judges', in his *Justice: Continuity and Change* (Oxford: Hart, 2018),
35; also Robert J. Sharpe, *Good Judgment: Making Judicial Decisions* (Toronto: University of Toronto
Press, 2018), 184; Susan Kiefel, 'The Academy and the Courts: What Do They Mean to Each Other
Today?' (2020) 44 *Melbourne Univ. L. Rev.* 447, 455.

[37] Lord Neuberger, 'Judges and Professors—Ships Passing in the Night?' (2013) 77(2) *Rabels
Zeitschrift für ausländisches und internationales Privatrecht* 233, 246; Lady Justice Carr, ' "Delicate
Plants", "Loose Cannons", or "A Marriage of True Minds"? The Role of Academic Literature in Judicial
Decision-Making' (2023) 23 *Oxford Univ. Commonwealth L. J.* 1, 15; also Alexandra Braun, 'Judges and
Academics: Features of a Partnership', in *From House of Lords to Supreme Court: Judges, Jurists and the
Process of Judging*, ed. J. Lee (Oxford: Hart, 2011), 227–253.

[38] Burrows, 'Judges and Academics' (n 32) 54.

[39] For examples from a massive field, see *United States v Vaello Madero*, 142 S. Ct 1539, 1552–1553
(2022) (Gorsuch J, concurring); *R v G* [2003] UKHL 50 at [34] (Lord Bingham) ('A decision is not, of
course, to be overruled or departed from simply because it meets with disfavour in the learned journals. But a decision which attracts reasoned and outspoken criticism by the leading scholars of the
day, respected as authorities in the field, must command attention'); *Members of the Yorta Aboriginal
Community v Victoria* (2002) 214 CLR 422 at paras 45–57 (Gleeson CJ, Gummow and Hayne JJ);
State of New York by Abrams v Brown, 721 F.Supp. 629, 642 (Distr. Ct NJ 1989) ('According to . . . an
influential law review article that has been followed by many courts [*sc.*, Phillip Areeda and Donald
F. Turner, "Predatory Pricing and Related Practices under Section 2 of the Sherman Act" (1975) 88
Harv. L. Rev. 697], pricing at or above reasonably anticipated average variable cost should be conclu-
sively presumed lawful, while pricing below that level should be conclusively presumed unlawful'); *R v
Shivpuri* [1987] AC 1, 23 (Lord Bridge).

[40] See e.g. Rodger, 'Savigny in the Strand' (n 31) 15; *Fulton v City of Philadelphia*, 141 S. Ct 1868,
1897–1898 (2021); *Kernan v Cuero*, 138 S. Ct 4, 8–9 (2017); *Huss Co. v Continental Casualty Co.*, 735
F.2d 246, 252–253 (7th Cir. 1984); also *National Hockey League Players' Association v Bettman*, No. 93
Civ. 5769 (KMW), 1994 WL 738835 1, 32 (SD NY Ct, 9 November 1994) ('[O]ne must be wary of attempting to develop or apply legal principles in a vacuum, divorced from the facts that give rise to the
controversy and not framed by adversary argument').

and they occasionally criticize other judges for being more enticed than they perhaps ought to be.[41] Bear in mind, Lord Macmillan cautioned his colleagues in *Read v Lyons* (1947), that our 'task in this House is ... not ... to rationalize the law of England'.[42] Instances of judges politely, or even staunchly, rebuffing academic legal argument are not uncommon.[43] Around the time that Macmillan issued his caution, a US federal court observed of a contentious precedent that it mattered not at all that it had 'been roundly criticized in ... [the] *Columbia Law Review*', because 'we are bound by the decision, not the criticism'.[44]

Judges, perhaps particularly US judges, have not exactly been shy about re-iterating this general sentiment.[45] The judicial line can be brusque—as when a court mentions scholarship only to draw attention to the fact that it is adrift on the relevant law.[46] Beware, judges warn, of over-estimating the influence of scholarship on the courts,[47] and bear in mind that work which once influenced judicial reasoning may now be past its shelf-life (the 'seminal article ... predi-cated ... on assumptions that simply do not accord with current reality').[48] It is not unusual for judges to remark on how their citation of, and even re-liance on, scholarship is not necessarily evidence of their opinions having been influenced by juristic analysis.[49] Or on how there is a difference between

---

[41] See e.g. *Indofood International v Morgan Chase* [2006] EWCA Civ 158, where there was clearly concern on the Court of Appeal that a lower court had been uncritically receptive of academic opinion. In *Roberts v SSAFA* [2019] EWHC 1104 (QB), the High Court judge was not enticed—'[t]he academic texts and articles provided no assistance' (ibid. at [80])—whereas one of the judges in the final court was: *Roberts v SSAFA* [2022] UKSC 29 at [73] (Lord Lloyd-Jones).

[42] *Read v Lyons* [1947] AC 156, 175.

[43] See e.g. *Thorner v Major* [2009] UKHL 18 at [31] (Lord Walker); *Williams v Natural Life Health Foods Ltd* [1998] 1 WLR 830, 837 (Lord Steyn) ('Distinguished academic writers have criticised the principle ... as often resting on a fiction.... In my view the general criticism is overstated'); *Saunders v Ford Motor Co.*, 879 F.3d 742, 752 (6th Cir. 2018); also Alan Paterson, *Final Judgment: The Last Law Lords and the Supreme Court* (Oxford: Hart, 2013), 219.

[44] *Phillips Petroleum Co. v Jones*, 76 F.2d 737, 739–740 (10th Cir. 1949).

[45] See e.g. *Steshenko v Gayrard*, 44 F.Supp.3d 941, 953 (ND Cal. 2014) ('Ninth Circuit case law—not law review articles—bind [*sic*] this Court'); *United States v Brown*, 677 F.2d 26, 27 (6th Cir. 1982) ('This court must follow Supreme Court precedent, not law review articles expressing contrary views').

[46] See e.g. *United States v Morison*, 844 F.2d 1057, 1072 (4th Cir. 1988); *Amalgamated Clothing and Textile Workers Union v NLRB*, 736 F.2d 1559, 1571 n 1 (DC Cir. 1984) (Bork J, concurring); *State of Illinois v General Paving Co.*, 590 F.2d 680, 683 n 7 (7th Cir. 1979).

[47] See e.g. Rodger, 'Judges and Academics' (n 7) 31 ('[In] a couple of cases in the House of Lords ... the speech of one of the Law Lords refers to a considerable number of academic articles. You would readily suppose that they had been influential in forming his decision. But, in fact, the draft of the speech was completed before the judge ever saw the articles.... There is therefore no reason to suppose that the articles in question had the slightest effect on the judge's decision in either case; indeed there is every reason to suppose that they had precisely none').

[48] *Garcia v San Antonio Metropolitan Transit Authority*, 469 US 528, 565 n 9 (1985) (Powell J, dissenting). See also *Andrew Robinson International, Inc. v Hartford Fire Insurance Co.*, 547 F.3d 48, 57 (1st Cir. 2008) ('musty lamentations ... subsequently rejected').

[49] See e.g. Beatson, 'Legal Academics' (n 4) 535 ('Citation by a court or its absence is not necessarily indicative of influence or its absence'); Posner, *Divergent Paths* (n 15) 28–29. For examples of judges co-opting academic terminology while explicitly eschewing the reasoning accompanying it, see *Jones v*

scholarship making an impression on a court and scholarship featuring in the submissions of legal representatives arguing before a court.[50] Or, furthermore, on how particular areas of law (usually areas where the law is basically settled) can be impervious to juristic influence or, indeed, to legal opinion contained in any type of secondary source.[51]

Judges now and again observe that even scholarship devised with an eye to assisting them is not really of their world and will often miss the mark. Guido Calabresi, soon after leaving full-time academia for his judicial career, realized that he had to resist 'the inclination . . . to write opinions as though they are law review articles', given that writing for publication in a law review, unlike writing a judicial opinion, involves no burden to provide reasons for a legal ruling: unlike legal scholars, he maintained, 'all judges write for the Law. We decide cases, we explain how we get to the result, and that's what the Law requires.'[52] Though '[j]udicial opinions are not law review articles', another federal judge remarked around the time that Calabresi was appointed to the bench, judges sometimes make the mistake of not keeping this in mind, and 'go astray (and lead litigants astray)' by 'seek[ing] to deal with issues that go beyond what is necessary to decide the case at hand'.[53] Even judges who judge for lawyers (see chapter 7, section (c)) need to think carefully about how far to venture. '[M]ost of the time, it is dangerous to do more than is required to decide the case in hand. It is even more dangerous if that is done in pursuit of some grand design.'[54]

Even if a judicial opinion does not constitute the court's decision it is still, in one way or another, a contribution to it. Unlike juristic argument, moreover, an opinion is not simply a matter of opinion, for judicial opinion-delivery concerns, first and foremost, the application of law rather than the articulation of a legal point of view. 'Depending on the level of court, a judgment has to make findings of fact, it has to decide what the relevant principles of law are, and it has to apply those legal principles to the facts as found. Unlike

---

Kernott [2011] UKSC 53 at [16] (Lord Walker and Lady Hale); *Delaware Tribal Business Committee v Weeks*, 430 US 73, 98 n 11 (1977) (Stevens J, dissenting).

[50] See e.g. *Skatteforvaltningen v Solo Capital Partners LLP* [2022] EWCA Civ 234 at [110]–[111]; *Sedima SPRL v Imrex Co., Inc.*, 741 F.2d 482, 486–487 (2nd Cir. 1984).

[51] See e.g. Daphne Barak-Erez, 'Writing Law: Reflections on Judicial Decisions and Academic Scholarship' (2015) 41 *Queen's L. J.* 255, 266; Rodger, 'Savigny in the Strand' (n 31) 9; also Nora Stappert, 'A New Influence of Legal Scholars? The Use of Academic Writings at International Criminal Courts and Tribunals' (2018) 31 *Leiden Jnl Int'l Law* 963, 979–980.

[52] Norman I. Silber, *Outside In: The Oral History of Guido Calabresi*, 2 vols (Oxford: OUP, 2023), II, 201–202.

[53] *McCullough v Brown*, 162 B.R. 506, 515 (ND Ill. 1993).

[54] Baroness Hale, 'A Minority Opinion?' (2008) 154 *Proc. Brit. Acad.* 319, 336.

a law review article, a judgment cannot, on the central questions, sit on the fence.'[55] Academic lawyers have liberties, by and large, where many judges do not. Legal scholars can choose their topics and write very much at their own pace.[56] They need not be confined, in the way that some common-law judges maintain that their judgments are confined, to evaluating and taking positions on the arguments and the points of law that litigants present to court.[57] They need not contemplate whether their pronouncements, once published, would withstand an appeal. Nor must they be mindful of running afoul of norms and conventions against unwarranted law making.[58] The common narrative about legal academics and judges being in partnership is not misleading, but nor is it the entire story.

The broader story need occupy us barely at all here, for it has been told many times before. As has been intimated already, citation—of scholarship, and especially of law review articles, by courts—features prominently in the story as typically recounted in the United States.[59] In other common law jurisdictions, the pre-eminent version of the story (related as often by judges as by academics) is more about how particular jurists have had the judiciary's ear—usually because judges find a jurist's argument to be especially cogent and pertinent (though sometimes it helps if the jurist is an indefatigable campaigner or is in with the relevant in-crowd).[60] Somewhat less analysed are the contours and the nature of scholarly influence in those instances where it is present. Academics influence judges, certainly, but—when they do, and when this influence is detectable—what forms does the influence take?

---

[55] Burrows, 'Judges and Academics' (n 32) 62.

[56] Richard A. Posner, How Judges Think (Cambridge, Mass.: Harvard UP, 2008), 206.

[57] See Flood v Times Newspapers [2012] UKSC 11 at [106] (Lord Phillips); Burrows, 'Judges and Academics' (n 32) 61. Some common-law judges, but not all: see chapter 7, section (c).

[58] See Beatson, 'Legal Academics' (n 4) 527; Christian Atias, 'Jurists, and Legal Knowledge' (1988) 74 Archiv für Rechts- und Sozialphilosophie 368, 387–390.

[59] See e.g. Tamara R. Piety, 'In Praise of Legal Scholarship' (2017) 25 William & Mary Bill of Rights Jnl 801, 821–824; Lee Petherbridge and David L. Schwartz, 'An Empirical Assessment of the Supreme Court's Use of Legal Scholarship' (2012) 106 Northwestern L. Rev. 995 (note that the authors, who argue against the notion that American judges and practitioners do not value legal scholarship, treat 'citation' and 'use' as synonymous (ibid. 1000)); Gregory Scott Crespi, 'Judicial and Law Review Citation Frequencies for Articles Published in Different "Tiers" of Law Journals: An Empirical Analysis' (2004) 44 Santa Clara L. Rev. 897. The argument tends to be that citation-analysis provides at best a rough proxy for the extent to which judges are influenced by legal scholarship.

[60] For instances, see Paterson, Final Judgment (n 43) 216 (F. A. Mann); Hale, 'Minority Opinion' (n 54) 323 n 18 (David Thomas); Burrows, 'Judges and Academics' (n 32) 53 (Peter Birks); Neil Duxbury, Frederick Pollock and the English Juristic Tradition (Oxford: OUP, 2004), 314–322; Jurists and Judges: An Essay on Influence (Oxford: Hart, 2001), 87–101 (Arthur Goodhart), 108–113 (J. C. Smith and Glanville Williams).

b) *Judges using scholarship*

When judges take account of legal scholarship, or indeed of scholarly expertise more generally, they use it mainly as a source of legal information. They might be relying on it in conjunction with, and in judgments and judicial opinions its contribution might be indistinguishable from that supplied by, other secondary sources. But in some instances, its epistemic function is distinct, typically because it addresses some important consideration, or set of considerations, pertaining to a case—context, history, relevant legal reasoning and doctrine, questions bearing on the interpretation of a legal text, central concepts or principles and their legal significance—which other sources either neglect entirely or handle inadequately. Reliance need not work to the good: injudicious use of scholarship might (just as a lack of discernment when drawing on other sources might)[61] result in the introduction of avoidable embellishment, technicality, or inaccuracy into an opinion.[62] Judges, moreover, sometimes turn out to be disputing scholarly accounts rather than relying on them.[63]

Rarely, however, are judges intent on using opinions and judgments as opportunities to take issue with jurists. Their normal objective in resorting to scholarship as an epistemic source is to make their reasoning more accessible or comprehensible than it would otherwise be. While a work of scholarship 'should clearly not be read as if it were a statute', the UK Supreme Court observed recently, it might provide a 'a helpful summary' and serve as 'a useful starting-point for analysis'.[64] Scholarship might assist an appeal court in providing lower courts—and prospective litigants—with direction on a point of law. It might enable a judge to canvass all the relevant legal authorities without overloading an opinion with detail.[65] It might be the key to clarifying an idea—possession, predatory pricing, and patient autonomy are three alliterative examples—which lawyers regularly confront and find challenging.[66] Or it

---

[61] See Maggie Gardner, 'Dangerous Citations' (2020) 95 *NYU L. Rev.* 1619.

[62] See Rodger, 'Judges and Academics' (n 7) 32; Beatson, 'Legal Academics' (n 4) 537.

[63] See e.g. *R v Jogee* [2016] UKSC 8 at [76]; *Westdeutsche Landesbank Girozentrale v Islington LBC* [1996] AC 669, 708–709 (Lord Browne-Wilkinson); *United States v Chesney*, 86 F.3d 564, 576 (6th Cir. 1996) (Batchelder J, concurring); *Wells v Wily* [2004] NSWSC 697 at paras 25–26 (Austin J).

[64] *Tindall v Chief Constable of Thames Valley Police* [2024] UKSC 33 at [42]–[43].

[65] See e.g. *London & S. E. Railway Ltd v Gutmann* [2022] EWCA Civ 1077 at [93]; *Furnes v Reeves*, 362 F.3d 702, 709 n 3 (11th Cir. 2004); *Carpet Fashions v Forma Holdings* [2003] NSWSC 460 at para. 147 (Einstein J); also Keith Stanton, 'Use of Scholarship by the House of Lords in Tort Cases', in Lee (ed.), *From House of Lords to Supreme Court* (n 37) 201–226 at 211.

[66] See *Secretary of State for the Environment, Food and Rural Affairs v Meier* [2009] UKSC 11 at [32], [34] (Lady Hale) and [60] (Lord Neuberger); *Matsushita Electric Industrial Co. v Zenith Radio Corp.*, 475 US 574, 589 (1986); *Chester v Ashfar* [2004] UKHL 41 at [18] (Lord Steyn).

might bring clarity to whatever happens to be the legal problem challenging the court. Even though the judge responsible for the Third Circuit's opinion in *In re Owens Corning* (2005) was a bankruptcy specialist, he was candid about finding the law of substantive consolidation—the circumstances in which a court exercising bankruptcy powers may consolidate affiliated entities—to be something of a mystery. The case authorities raised as many questions as they answered,[67] and '[n]o treatise . . . was of much help'.[68] But there was scholarship in the law reviews that helped him through the thicket.[69]

Generally more interesting than examples of judges valuing scholarship as information are those instances in which they value it as argument. Cardozo CJ appeared to have the persuasive as well as the epistemic value of law review literature in mind when, in 1931, he wrote of 'the [United States] courts . . . turning more and more to the great scholars of the law schools', a development which 'has stimulated a willingness to cite the law review essays in briefs and in opinions in order to buttress a conclusion'.[70] When, in 1970, the US Supreme Court expanded the Fourteenth Amendment meaning of 'property' to include welfare benefits, the opinion of the majority relied directly on Charles Reich's explanation of social welfare as an entitlement to claim on, rather than as a gratuitous disbursement made from, government funds.[71] When, in 2022, the Court reversed its own precedent (precedent which some had thought unassailable)[72] and abrogated the constitutional right to abortion, the majority sought to fortify its position by citing works by numerous legal scholars who, unlike the justices in the majority, were not perceived to be conservatives but who, like those justices, 'were unsparing in their criticism' of what they considered to be the main precedent's 'exceedingly weak' reasoning.[73] The legal

---

[67] See *In re Owens Corning*, 419 F.3d 195, 208–209 n 14 (3rd Cir. 2005).

[68] Thomas L. Ambro, 'Citing Legal Articles in Judicial Opinions: A Sympathetic Antipathy' (2006) 80 *Am. Bankruptcy L. J.* 547, 549.

[69] One article in particular 'laid out the backdrop so well . . . that . . . I felt I had found the Rosetta Stone'. Ibid. 549–550.

[70] Benjamin N. Cardozo, 'Introduction', in *Selected Readings on the Law of Contracts from American and English Legal Periodicals* (New York: Macmillan, 1931), vii–xi at ix.

[71] *Goldberg v Kelly*, 397 US 254, 262 (1970) (Brennan J); and see Charles A. Reich, 'Individual Rights and Social Welfare: The Emerging Legal Issues' (1965) 74 *Yale L. J.* 1245, 1255–1256; also Reich, 'The New Property' (1964) 73 *Yale L. J.* 733, 787.

[72] Ronald Dworkin, *Religion Without God* (Cambridge, Mass.: Harvard UP, 2013), 144; Anthony Dutra, 'Men Come and Go, But *Roe* Abides: Why *Roe v Wade* Will Not Be Overruled' (2010) 90 *Boston Univ. L. Rev.* 1261; and cf—the dawning realization that there may be writing on the wall—G. Alexander Nunn and Alan M. Trammell, 'Settled Law' (2021) 107 *Va L. Rev.* 57, 89 ('[P]redicting that the current Supreme Court will continue to uphold the central tenets of *Roe* and *Casey* seems less certain than in past decades').

[73] *Dobbs v Jackson Women's Health Org.*, 597 US 215, 278 (2022) (Alito J). For the majority's similar assessment, see ibid. 218 ('*Roe* [v Wade, 410 US 113 (1973)] was . . . egregiously wrong and on a collision course with the Constitution from the day it was decided'). *Dobbs* also overturned *Planned Parenthood v Casey*, 505 US 833 (1992), which in essence had reaffirmed *Roe*. Not all of the scholars enlisted by

difficulty before a court might be unanswered by, or be a thorn in the side of, the legislature and the jurisdiction's other courts; existing law might yield an impasse, or be shown to contain a gap, or be binding but unsatisfactory, as when a rule applies to the facts of a case so as to settle it in a way that no reasonable person would consider fair. A case might bring to the fore a perennial but essentially unresolvable legal debate—over the proper scope of constitutional adjudication, say, or the correct approach to interpreting ambiguous statutes. A court might be at a loss as to how to decide a case currently before it without confronting one of these, perhaps more than one of these, conundrums. And it might transpire—perhaps because one or another legal representative suggests to the court—that a compelling, possibly the most compelling, argument as to how the case should be handled is to be found in a work or body of scholarship.

There is a distinct risk, in recounting instances where judges turn to normative scholarship when addressing legal dilemmas, of simply ending up with a collection of cases which go to prove nothing apart from that courts can benefit from taking on board arguments made by academics. The challenge is to discern from identified instances the distinctive as well as the regular modes of judicial reliance: not just the persistent tendencies and overarching preoccupations but also the idiosyncratic, perhaps unexpected, ways in which judges put normative scholarship to use. Perhaps the most obvious mode of reliance is the turn to scholarship in order to justify a fresh interpretation of a legal rule or a decision to extend or revise some aspect of legal doctrine. A well-known English-law example is *Hunter v Canary Wharf* (1997), in which the House of Lords had to decide if interference with television signal-reception was the basis for a private nuisance action. The House decided that it was not— that there must be interference with an interest in land for the action to arise. Lord Goff thought some torts scholars moved too quickly to the conclusion that interference with mere enjoyment of land sufficed to establish the action.[74] But he was in no doubt, not for the first time,[75] that Francis Newark was an honourable exception—that the core argument of Newark's seminal article on the categorization of nuisance as a tort directed against land rights was on a

the *Dobbs* majority as liberal critics of the reasoning in *Roe* were critical of the reasoning in *Casey*. John Hart Ely, the constitutional law scholar on whom the majority in *Dobbs* seem most reliant—see Caitlin B. Tully, 'The Liberal Giant Who Doomed *Roe*', *Slate*, 25 June 2023 at https://slate.com/news-and-politics/2023/06/john-hart-ely-dobbs-roe-legacy.html (accessed 28 July 2023)—lauded the plurality opinion in *Casey*: John Hart Ely, 'Letter to Justices Kennedy, O'Connor, and Souter Concerning *Planned Parenthood v Casey* (1992)', in his *On Constitutional Ground* (Princeton, NJ: Princeton UP, 1996), 304–306 at 305 ('Your joint opinion is excellent . . .').

[74] *Hunter v Canary Wharf Ltd* [1997] AC 655, 694.
[75] See *Cambridge Water Co. v Eastern Counties Leather* [1994] 2 AC 264, 297–298.

par with even the weightiest judicial *dicta* on the subject.[76] Judges in English courts have regularly echoed this sentiment ever since *Hunter* was decided.[77] In another House of Lords case, *The Achilleas* (2008), a bare majority considered the facts at issue to be 'not squarely covered by precedent'[78] because the contractual loss caused by delay in delivery called for the application of a more nuanced remoteness of damages test than the one set down in *Hadley v Baxendale* (1854).[79] The pertinent question in *The Achilleas*, Lord Hope observed, is not whether the loss was reasonably foreseeable at the time the parties entered into the contract, but rather 'whether the loss was a type of loss for which the party [responsible for the delay] can reasonably be assumed to have assumed responsibility'.[80] Two other law lords, reaching the same conclusion, took account of analyses by three contracts professors who, in law review articles not cited in arguments before the court, had independently critiqued the *Hadley v Baxendale* rule in ways which served to 'demonstrate that foreseeability by itself is not a satisfactory test'.[81]

Hunter v Canary Wharf and *The Achilleas* illustrate how academic-legal arguments can support, even prompt, judicial creativity. Sometimes, however, the work of academic lawyers will tug in a different direction. The difficulty for the Ninth Circuit in *Carman Tool v Evergreen* (1988) was its own precedents on liability for damage to goods in transit. Carman's goods, on arriving at their destination, were found to be damaged to the tune of $115,000. Carriage of goods legislation limited a carrier's liability to $500 per package. But Carman could cite Ninth Circuit judgments holding that this limitation only applied if the shipper had provided the carrier with fair opportunity to declare the nature and value of the goods itemized on the bill of lading. Carman contended that since the shipper, Evergreen, had not provided it with the bill of lading till

---

[76] See *Hunter v Canary Wharf* (n 74) at 687–688. The core argument of the article (F. H. Newark, 'The Boundaries of Nuisance' (1949) 65 *LQR* 480) is that personal injury damages are recoverable not in public nuisance but rather in negligence.

[77] See e.g. *Fearn v Board of Trustees of the Tate Gallery* [2023] UKSC 4 at [9]-[11] (Lord Leggatt); *Coventry v Lawrence* [2014] UKSC 46 at [76]-[77] (Lord Neuberger); *Corby Group v Corby BC* [2008] EWCA Civ 463 at [31] (Dyson LJ) (though note also Dyson's qualifying remarks at [20]).

[78] *Transfield Shipping v Mercator Shipping (The Achilleas)* [2008] UKHL 48 at [65] (Lord Walker). On the bareness of the majority (a 2-2 split and an opinion containing elements of each side's reasoning, see *Sylvia Shipping Ltd v Progress Bulk Carriers Ltd* [2010] 1 CLC 470 at [36]-[39] (Hamblen J).

[79] *Hadley v Baxendale* (1894) 9 Exch. 341, 344–345 (Alderson B).

[80] *The Achilleas* (n 78) at [32].

[81] Ibid. at [79] (Lord Walker). See also ibid. at [11], [19] (Lord Hoffmann), though cf [92]–[93] (Lady Hale) ('[This] interesting but novel way in which the question of remoteness of damages in contract is to be answered ... was not explored before us [in arguments made by counsel], although it is explored in academic ... writings. ... [H]owever, ... I am not immediately attracted to the idea of introducing into the law of contract the concept of the scope of duty which has perforce had to be developed in the law of negligence').

after the goods were shipped, the package liability limitation could not apply. The judge who wrote the Ninth Circuit's opinion drew on an article written by a professor of admiralty law, Michael Sturley, which made the case that the statutory liability limitation imposed no notification duty on carriers. Sturley had demonstrated, the judge wrote, that the notification duty was attributable to the court's own unfortunate precedents, to 'a judicial encrustation' that 'has been criticized for introducing uncertainty into commercial transactions'.[82] To rule in Carman's favour, the court concluded, would 'greatly magnify' the error.[83] The judge sent a copy of the slip opinion to the professor,[84] who then wrote a further article, commending the court for doing as much as it could to rein in (in *Carman* the panel, not being en banc, could not overrule) circuit precedent.[85]

Often, when judges invoke juristic work as persuasive authority, their objective is to develop, or to justify some new and more expansive interpretation of, the law they deem applicable to the facts of a case. In *Carman*, however, legal scholarship convinced the Ninth Circuit that a correct reading of the applicable law required the court not to be creative but rather to backtrack on its own creativity. Academic-legal argument also operated as a spur to judicial restraint, albeit in a somewhat circuitous fashion, in *Lexecon v Milberg Weiss* (1998), a case heard on appeal from the Ninth Circuit by the Supreme Court. *Lexecon* concerned whether, in litigation covering multiple districts, a judge selected to preside over pre-trial proceedings is permitted to keep the case and conduct the trial—what is known as self-transfer—or whether the trial has to be conducted by a judge in the district where the case was filed.[86] Allowing judges to self-transfer means that petitioners will often be denied trial in their preferred forum. But insisting that cases be remanded to the districts where they were originally filed creates an extra layer of court bureaucracy. Federal circuit court precedent stretching back to the early 1970s endorsed self-transfer. But the consensus among academic commentators over the same period was that legislation governing multi-district litigation definitely did not authorize self-transfer.

Before *Lexecon* reached the Supreme Court, the Ninth Circuit heard it twice. A majority held in favour of self-transfer in each instance, and—since

---

[82] *Carman Tool & Abrasives, Inc. v Evergreen Lines*, 871 F.2d 897, 900 (9th Cir. 1989).
[83] Ibid.
[84] Alex Kozinski, 'Who Gives a Hoot about Legal Scholarship?' (2000) 37 *Houston L. Rev.* 295, 297.
[85] Michael F. Sturley, 'The Future of the COGSA Fair Opportunity Requirement: Is There Life After *Carman Tool* and *Chan*?' (1989) 20 *J. Maritime Law & Commerce* 559, 563–566.
[86] *Lexecon, Inc. v Milberg Weiss Bershad Hynes & Lerach*, 523 US 26 (1998).

precedent across the circuits completely supported the court's decisions—the court denied Lexecon's petition for mandamus. But on both occasions that the case was heard, Kozinski J dissented. In his first dissent, he made no mention of the vast body of academic commentary that maintained that the courts persistently misinterpreted multi-district litigation legislation, though he neatly summarized the argument that academics had advanced.[87] In his second one, he cited a federal courts treatise and numerous law review articles to make his case against the case law in a somewhat more strident fashion:

> commentators ... [w]ith remarkable unanimity ... have questioned whether, and under what circumstances, district judges to whom cases are entrusted for purposes of discovery may hold on to them for trial.... Research discloses not a single commentator who has examined the question and found statutory support for the position taken by the federal courts.[88]

'I dissented', Kozinski quipped some years later, 'saying, essentially, forty million academics can't be wrong'.[89] After the Ninth Circuit had finished with the case, one of the academics on whose work Kozinski had relied filed a pro se *amicus* brief supporting Lexecon's petition for certiorari.[90] The Supreme Court agreed to hear the case and unanimously reversed the Ninth Circuit, holding that legislation governing multi-district litigation did not authorize self-transfers. The opinion not only accorded with Kozinski's dissents but also included a redacted (though also slightly supplemented) version of the list of juristic sources that he had included in his second dissent. '[A]cademics', Kozinski reflected, 'over the course of three decades, simply refused to grant legitimacy to the commonly accepted judicial wisdom'.[91] Jurists, with Kozinski serving as their intermediary, had played a significant part in re-shaping federal court jurisprudence—a re-shaping which, rather than affirming judicial creativity, reinstated the letter of the law.

---

[87] *Lexecon, Inc. v United States District Court for District of Arizona*, 61 F.3d 911 (Table), 1995 WL 432395 (4 pp), at 2 (Kozinski J, dissenting).

[88] *In Re American Continental Corporation/Lincoln Savings & Loan Securities Litigation*, 102 F.3d 1524, 1542 (9th Cir. 1996) (Kozinski J, dissenting).

[89] Alex Kozinski, 'Who Gives a Hoot about Legal Scholarship?' (n 84) 306.

[90] 'Brief of Charles Alan Wright as *Amicus Curiae* Supporting Petitioner' (filed 11 April 1997), at https://www.proquest.com/briefs (accessed 10 November 2023). Wright, when making the case against self-transfer, relied on the second of Kozinski's dissents: ibid. 6. The Supreme Court didn't address Wright's brief because his main argument (concerning the propriety of a Ninth Circuit's decision to allow the respondent's claim to go forward) fell outside the question on which the Court granted certiorari.

[91] Kozinski, 'Who Gives a Hoot about Legal Scholarship?' (n 84) 306.

Whereas, in *Hunter v Canary Wharf* and *The Achilleas*, legal scholarship contributed to judicial efforts to make modest alterations to the law, in *Carman* and *Lexecon* it led judges to retreat from alterations. Juristic work occasionally leads judges to see the law afresh, but the new perspective entails neither an alteration nor a retreat. In *Oppenheimer v Cattermole* (1975), the House of Lords had to determine if Oppenheimer, a German-born UK resident who left Germany in 1939 and who became a naturalized British citizen in 1948, was liable to pay UK income tax on pensions which he received from the German government between 1953 and 1968 as compensation for assets having been appropriated from him under Nazi legislation authorizing the confiscation of property from Jews.[92] A Nazi decree of 1941 purported to strip Jewish émigrés of German citizenship. If the UK recognized this decree as valid law, Oppenheimer incurred the tax liability as a UK national. If it did not, he had dual nationality and so was exempt from the liability by virtue of an Anglo-German double taxation convention. A majority in the Court of Appeal ruled that he was a UK national by virtue of the 1941 decree and so had to pay tax on his pensions. The House of Lords heard the case, remitted it for further consideration by the tax commissioners, and then heard it again before holding, as had the Court of Appeal, that Oppenheimer was not a dual national.

The House of Lords' reasoning was influenced by legal scholarship and was very different from the reasoning presented by the Court of Appeal. A German-born British jurist, F. A. Mann, had argued in an article criticizing the Court of Appeal's judgment that a German nationality law of 1913—providing that nationals resident abroad were, unless exempted, no longer German nationals once they acquired a foreign nationality—rendered the question of the 1941 decree's validity an irrelevance: Oppenheimer had renounced his German nationality when he became British. The House prolonged proceedings in *Oppenheimer* because Mann's article was brought to the law lords' notice during arguments at first hearing.[93] On learning of the content of this article, Lord Cross acknowledged, '[w]e . . . put the appeal back into the list for further argument and, as a result of the discussion which then ensued, it became clear—and was accepted by counsel on both sides—that the case ought to be sent back to the Commissioners for further findings as to the relevant German law'.[94] The law lords decided the appeal 'contrary to the way they would have done had the article not come to their attention'.[95] Mann reports in his

---

[92] *Oppenheimer v Cattermole* [1976] AC 249. (Case decided 5 February 1975.)
[93] See J. G. Merrills, 'Oppenheimer v Cattermole—The Curtain Falls' (1975) 24 *ICLQ* 617, 619.
[94] *Oppenheimer v Cattermole* (n 92) 268.
[95] Paterson, *Final Judgment* (n 43) 216.

posthumously published, unfinished autobiography that two of the law lords involved in the appeal gave him the impression that, but for his article, the House would have reversed the Court of Appeal's decision.[96]

Although, in these examples, scholarship can be seen to lead judges to think differently about the law, it does not, in every instance, lead them to make new law. Quite what it means, in any event, to speak of judges making law is not entirely straightforward. Judges in England—perhaps particularly those whose careers overlapped with that period when the final court would not overrule its own precedents—have now and again been minded to emphasize a form of judicial creativity which they consider almost, though not quite, tantamount to law-making. (Judges in other jurisdictions, though less overtly preoccupied with this phenomenon, are hardly oblivious to it.)[97] 'The judges', Lord Devlin claimed in 1962, 'always have been and still are fashioners of law, not creators, out of the material that is supplied to them.'[98] 'Even if we do not greatly relax the doctrine of precedent and if we do not encroach on the sphere of Parliament', Lord Reid ventured a decade later, 'there is still considerable scope for judges to mould the development of the common law.'[99] Judges, when engaged in this exercise, are adding and removing features rather than creating from scratch.

Of course, judges have been known to deny that they perform even this modest creative function—to insist that they are but mouthpieces of the law and never fashioners of it. A court may well intend not to shape the common law's development but simply to restate a common-law rule-formulation in a way that has no bearing on the rule's applicability—as when judges 'review the authorities' and clarify or summarize them while leaving them unaltered in substance,[100] or re-articulate a precedent's *ratio* or holding without doing anything that could be read as altering the *ratio*'s scope.[101] As Benjamin Cardozo observed, however, this is rarely if ever a straightforwardly reiterative manoeuvre, for when lawyers 'state the law today as well as human minds can state it, new problems, arising almost overnight, ... encumber the ground again', so that 'the changing combinations of events ... beat upon the walls of ancient

---

[96] Frederick Alexander Mann, *Life and Cases: Manuscript of an Autobiography*, ed. W. Ernst (Bonn: Bonn UP, 2021), 214.

[97] See e.g. Posner, *How Judges Think* (n 56) 209 ('The knack ... of reading cases and statutes creatively ... and an ineffable sense ... of just how far one can go as a judge in changing the law ...').

[98] Patrick Devlin, *Samples of Lawmaking* (London: OUP, 1962), 3.

[99] Lord Reid, 'The Judge as Law Maker' (1972) n.s. 12 *JSPTL* 22, 25; see also *Indyka v Indyka* [1967] P. 233, 262 (Diplock LJ) ('It is the function of the courts to mould the common law and to adapt it to the changing society for which it provides the rules of each man's duty to his neighbour').

[100] See e.g. *Tomlinson v Congleton BC* [2002] EWCA Civ 309 at [12]–[18] (Ward LJ); *Neuhoff, Inc. v Neuhoff Packing Co.*, 167 F.2d 459, 465–466 (6th Cir. 1948).

[101] See e.g. *Lloyd v Sadler* [1978] QB 774 (CA), 788–790; *Texas v Mead*, 465 US 1041, 1046 (1984) (Stevens J) ('I believe this Court has an obligation to clarify its holding ... and to resolve these conflicts').

categories.[102] It is something of a modern judicial commonplace that 'each new application of a precedent ... modifies the law',[103] that a court fashions the law afresh even when it confines itself to re-stating what judges have already declared the law to be, that '[j]udges cannot adhere to the declaratory principle even if they would.'[104] '[T]here was never a more sterile controversy than that upon the question whether a judge makes law', Lord Radcliffe remarked. 'Of course he does. How can he help it?'[105] Judicial legislation is inevitable, he thought, because even the judge committed to 'the most rigid principle of adherence to precedent' will find that 'when he repeats' what 'his predecessors ... decided before him ... their words ... mean something materially different in his mouth. ... The context is different; the range of reference is different; and, whatever his intention, the hallowed words of authority themselves are a fresh coinage newly minted in his speech.'[106] Courts develop the common law when they distinguish precedent. But even when they follow precedent, the common law might not be left unaltered.

The relationship between scholarship and judicial reasoning is a source of especial curiosity in cases where judges fashion the law, not because they seek to distinguish or overrule precedent—or to depart, indeed, from any kind of relevant legal authority—but because they cannot find in the primary sources of law a satisfactory, or perhaps any, answer to the question before them. It is never in the nature of a common-law judgment, it seems fair to say, that a court applies scholarship to the facts of a case as it would apply law derived from a primary source. But there certainly are cases where judges fail to find in the primary sources the material, or all of the material, that they need in order to deliver a legal judgment on the matter at hand, and where scholarship does at least some of the work in filling the void. Scholarship, in these instances, is not operating as a primary source of law, but nor is it necessarily serving as a conventional—epistemic or persuasive—secondary source either.

Consider how the Coase theorem has fared in the US courts. The theorem postulates that the impact of legal rules will be largely or entirely eradicated when transaction costs are either absent or are so low as not to deter disputing parties from negotiating an efficient allocation of resources for themselves.[107]

---

[102] Benjamin N. Cardozo, *The Growth of the Law* (New Haven: Yale UP, 1924), 19.

[103] Wilfrid Normand, *Scottish Judicature and Legal Procedure* (Birmingham: Holdsworth Club, 1941), 41. In a similar vein, see Lord Wright, *Legal Essays and Addresses* (Cambridge: CUP, 1939), 204.

[104] Tom Bingham, *The Business of Judging: Selected Essays and Speeches* (Oxford: OUP, 2000), 29.

[105] Lord Radcliffe, *Not in Feather Beds* (London: Hamish Hamilton, 1968), 215.

[106] Ibid. 271.

[107] See Ronald H. Coase, 'The Problem of Social Cost' (1960) 3 *Jnl Law & Econ.* 1.

There are cases in which judges declare the theorem irrelevant to dispute-resolution: their reasoning, in essence, is that since transaction costs are nearly always a material consideration, the idea of chaining litigants to a hypothetical bargain—of determining their rights and liabilities on the basis of the allocation that they would have agreed to if these costs were absent or inconsequential—is for the birds.[108] 'Although it is theoretically possible' that the litigants, left to their own devices, could have found their way to a Coasean solution, Henry Friendly remarked in 1968, 'this would seem unlikely to occur in real life'.[109] But judges (some of them, admittedly, invested in law-and-economics) can now and again be seen turning to the theorem on the basis that it enables them to explain their rulings regarding particular resource-allocation disputes in light of how the litigants would likely have behaved had transaction costs not been a relevant factor.[110] US courts, when they resort to law professors' law-and-economics scholarship (even work that bears affinities to Coase's), tend to rely on it as a conventional secondary source.[111] But Coase—an economist who was not writing for, who professed no interest in how or whether his work was received by, lawyers[112]—is somehow *sui generis*. Judges, on the occasions that they do invoke his theorem, are inclined to treat it as not so much addressing a legal problem as explaining, or as at least contributing to an explanation of, a legal perspective or outcome that primary and conventional secondary legal sources do not readily or fully support.

When judges turn to scholarship for its heuristic value, the broader objective will occasionally be the justification of a position which, though legally supportable, encounters strong opposing arguments (or has previously been

---

[108] See e.g. *Quirin v City of Pittsburgh*, 801 F.Supp. 1486, 1489 (WD Pa 1992); *Bowden v Wal-Mart*, 124 F.Supp.2d 1228, 1238 (MD Ala 2000); *Michigan v United States EPA*, 213 F.3d 663, 676 (DC Cir. 2000) ('If transaction costs were zero, . . . firms with high emission-reduction costs would buy allowances from those with low costs and thereby transfer wealth to them. . . . But transaction costs notoriously are not zero; so the likely effect of the proposed statutory interpretation would be that any aggregate cutback would be achieved at considerably higher cost . . . with absolutely no offsetting environmental benefit to the public').

[109] *Bushey & Sons v United States*, 398 F.2d 167, 171 n 7 (2nd Cir. 1968).

[110] See e.g. *Davis v Echo Valley Condominium Association*, 945 F.3d 483, 494–495 (6th Cir. 2019); *Sheridan v IHeartMedia*, 255 F.Supp. 3d 767, 773 (ND Ill. 2017); *Reyes v Remington Hybrid Seed Co.*, 495 F.3d 403, 408–409 (7th Cir. 2007); *International Brotherhood of Teamsters v Philip Morris, Inc.*, 196 F.3d 818, 824–825 (7th Cir. 1999); *Chrysler v Kolosso Auto Sales*, 148 F.3d 892, 894 (7th Cir. 1998); *In re Envirodyne Industries*, 174 B.R. 986, 995 (ND Ill. 1994).

[111] See e.g. *Air and Liquid Systems Corp. v DeVries*, 139 S. Ct 986, 997 (2019) (Gorsuch, Thomas, and Alito JJ, dissenting); *Mutual Pharmaceutical Co. v Bartlett*, 570 US 472, 491 (2013); *Behrens v Pelletier*, 516 US 299, 315 (1996) (Breyer and Stevens JJ, dissenting); *American Airlines, Inc. v Wolens*, 513 US 219, 230 (1995); *Commonwealth Edison Co. v Montana*, 453 US 609, 649 (1981) (White J, concurring).

[112] 'I have no interest in lawyers or legal education. . . . My interest is in economics'. Ronald Coase, quoted in Edmund W. Kitch (ed.), 'The Fire of Truth: A Remembrance of Law and Economics at Chicago, 1932–1970' (1983) 26 *Jnl Law & Econ*. 163, 192.

poorly defended by reliance on weak argument), and which therefore warrants careful explanation or articulation. This scholarship may shape judicial thinking but not judicial conclusions; resort to it might be attributable to the fact that it prompts or helps judges to finesse their own reasoning, even though it neither anticipates nor affirms that reasoning. In recent years in the United States, judicial reflections on the efficacy of *Miranda* warnings attest to how academic interventions on a legal subject can make an impact on, without necessarily altering, the way judges generally conceive of it.[113] A similar observation might be made about Second Amendment jurisprudence, which in certain instances can be seen to have been influenced, even if not entirely reconfigured, by late-twentieth-century scholarship advancing the case that the Constitution protects an individual's right to bear arms.[114] A particularly vivid illustration of scholarly intervention bearing on but not determining judicial thinking can be found in Canadian final court jurisprudence from the 1980s, on spousal support agreements: Canada's Supreme Court imposed a stringent test for re-opening support agreements,[115] academic lawyers took issue with the test as applied in the lower courts,[116] whereupon the Court reviewed the academic writings and, while sticking to its test, accepted that the terrain was more complex than it had originally appreciated.[117] In instances of this kind, judges are not prioritizing scholarship over law. Nor are they resorting to scholarship because they find the law to be silent in the face of some controversy. Their point, rather, is that the law speaks to a controversy either ambiguously or incompletely, or that existing judicial interpretations of the relevant law could benefit from refinement, and that the key, or one of the keys, to devising a satisfactory or improved legal answer rests in the realm of scholarship.

A striking illustration of scholarship functioning in this fashion can be found in a classic, very unsettling, modern English case. Doing justice to this unusual instance is impossible without (at the risk of a slight *longueur*) some scene-setting. The fact that the same conclusion was reached by all nine judges

---

[113] See e.g. *United States v Rang*, 919 F.3d 113, 119–120 (1st Cir. 2019); *United States v Dickerson*, 166 F.3d 667, 687 (5th Cir. 1999).

[114] See e.g. *Printz v United States*, 521 US 898, 938 n 2 (1997) (Thomas J, concurring); *Nordyke v King*, 563 F.3d 439, 457 (9th Cir. 2009); also David Cole, *Engines of Liberty* (New York: Basic Books, 2016), 116–124, where *District of Columbia v Heller*, 554 US 570 (2008) is identified as the pinnacle of this development.

[115] *Pelech v Pelech* [1987] 1 SCR 801; *Richardson v Richardson* [1987] 1 SCR 857; *Caron v Caron* [1987] 1 SCR 892.

[116] See e.g. Carol J. Rogerson, 'The Causal Connection Test in Spousal Support Law' (1989) 8 *Can. Jnl Fam. L.* 95; Thomas A. Heeney, 'The Application of *Pelech* to the Variation of an Ongoing Support Order: Respecting the Intention of the Parties' (1989) 5 *Child and Fam. L. Q.* 217.

[117] *Moge v Moge* [1992] 3 SCR 813; *G.(L.) v B.(G.)* [1995] SCR 370; also, for Supreme Court judicial reflections, see Claire L'Heureux-Dubé, 'It Takes a Vision: The Constitutionalization of Equality in Canada' (2002) 14 *Yale Jnl Law & Feminism* 363, 372; Michel Bastarache, 'The Role of Academics and Legal Theory in Judicial Decision-Making' (1999) 37 *Alberta L. Rev.* 739, 742–745.

throughout the three courts that heard *Airedale NHS Trust v Bland* (1993) suggests that the decision did not especially trouble them.[118] But nothing could be further from the truth. Scattered among the opinions—all the judges delivered their own—are confessions of unease that would not be out of place in Fuller's classic parable about the cannibals trapped in the cave.[119] The question at the heart of *Bland* was whether, when a patient has lost consciousness without hope of recovery, physicians might lawfully discontinue life-sustaining treatment (which, in Bland's case, meant ceasing to provide fluid nutrition via a naso-gastric tube and antibiotics to treat infections). Bland had not consented, could not consent, to the withdrawal of treatment, and his family—though of the view that he would have favoured discontinuation—was not legally entitled to consent on his behalf.

The House of Lords had already decided, four years before hearing *Bland*, that doctors had a duty to treat (in the particular instance, treatment meant sterilizing) a mentally ill patient on the basis that it would be in the patient's best interests.[120] But in *Bland*, determining the patient's best interests posed a quandary. Bland had no cognitive capacity and was judged to have no hope of recovery, so whether he lived or died was a matter of indifference to him. Neither the continuation nor the discontinuation of treatment seemed readily justifiable on the basis of his best interests. A physician would certainly face criminal liability for administering a treatment so as to cause his death. But how was discontinuation of treatment different? Was it not 'hypocrisy' for a court to rule that the same liability does not arise if this physician is not administering but rather ceasing treatment to cause death?[121] The conclusion of all three courts was that the termination of Bland's life-support was justifiable. 'The question', Lord Goff stated, 'is whether the doctor should or should not continue to provide his patient with medical treatment or care which, if continued, will prolong his patient's life'.[122] Prolonging Bland's life was judged to be of no benefit to him.

The case clearly discombobulated some of the judges involved in it. A decision of this nature, one of the law lords remarked, was really for the

---

[118] The judgments of all three courts, along with the originating summons and the legal submissions to the House of Lords, are reported together as *Airedale NHS Trust v Bland* [1993] AC 789 (hereafter, *Bland*).

[119] See Lon L. Fuller, 'The Case of the Speluncean Explorers' (1949) 62 *Harv. L. Rev.* 616 and see esp. at 626 and 631 ('I [Tatting J] have been wholly unable to resolve the doubts that beset me about this case …'); and cf e.g. *Bland* (HL) 899 (Lord Mustill) ('I must admit to having felt profound misgivings about almost every aspect of this case').

[120] *Re F (Mental Patient: Sterilisation)* [1990] 2 AC 1. (Case decided 24 May 1989.) See also *Bland* (HL) 858 (Lord Keith).

[121] *Bland* (HL) 865 (Lord Goff).

[122] *Bland* (HL) 868.

legislature; 'judge-made law . . . is not the best way to proceed'.[123] Another agreed: 'I have felt serious doubts about whether this question is . . . a proper subject for legal adjudication. The whole matter cries out for exploration in depth by Parliament'.[124] He worried that although 'the law is there and we must take it as it stands', the decision would 'only emphasise the distortions of a legal structure which is already both morally and intellectually misshapen'.[125] After all, Lord Browne-Wilkinson confessed, the decision

> will appear to some to be almost irrational. How can it be lawful to allow a patient to die slowly, though painlessly, over a period of weeks from lack of food but unlawful to produce his immediate death by a lethal injection, thereby saving his family from yet another ordeal to add to the tragedy that has already struck them? I find it difficult to find a moral answer to that question. But it is undoubtedly the law . . .[126]

It was on the basis of common law, not statute, that the lawfulness of discontinuing Bland's treatment was determined. The dominant judicial sentiment in *Bland* is that the decision demanded the law-fashioning instinct— demanded that the judges 'think more deeply about the applicable principles of law' so as 'to formulate those principles more accurately',[127] or even 'develop new law to regulate the new circumstances'.[128] Secondary sources supplied reasoning and information that helped some of the judges act on this sentiment. There were foreign judicial opinions (not always majority opinions) presented to court which supported the view that treatment could be withdrawn without undermining sanctity of life, or Bland's best interests, or the duty of care owed by physicians to patients.[129] And writings by medical law and criminal law scholars were relied on for the purpose of explaining or defining legal concepts at the heart of the case.[130] But in the Court of Appeal, the resort to scholarship by one of the judges was markedly less conventional.

The Court of Appeal considered the legal and moral elements of *Bland* to be intertwined. 'This is not an area', Hoffmann LJ observed, 'in which any

---

[123]   *Bland* (HL) 880 (Lord Browne-Wilkinson).
[124]   *Bland* (HL) 891 (Lord Mustill).
[125]   *Bland* (HL) 887.
[126]   *Bland* (HL) 885.
[127]   *Bland* (HL) 862 (Lord Goff).
[128]   *Bland* (HL) 880 (Lord Browne-Wilkinson).
[129]   See e.g. *Bland* (CA) 809–812 (Bingham MR); 821–822, 823 (Butler-Sloss LJ); (HL) 863–864, 867 (Lord Goff). Cited foreign positions were not always accepted: see e.g. ibid. (CA) 817 (Butler-Sloss LJ); (HL) 872 (Lord Goff).
[130]   See e.g. *Bland* (HL), 863, 868 (Lord Goff); 882 (Lord Browne-Wilkinson). Again, cited positions were not always accepted: see ibid. (HL) 895 (Lord Mustill).

difference can be allowed to exist between what is legal and what is morally right'.[131] '[W]hether . . . the termination of life-support would be justified as being in the best interests of the patient . . . is a . . . legal (or moral) decision'.[132] Hoffmann deliberately devoted very little attention (only one paragraph) to 'the authorities' pertaining to the case,[133] as the three judges in the Court of Appeal had settled on a division of labour: two of them would write opinions addressing the relevant domestic and foreign sources and Hoffmann would produce an opinion examining the moral principles underlying the Court's decision to withdraw treatment.[134] The approach that he took to writing his opinion—'argu[ing] from moral rather than purely legal principles' so as to 'clarify my own thought and perhaps help others'—was, he accepted, 'somewhat unusual'.[135] It is no less unusual for a judge to turn to philosophers for help with the task. But this is what Hoffmann did. 'I must acknowledge the assistance I have received', he states early in his opinion, 'from reading the manuscript of Professor Ronald Dworkin's forthcoming book *Life's Dominion* and from conversations with him and Professor Bernard Williams'.[136] Hoffmann made use of Dworkin's manuscript—a scholarly work by a law professor—as a secondary source.[137] But its influence on him was not so much epistemic or persuasive as dialectical.

Dworkin's central argument in *Life's Dominion* is that it is a mistake to frame decisions about whether to withdraw treatment from patients in a position like Bland's as decisions about patients' direct interests. The decisions, whichever

---

[131] *Bland* (CA) 825.

[132] *Bland* (CA) 834.

[133] *Bland* (CA) 833.

[134] The division of labour was, apparently, a consequence of the timetable. The then President of the Family Division of the High Court, Sir Stephen Brown, heard *Bland* in November 1992. He handed down his judgment on Thursday, 19 November. Proceedings commenced in the Court of Appeal less than two weeks later, with hearings on 1–3 December and delivery of the judgment on Wednesday, 9 December. The House of Lords began hearing the final appeal on Monday, 14 December, delivering its judgment on Thursday, 4 February 1993. The House of Lords had made clear to the Court of Appeal that final appeal proceedings would commence on the 14th and that the Lords would need the Court of Appeal's judgment by no later than then. To meet the deadline, the three Court of Appeal judges took responsibility for different elements of the judgment: Bingham MR for the English case law, Butler-Sloss LJ for the foreign case law, and Hoffmann LJ for the moral philosophy. See 'An Interview with Lord Hoffmann: In Conversation with a Reasonable Man', Bryan Cave Leighton Paisner event (Cockerill J, chair), London, 25 January 2023 (https://www.youtube.com/watch?v=jDjYNmiIxH4) at 31:45–32:45 (accessed 1 June 2023).

[135] *Bland* (CA) 825–826.

[136] *Bland* (CA) 826. At this point, Williams held the White's Chair of Moral Philosophy at Oxford. Hoffmann drove to Oxford to talk to Williams over the weekend separating the beginning of the Court of Appeal Hearings and the delivery of the Court's judgment: 'An Interview with Lord Hoffmann' (n 134) at 32:50–33:12.

[137] *Life's Dominion* was published on 20 May 1993. Dworkin and Williams 'taught a seminar on the manuscript . . . in Oxford in 1992'. Ronald Dworkin, *Life's Dominion* (London: HarperCollins, 1993), 261.

way they go, are really decisions about the intrinsic value of human life. A decision either way cannot be justified in accordance with the patient's interests in experiencing life if the patient no longer has experiential preferences.[138] However, decisions in either direction *can* be justified in terms of sanctity of life. The obvious novelty in Dworkin's argument is the proposition that a commitment to sanctity of life does not rule out the withdrawal of life-sustaining treatment.

> Anyone who believes in the sanctity of human life believes that once a human life has begun it matters, intrinsically, that that life go well. . . . Someone who thinks his own life would go worse if he . . . stayed biologically alive for years as a vegetable believes that he is showing more respect for the human contribution to the sanctity of his life if he makes arrangements in advance to avoid that, and that others show more respect for his life if they avoid it for him.[139]

Counsel for the Official Solicitor in *Bland*—the barrister who presented the case against withdrawing treatment—subsequently observed that Hoffmann was a judge attracted to Dworkinian reasoning.[140] The observation would not have been intended as revelatory—long before *Bland*, Hoffmann had admitted to the attraction (and claimed that other judges were similarly attracted).[141] Dworkinian jurisprudence, he maintained, helped him, as a judge, to understand

> what scope I had for making choices; when I was constrained by the need for fidelity to the language of the statute or . . . to the long history of the common law; and when I was free to choose the way forward. It explained how I should make that choice, by interpreting the rule in a way I thought best calculated to promote the values of the . . . society in which I lived.[142]

Dworkin is 'someone who has not only been a great friend for many years', he remarked in 2006, 'but, for good or ill, has had more influence upon my

---

[138] See *Life's Dominion* (n 137) 201–202, 208–209.

[139] Ibid. 215–216. For his later elaborations of the argument, see Ronald Dworkin, *Is Democracy Possible Here? Principles for a New Political Debate* (Princeton, NJ: Princeton UP, 2006), 79; *Religion Without God* (n 72) 10–11.

[140] *R (Smeaton) v Secretary of State for Health* [2002] EWHC 610 (Admin) at [324] and [338] (Munby J); also *A v East Sussex CC* [2003] EWHC 167 (Admin) at [95].

[141] '[J]udges are attracted by the arguments of Dworkin, which not only accept at face value what they are saying but assume that there is a point to what they are trying to do. . . . Dworkin is one of the few writers on general jurisprudence who accepts and engages with the reality of what judges have to do.' L. H. Hoffmann, Book Review (1989) 105 *LQR* 140, 144.

[142] Lord Hoffmann, 'Ronald Dworkin' (2013) 17 *Oxford Law News* 8, 8.

professional life than any other legal writer'.[143] The admiration ran both ways. Whereas, in the published version of *Life's Dominion*, some of the law lords' contributions to *Bland* met with criticism, Hoffmann was lauded for having delivered 'a strikingly philosophical opinion'.[144] There are commentators on *Bland* who make a point of drawing attention to what they consider to be a philosophical alignment between the professor and the judge[145]—which is understandable, considering that Hoffmann's opinion contains reflections on constructive interpretation and human dignity that are not a million miles from Dworkin's own.[146]

But Hoffmann's reasoning in support of withdrawal of treatment neither invokes nor accepts Dworkin's sanctity of life argument. Concern for sanctity of life and the protection of individual dignity, Hoffmann maintained, 'are not at all the same thing'—the principles have to be balanced against one another, and sometimes prove irreconcilable.[147] The notion—Dworkin's notion—that one can 'smooth away the differences [between the principles] by interpretation' runs afoul, he thought, of Isaiah Berlin's *dictum* that 'we encounter in ordinary experience . . . choices between ends equally ultimate, and claims equally absolute, the realization of some of which must inevitably involve the sacrifice of others'.[148] We can (like Dworkin) choose

> to qualify the meaning of the sanctity of life by including . . . concepts of dignity and fulfilment as part of the essence of life. In this way one could argue that,

---

[143] Lord Hoffmann, 'Tribute to Ronald Dworkin' (2007) 63 *NYU Ann. Surv. Am. L.* 1, 3 (address delivered April 2006); and see also his comments in *Jones v Saudi Arabia* [2006] UKHL 26 at [63].

[144] *Life's Dominion* (n 137) 188. For criticism of some of the opinions in the House of Lords, see ibid. 208–209.

[145] See e.g. Samantha Halliday, 'Comparative Reflections upon the Assisted Dying Bill 2013: A Plea for a More European Approach' (2013) 13 *Medical Law International* 135, 142; Bradley W. Miller, 'A Time to Kill: Ronald Dworkin and the Ethics of Euthanasia' (1996) 2 *Res Publica* 31, 48.

[146] On constructive interpretation, see *Bland* (CA) 829–830 ('[I]f he is unable to express his choice, we should try our honest best to do what we think he would have chosen'); also Hoffmann, 'Tribute to Ronald Dworkin' (n 143) 2 ('One of Ronald's ideas that has had particular resonance with me is the notion that judicial development of the law must fit with the legal system as a whole'); and compare Dworkin, *Law's Empire* (London: Fontana, 1986), 52–53, 239, 255, 335–337, 349, 400. On human dignity, see Dworkin, *Life's Dominion* (n 137) 217 ('Making someone die in a way that others approve, but he believes a horrifying contradiction of his life, is a devastating, odious form of tyranny') and, for similar reasoning applied in the opposite direction, compare *Bland* (CA) 830 ('Normally we would unquestioningly assume that anyone would wish to live rather than die. But in the extraordinary case of Anthony Bland, we think it more likely that he would choose to put an end to the humiliation of his being and the distress of his family. Finally, Anthony Bland is a person to whom respect is owed and we think that it would show greater respect to allow him to die and be mourned by his family than to keep him grotesquely alive'). See also *R (Nicklinson) v Ministry of Justice* [2013] EWCA Civ 961 at [50]–[52].

[147] *Bland* (CA) 830.

[148] Isaiah Berlin, *Four Essays on Liberty* (Oxford: OUP, 1969), 168, quoted by Hoffmann in *Bland* (CA) 830 (and rejected in favour of 'abstract agreement' by Ronald Dworkin, *Justice in Robes* (Cambridge, Mass.: Belknap Press, 2006), 114).

properly understood, Anthony Bland's death would not offend against the sanctity of life. But I do not think that this would satisfy the many people who feel strongly that it does. I think it is better to accept this and confront it.[149]

At no point in his opinion does Hoffmann explicitly distinguish his reasoning from Dworkin's; indeed, his only reference to Dworkin is his acknowledgment of having benefited from reading the typescript of *Life's Dominion*. But note the nature of the benefit: Hoffmann did not co-opt or draw upon Dworkin's argument, nor does it seem entirely accurate to claim that he was influenced by it. Rather than shape Hoffmann's reasoning, it helped him settle on how to shape it for himself: it served as a counterweight or catalyst rather than as a source of influence. When judges resort to scholarship as a secondary source, they are sometimes not persuaded by or drawing information from it, but critically—which need not mean negatively—reacting to it: there are instances, that is, when scholarship proves stimulating or inspirational to judges even though it does not supply the actual reasons underpinning—or even necessarily support—their effort to shape the law in some particular way.

c) *Coda: judges and attribution to scholarship*

We saw in chapter 4 that, sometimes, judges and lawyers are only conditionally permitted—and might indeed, paradoxically, not be permitted—to draw on permissive authority. The point is illustrated by those bygone English conventions forbidding references in court to living jurists and to legislative history, though perhaps the simplest way to capture the point is to observe that, apart from in very exceptional instances, judges cannot elect to forgo deciding cases according to applicable laws because they prefer decisions that they could justify were they to apply secondary source material instead. Primary source material cannot simply be swapped out for secondary source material, and there can be constraints on judges relying on secondary source material even for purely secondary purposes.

What are these constraints? In English law, reference to legislative history as an interpretive aid is still only qualifiedly endorsed.[150] Reliance on other

---

[149] *Bland* (CA) 827.
[150] See e.g. *R (O) v Secretary of State for the Home Department* [2022] UKSC 3 at [32] (Lord Hodge); *R (Coughlan) v Minister for the Cabinet Office* [2022] UKSC 11 at [14] ('[S]uch references are not a legitimate aid to statutory interpretation unless the . . . conditions set out . . . in *Pepper v Hart* are met').

secondary sources (as secondary sources) is relatively unencumbered—certainly no explicit conditions attach to the introduction of *dicta*, foreign judgments, or (nowadays) scholarship into arguments to court and judicial opinions—though it is fairly standard for common law judges to refer to factors such as the persuasiveness, provenance, weight, approval, or relevance of a pronouncement as reasons for choosing, or declining, to rely on it. Judicial negotiation of scholarship is particularly intriguing, because tacit engagement norms do seem to exist. Generalization on the topic is hazardous, given that judicial conventions and judgment (particularly appellate judgment) delivery-styles differ quite significantly among common-law jurisdictions. And postulating plausible reasons for judges citing, or forgoing citation of, academics is not the same as identifying canons by which those judges abide. Recently in the United Kingdom, for example, there have been judgments on politically controversial legal questions in which legal scholarship makes no appearance, even though the questions have prompted an abundance of academic commentary.[151] It is not beyond fantasy to surmise that judges might occasionally opt not to cite such commentary, even if they find it valuable, should they believe that doing so might unnecessarily align them, or the court, with one side of an academic dispute ('the selection of some in preference to others would be invidious'),[152] or if they fear that it would inappropriately associate a contemporary academic, or academic cohort, with a highly controversial or unpopular ruling or opinion. But then judges could have all sorts of reasons for not citing academic commentary, and it is not as if there is a dearth of politically contentious cases where they do cite it.[153] To maintain that there must be an implicit judicial *convention* against citation in instances of this kind—rather than individual, *ad hoc* forbearance—would be far-fetched.

[151] The most high-profile being *Miller 2* (*Miller v The Prime Minister* [2019] UKSC 41), where no academic works are mentioned apart from a textbook which appears in a passage quoted from another case.

[152] *White v Jones* [1992] 2 AC 207, 292 (Lord Mustill). For similar *dicta* from other jurisdictions, see *Feeney v Alberta* (2021) ABCA 398 (Alberta CA) at para. 11 (Watson JA) ('[C]ourts are to administer equal justice under law, and ... justice must also remain neutral. Associated with that, courts ... must not occupy themselves with academic matters of legal or procedural argument ... which adversely impact other parties or the system'); *Benjamin v Jacobson*, 124 F.3d 162, 169 n 11 (2nd Cir. 1997) (Calabresi J) ('In order to decide the constitutionality of the termination provision, it is unnecessary to take sides in the academic debate about whether Congress has the power to eliminate *all* federal jurisdiction in a particular area'). (Emphasis in original.)

[153] The most high-profile (in recent years) being *Miller 1* (*R (Miller) v Secretary of State for Exiting the European Union* [2017] UKSC 5), where the majority cite two modern textbooks (and Blackstone), and two of the dissenting judges cite law review articles published shortly before the case was decided.

Might it nevertheless be convention, at least in some common-law jurisdictions, that when judges do rely on scholarship, they need not adhere as rigorously to attribution norms as academics generally do? Even this question needs to be treated with care. Some judicial conventions seem obvious till one starts to scrutinize them; what looks like convention can turn out to be unsettled practice. *Sua sponte* judicial reliance on authority is illustrative in this regard. There was certainly a time when the UK legal convention seemed to be that apex court judges should not deliver judgments that are dependent on authorities which neither party included in submissions and arguments to court. Research conducted in the 1970s found that most barristers considered the convention operative when they argued before the House of Lords.[154] Much the same opinion was shown to prevail when the research was updated some four decades later.[155] Yet, as we saw in the final section of the last chapter, final court judges have never quite settled on a convention. For some of them, unless the court provides counsel with the opportunity to present fresh arguments in response to authority which the court will otherwise be applying out-of-the-blue—thereby delaying proceedings and very likely adding to litigants' costs—its introduction will benefit one party while leaving the other with reason to feel aggrieved that their case was disadvantaged by judicial intervention. For others, it would be remiss of the final court not to take account of the authority, even if that means springing it upon the parties by surprise, given that a core element of the court's remit—resolving matters of legal principle and settling points pertaining to the interpretation and application of laws—demands comprehensiveness. Nor, in English law, would it be accurate to claim that convention clearly abjures against dispositive reliance in the lower courts, where judges quite regularly invoke authority which they think not only should have been referred to in submissions but which they consider to be so pertinent to a case that the court's judgment would be very obviously vulnerable to appeal or a re-trial petition if it were not taken into account.[156] As with judicial reliance on authorities not mentioned in arguments to court, so too with how judges acknowledge—and omit to acknowledge—scholarship: that practice is governed by a distinct convention seems questionable.

The perils of proclaiming conventions aside, it is worth noting too that, while it may well be the case that judges, when relying on scholarship, are not as beholden

---

[154] Alan Paterson, *The Law Lords* (London: Macmillan, 1982), at 20–21, 38.

[155] Paterson, *Final Judgment* (n 43) 20.

[156] See e.g. *Allan v Nolan* [2002] EWCA Civ 85 at [49]–[51]; *R (Richardson) v N Yorkshire CC* [2003] EWHC 764 (Admin) at [47]–[48]; *Normandy v Ind Coope & Co. Ltd* [1908] 1 Ch. 84, 106–107.

to formal attribution practices as academics are, it would be wrong to maintain that reliance without ascription might be acceptable to judges but is always anathema to scholars. Fred Rodell commented on Thurman Arnold's insouciance—'forget[ting] his footnotes as though to say that if people do not believe or understand him that is their worry and not his'—not when Arnold was a judge on the DC Circuit in the mid-1940s but when they were bad-boy realist colleagues at Yale Law School a decade earlier.[157] At the end of the Preface to the *Philosophy of Right*, Hegel observes that '[t]he owl of Minerva spreads its wings only with the falling of the dusk'.[158] Judges have occasionally adopted or paraphrased this observation, acknowledging its provenance in the process—even if not necessarily supplying a detailed source.[159] But, in the course of a landmark English proprietary estoppel case, a judge who has already featured prominently in this chapter, Lord Hoffmann, replicated the sentence (and other judges subsequently quoted his replication) without indication as to its source.[160] No footnote, no quotation-marks, no in-text clue as to its origin—nothing. A US law school law review editor would be aghast. Yet it would be a mistake to regard Hoffmann's replication as evidence of a difference in judicial and academic attitudes to attribution, for academics across a range of disciplines regularly invoke Hegel's *dictum* without so much as mentioning him.[161] Presumably they envisage—presumably Hoffmann envisaged— readers spotting a line from a classic work of philosophy (with a reference to Greek mythology to boot!), and enjoying the feeling of doing so unaided.

There are, nevertheless, ways of engaging with scholarship which are suited to judicial decision-making even though they make for irregular, or even inappropriate, academic practice. Of late, the UK's final court has been predisposed, for example, to introducing into judgments CLS-redolent paragraphs acknowledging, often without further reference or discussion, scholarship from which some or all of the contributing judges 'derived assistance'.[162] Richard Posner had an explanation for casualness of this kind, and indeed for

---

[157] Fred Rodell, 'Goodbye to Law Reviews' (1936) 23 *Va L. Rev.* 38, 41. Rodell was commenting not specifically on Arnold but on Arnold and law professors like him ('Once in a while a Thurman Arnold forgets his footnotes as though to say ...').

[158] G. W. F. Hegel, *Philosophy of Right*, trans. T. M. Knox (London: OUP, 1952 [1821]), 13.

[159] See e.g. *Guest v Guest* [2022] UKSC 27 at [243]; *Merricks v Adkisson*, 785 F.3d 553, 562 (11th Cir. 2015).

[160] *Thorner v Major* (n 43) at [8]. For bare replications, see *Trentelman v Owners of Strata Plan No. 76700* (2021) 106 NSWLR 227 at para. 138; *Sabey v von Hopffgarten Estate* [2013] BCSC 642 (Brit. Columb. SC) at para. 48; *Murphy v Rayner* [2011] EWHC (Ch) 1 at [267].

[161] For recent examples, see Paul A. Roth, 'Undisciplined and Unpunished' (2018) 57 *History and Theory* 121, 132; Samuel Moyn, 'The End of Human Rights History' (2016) 233 *Past & Present* 307, 309.

[162] See e.g. *R (Officer W80) v Director General of the Independent Office for Police Conduct* [2023] UKSC 24 at [85] ('we have found great assistance from ...'); *Trustees of the Barry Congregation of*

judges not so much as mentioning the scholarship to which they resort. It was observed in section (a) of this chapter that one of Posner's books, *Divergent Paths*, belongs to a line of modern American judicial observation lamenting the absence of incentive for, and therefore a general disinclination on the part of, ambitious US law professors to produce scholarship that judges will find useful.[163] In an earlier book, on the concept of plagiarism, he approached the general topic of juristic writing and judicial reliance on it from a different, slightly more elaborate angle.

Even when judges find scholarship valuable, Posner maintained, their reliance—particularly their explicit reliance—on it is mediated by the judicial function and by the nature of the judicial opinion. 'In modern America, . . . publishing a judicial opinion under the name of a judge who did not write it is not plagiarism, but a professor's publishing an article actually written by his research assistant is.'[164] Academics are unjustly enriched if they make money from publishing work which plagiarizes other sources, but, so far as financial reward in concerned, the most that plagiarizing judges—who 'are not permitted to copyright their opinions and so obtain no royalties from them'[165]—can hope for is that their reliance on scholarship improves their opinions, enhancing their judicial reputations, resulting in promotion.

Posner's argument seems disputable. For academics, plagiarism is solecism whether or not they financially benefit from the practice, as is plagiarism from which a plagiarist might derive only indirect advantage. It would be mistake, too, to maintain that judges are entitled to be casual about plagiarizing if they face time pressures or if they deliver opinions orally; all manner of plagiarists contend with deadlines, after all, and ex tempore delivery does not preclude reference to sources. This is not to maintain, however, that there are no valid

---

Jehovah's Witnesses v BXB [2023] UKSC at [7]; *Byers v Saudi National Bank* [2023] UKSC 51 at [104] (and also [103], for scholarship considered 'helpful on the debate' over whether the concept central to the case (the equitable property right) should be 'recast', but not relevant 'as a practical matter . . . to the correct application or understanding of the law'); *Guest v Guest* (n 159) at [170]; *R (Miller) v Secretary of State for Exiting the European Union* (n 153) at [11] (where the majority acknowledges being 'assisted by a number of illuminating articles written by academics' but does not identify articles or authors); *BNY Corporate Trustee Services Ltd v Eurosail-UK* [2013] UKSC 28 at [26]; *OBG v Allan* [2007] UKHL 21 at [195]. Early US Critical Legal Scholars would often begin an article by name-checking the authors and works they considered to have most influenced them in writing it. These authors and works would not necessarily appear more than the once. See e.g. Duncan Kennedy, 'The Structure of Blackstone's *Commentaries*' (1979) 28 *Buffalo L. Rev.* 209, 210; Gerald E. Frug, 'The City as a Legal Concept' (1980) 93 *Harv. L. Rev.* 1057, 1059–1060 n 1.

[163]   That they will find useful, that is, rather than—to draw on his (not exactly timorous) description of modern US constitutional theory—'stifling in . . . its pretentious obscurantism, its inconclusiveness, its unhelpfulness, its occasional frivolousness'. Posner, *Divergent Paths* (n 15) 29.

[164]   Richard A. Posner, *The Little Book of Plagiarism* (New York: Pantheon, 2007), 49.

[165]   Ibid. 22.

reasons for judges being relaxed about acknowledging the influence of scholarship when they write opinions. Academics misrepresent themselves as having produced original scholarship if their research plays down or neglects to acknowledge how much it is derived from work done by others. But judges, when writing opinions, are not striving for scholarly originality—and so are not required to observe attribution conventions so that the originality of their own pronouncements is discernible—in the way that academics commonly are.[166]

Judges seeking to ensure minimal distraction from their reasoning, or to establish clarity on points of law, might regard source-provenance details as unnecessary encumbrances.[167] They might also want to maintain an element of distance between the opinions they produce and the legal scholarship on which they rely. Judicial citation of a jurist's work, Posner argues, can be 'the equivalent of a celebrity endorsement of a product'.[168] Judges mindful of this fact could value a jurist's work and rely on it but decline to refer to it out of concern that other jurists with alternative products might be left with their noses out of joint. The real judicial inclination might be to respond to, rather than to rely on, academic work—as when the work contains criticisms of *dicta* set forth or endorsed by judges in an earlier case and which they now have an opportunity to develop or integrate into a binding *ratio*. But judicial rules of conduct may constrain them from responding. Judges in England and Wales, for instance, are prohibited from answering public criticism of their legal opinions.[169]

Common-law judgments regularly draw verbatim on other legal documents—written submissions to court, for example, or first-instance findings of fact—with negligible or no attribution.[170] The practice is not without its

[166] See ibid. 71–72.
[167] 'Judges at the highest level appreciate the help that they can derive from academic scholarship, particularly doctrinal scholarship. I am afraid we do not often acknowledge it in our judgments, essentially because we are trying (or perhaps I should say struggling) to keep our judgments as short as we can—believe it or not—and are more concerned to set out our analysis of the issues than to explain the process of research and thought which led us to it.' Lord Reed, 'Triremes and Steamships: Scholars, Judges, and the Use of the Past', Scrymgeour Lecture, University of Dundee, 30 October 2015 (www.supremecourt.uk/docs/speech-151030.pdf) at 1 (accessed 24 July 2023). See also Beatson, 'Legal Academics' (n 4) 538.
[168] Posner, *The Little Book of Plagiarism* (n 164) 26.
[169] *Guide to Judicial Conduct* (London: Courts and Tribunals Judiciary, 2020), 14 ('Judges should refrain from answering public criticism of a judgment or decision . . .'). See also HL Deb., 21 May 2003, vol. 648 col. 882 (Lord Woolf) ('Members of the judiciary . . . are dependent upon the reasoning set out in their judgments to explain their decisions. . . . If judgments are not understood or are misrepresented, the judiciary is inhibited from responding because of the very important convention that judges do not discuss individual cases'); Burrows, 'Judges and Academics' (n 32) 59.
[170] See e.g. *Re Merck & Co.* [2007] EWHC 3842 (Ch) at [2] (Warren J) ('Norris J had a similar application at the end of last week . . . and he reviewed in his admirable concise ex tempore judgment the relevant provisions and rehearsed the arguments that . . . are put before me. . . . I hope I will be

critics,[171] though tacit presumptions about fair use tend to apply to replications of this kind.[172] The waters become muddier when judges appropriate legal reasoning rather than summaries of information or statements of fact. Seldom is reasoning derived from legal scholarship actually plagiarized in judicial opinions. In 1996 a US law professor, Jaime Dursht, solemnly condemned judicial plagiarism as 'undermin[ing] the integrity of the judiciary'[173] and argued for its being classified as a contravention of court rules. Yet she identified only one instance of its occurrence, a case concerning a judge who admitted to plagiarising two law review articles in a law review article of his own (published three years after his becoming a judge).[174]

Since Dursht's article was published, cases of this kind have hardly proliferated, and judicial opinions in which plagiarism is proved to be present are close to non-existent. In 2001, a judgment of the Federal Court of Australia was amended to acknowledge that sections of it had 'been drawn' from a law professor's 'very valuable summary of the [relevant legal] principles' in a chapter of *Halsbury's Laws of Australia* after the professor alleged plagiarism and the judge who had written the judgment stated that his footnotes citing the chapter had been omitted in error.[175] In 2011, a judge of the Philippines Supreme Court successfully defended his failure to attribute in an opinion passages replicated from two academic works. His defence was that he didn't spot that his assistant had accidentally deleted his citations to the works.[176] Allegations that a judicial opinion plagiarizes scholarship are rare. Instances in which an allegation is upheld are extremely rare.

---

forgiven if I shamelessly plagiarise what he has to say'); *Conant v Walters*, 309 F.3d 629, 641 n 3 (9th Cir. 2002) (Kozinski J, concurring); *Bowen v Celotex Corp.*, 292 F.3d 565, 566 (8th Cir. 2002) (Bye J); *Daryanani v Kumar & Co.* [2001] C.P. Rep. 27 (CA) at [4] (Mantell LJ); *Schultz v Instant Handling, Inc.*, 418 F.2d 1019, 1020 n* (5th Cir. 1969) (Rives J).

[171] See e.g. *Parlak v Holder*, 578 F.3d 457, 476 (6th Cir. 2009) (Martin J, dissenting).
[172] See Posner, *The Little Book of Plagiarism* (n 164) 21; also Adam Feldman, 'All Copying is Not Created Equal: Borrowed Language in Supreme Court Opinions' (2016) 17 *Jnl Appellate Practice & Process* 21; Simon Stern, 'Copyright Originality and Judicial Originality' (2013) 63 *UTLJ* 385, 413.
[173] Jaime S. Dursht, 'Judicial Plagiarism: It May be Fair Use but is it Ethical?' (1996) 18 *Cardozo L. Rev.* 1253, 1293.
[174] *Matter of Brennan*, 447 N.W.2d 712 (Mich. 1989). See Dursht, 'Judicial Plagiarism' (n 173) 1287–1288, 1293–1294.
[175] *SVI Systems Pty Ltd v Best & Less Pty Ltd* [2001] FCA 279 at para. 113. See also ibid. at para. 106 and Robert Nicholson, 'Plagiarism and the Law' (2009) 14 *Angelaki* 21, 24.
[176] The case in relation to which the plagiarism allegation was made is *Vinuya v Romulo* [2010] PHSC 450 (SC Philippines, en banc). The Supreme Court dismissed a judicial impeachment motion (and a subsequent motion for reconsideration) initiated by the University of Philippines College of Law: *In the Matter of the Charges of Plagiarism, Etc, against Associate Justice Mariano C. Del Castillo* [2011] PHSC 143 (SC Philippines, en banc) (per curiam). See also Stern, 'Copyright Originality and Judicial Originality' (n 172) 414–415.

But this does not mean that judges never sail close to the wind. In English law, examples adduced in support of this claim—examples, intriguingly, provided as often as not by judges—usually indicate that reasoning contained in a work of legal scholarship has been reformulated and adopted, but not credited, in a judgment or judicial opinion.[177] Very occasionally, a judicial and an academic pronouncement will be near-indistinguishable. A UK Supreme Court judgment of 2018 states that '[i]n the ordinary run of cases, courts consider what has been decided previously and follow the precedents', and that a negligence test established in 1990 by the House of Lords, '[p]roperly understood, . . . achieves a balance between legal certainty and justice'.[178] An article concerning the test is referenced later in the judgment, though these passages aren't attributed to it—even though the article states that '[i]n the normal run of cases, one looks to what has been decided previously and follows those decisions',[179] and that, '[p]roperly understood',[180] the test 'reaches an appropriate balance between certainty and justice'.[181] A few years after an eminent commercial law professor had published a monograph in which he maintained that it is 'inherently impossible' for a bank to take a charge over the credit balance of one of its own customers, thereby 'mak[ing] the bank its own creditor',[182] a High Court judge decided 'that a charge in favour of a debtor of his own indebtedness to the chargor is conceptually impossible'.[183] Another judge would write of how the decision—reached 'using substantially the same language as' the professor had used, 'but without citing him, apparently on the ground that counsel had not referred to the book'—illustrates how, in a judgment, 'an academic . . . contribution can be unacknowledged or forgotten'.[184] (That the language used in

---

[177] For some convergent qualms, see William Day, 'Further Narrowing the Scope of Unjust Enrichment' (2019) 78 *CLJ* 24, 27 ('[T]he judgments in *Prudential Assurance* did not really engage with academic writings at all despite a striking similarity between the Supreme Court's application of *Investment Trust Companies* to the question of compound interest and the arguments contained in R. Stevens (2018) 134 *LQR* 574 (an unpublished version of which had been read by members of the Supreme Court)'); P. S. Davies 'One Step Backwards: Restricting Negotiating Damages for Breach of Contract' [2018] *Lloyd's Maritime and Commercial L. Q.* 433, 437–438; Andrew Burrows, 'Narrowing the Scope of Unjust Enrichment' (2017) 133 *LQR* 537, 541–542. And for some judicial push-back, see Andrew Baker, 'Unjust Enrichment Scholarship in the Courts: Use and Utility' [2023] *Lloyd's Maritime and Commercial L. Q.* 624.

[178] *Robinson v Chief Constable of West Yorkshire Police* [2018] UKSC 4 at [29].

[179] Craig Purshouse, 'Arrested Development: Police Negligence and the *Caparo* "Test" for Duty of Care' (2016) 23 *Torts L. J.* 1, 8.

[180] Ibid. 23.

[181] Ibid. 8.

[182] R. M. Goode, *Legal Problems of Credit and Security* (London: Sweet & Maxwell, 1982), 86.

[183] *Re Charge Card Services Ltd* [1986] 3 All ER 289, 308.

[184] Beatson, 'Legal Academics' (n 4) 524.

the judgment was substantially the same as that used in the monograph seems, if one compares the relevant passages, somewhat debatable.)[185]

It is quite common for judges to observe of their own profession that although they need not meticulously attribute to scholarship when relying on it in opinions, they might still fail to credit it sufficiently—even if they cannot be said to have plagiarized it.[186] *Woolwich Equitable Building Society v IRC* (1988) was concerned with whether citizens have an automatic right to restitution if they pay money to a public body which issued the payment demand without lawful authority.[187] When the case was heard in the High Court, the judge decided that there was no such right, and in doing so cited in support of his conclusion a passage from Peter Birks' book, *An Introduction to the Law of Restitution*.[188] Birks then produced an essay in which he criticized the High Court judgment. Since the publication of his book, Birks confessed, his 'position had changed considerably'.[189] Whereas once he had thought that judges, when ruling on restitution claims, had to be mindful of 'the need to safeguard public funds',[190] he now believed that 'confidence in legality'[191] demanded that judges had to set concerns about 'fiscal disruption' to one side: 'the principle of legality outweighs those dangers and requires that judges leave it to legislatures to impose what restrictions on the right of restitution they think necessary, wise and proper.'[192] For Birks, there was an automatic right to restitution after all, even if restrictions could be placed on the availability of that right.

[185] Compare *Re Charge Card Services* (n 183) at 308 (Millett J) ('If the right of retention constitutes a charge, there is no doubt that it is ... a charge created by the company. But is it a charge at all? The sum due from Commercial Credit [*sc.*, the respondent] to the company under the agreement is ... a ... debt of the company which the company can charge to a third party. In my judgment, however, it cannot be charged in favour of Commercial Credit itself, for the simple reason that a charge in favour of a debtor of his own indebtedness to the chargor is conceptually impossible') with Goode, *Legal Problems of Credit and Security* (n 182) 86–87 ('A customer's credit balance ... is ... an asset which he can charge to a third party. But can he charge it ... to secure a contingent liability? ... [M]any lawyers see no legal obstacle to this. Yet ... others ... stoutly maintain that a charge over the customer's credit balance in favour of the bank holding the balance is inherently impossible, for the effect of the charge is to make the bank its own creditor.... [H]ere the debtor is the bank, which cannot legally sue itself. It follows that the customer's assignment to the bank of his own right of action against the bank is a nullity, for it transfers nothing').

[186] See e.g. Kiefel, 'The Academy and the Courts' (n 36) 452; Rodger, 'Judges and Academics' (n 7) 32 ('When it comes to using academic writing, judges must, of course, be careful not to plagiarise. In other words, if they are really just adopting some argument from an academic article, then it would be wrong for them not to acknowledge the source. I think they do, on the whole. But judges always have to remember that they are writing a judgment, not an academic article').

[187] *Woolwich Equitable Building Society v IRC* [1989] 1 WLR 137. (Case decided 10 March 1988.)

[188] Ibid. 140–141, quoting Peter Birks, *An Introduction to the Law of Restitution* (Oxford: Clarendon Press, 1985), 295.

[189] Peter Birks, 'Restitution from the Executive: A Tercentenary Footnote to the Bill of Rights', in *Essays on Restitution*, ed. P. D. Finn (Sydney: Law Book Company, 1990), 164–205 at 168 n 29.

[190] Ibid.

[191] Ibid. 203.

[192] Ibid. 204.

A three-judge Court of Appeal overruled the High Court. One of the two judges in the majority, observing that the issues at the heart of the case had been 'discussed by distinguished academic commentators',[193] concluded that, 'subject to . . . limitations', there 'should, in the interests both of justice and good government, be such a general restitutionary principle as that for which Woolwich contends'.[194] The other majority judge agreed.[195] Both reasoned just as Birks had in his essay, yet—a fact which another judge deemed 'unfortunate and possibly discourteous'[196]—neither saw fit to mention him. When the case went to the House of Lords, the law lord who delivered the lead judgment pointedly awarded Birks juristic restitution: 'I have little doubt that this essay . . . provided the main inspiration for . . . the judgments of the majority of the Court of Appeal'.[197] Outright plagiarism of scholarship by judges is unusual. Even when it is reasonable to look askance at absence of attribution, there may be factors raising the benefit of the doubt. There are, nevertheless, instances, as judges themselves are occasionally minded to observe, when it is near impossible to draw any conclusion other than that a source should have been acknowledged.

---

[193] *Woolwich Equitable Building Society v IRC* [1991] 4 All ER 577, 583 (Glidewell LJ).

[194] Ibid. 599.

[195] Ibid. 637 (Butler-Sloss LJ) ('I consider that there is a general principle of repayment of tax unlawfully demanded . . . subject to limitations').

[196] Beatson, 'Legal Academics' (n 4) 536.

[197] *Woolwich Equitable Building Society v IRC* [1993] AC 70, 166 (Lord Goff).

Conclusion

The case was made in chapter 3 that Ronald Dworkin's legal theory is not a wholesale rejection of the thesis that norms are legal norms because they are attributable to sources which law-enforcing officials recognize to be sources of law. But he very clearly did think that judges motivated by integrity will not be especially preoccupied with the implications of the thesis, even if they cannot turn a blind eye to the brute facts of legal history. Late in *Law's Empire*, in the chapter on the United States Constitution, Dworkin's thinking becomes startlingly clear when he ponders whether—in truth, how—an integrity-minded judge might conclude that the framers of the Constitution supported racial integration. Legal history presents this judge with, to say the least, an uphill task. Anyone who 'limits eligible interpretations of the Constitution to principles that express the historical intentions of the framers . . . will not accept that the equal protection clause [of the Fourteenth Amendment] outlaws state-imposed segregation unless . . . he is satisfied that the framers did not think the clause did not outlaw segregation'.[1] The Chairman of the House Judiciary, James Wilson, assured the congressmen and legislators who passed the Fourteenth Amendment bill that they were not voting to outlaw racially segregated schools. After the bill entered the Constitution, Congress continued to segregate the schools of the District of Columbia. Even if the abstract conviction of these statesmen was 'that the Constitution should require the law to treat all citizens as equals', Dworkin concedes, there is no doubt that '[m]any of them had the further concrete conviction that racial segregation did not violate that requirement'.[2] A judge with Herculean aspirations, interpreting the equal protection clause, has to contend with this brute fact.

And yet—lo and behold—this judge need not ultimately be constrained by this fact. For he might be able to interpret the source in accordance with the 'more abstract . . . conviction that America should . . . treat everyone as equal before the law'.[3] Rather than heed the fact that barring racial segregation, certainly segregation in schools, was not on the framers' minds,

---

[1] Ronald Dworkin, *Law's Empire* (London: Fontana, 1986), 360.
[2] Ibid. 362.
[3] Ibid.

he would do better to look directly to the overall structure of the post-Civil War amendments . . . seen as part of the more general constitutional system they left in place, and to ask what principles of equality are necessary to justify that structure. Only when he has identified and refined these principles can he sensibly decide whether, in his opinion, the framers' concrete opinion about segregation is consistent with their more abstract convictions about equality. If he decides they are not, . . . he is led steadily away from relying exclusively on what the framers thought about this particular issue.[4]

Dworkin had a knack for developing arguments which are at once clever and elusive, ingenious and exasperating; the constitutional historian on whom he draws in *Law's Empire* when accepting that the passing of the Fourteenth Amendment was not motivated by a desire to outlaw racially segregated education would subsequently write in far from complimentary terms about Dworkin's choice to emphasize more abstract convictions.[5] Yet Dworkin's reasoning, however one evaluates it, proves highly instructive on the subject of law's sources. The early chapters of this book provide what is, essentially, the story of the idea that a law is binding authority by virtue of its being attributable to a primary source. Crucial to this story is H. L. A. Hart (along with his somewhat neglected precursor, John Salmond) and the re-configuration of source-focused analyses so that questions about legal authority are formulated in terms of the practices of legal officials, particularly judges, as distinct from the attitudes and the compliance of citizens. Although Dworkin features in this story, while he never completely extricates his legal philosophy from the implications of the sources thesis, he was primarily interested—as is evident from his observations on how best to read the equal protection clause—in what authorities are understood to be authorities for, rather than in what makes them authorities in the first place. Legal authorities constrain the decision-making of judges, and judges often will not like the constraints. But if they search hard enough, they might find within the law itself—Dworkinian judges, it seems,

---

[4] Ibid. 363.

[5] 'Dworkin's imaginary framer must have lived in an airtight cocoon'. Raoul Berger, *Government by Judiciary: The Transformation of the Fourteenth Amendment*, 2nd edn (Indianapolis: Liberty Fund, 1997), 28. (Dworkin relies on the first edition: *Law's Empire* (n 1) 450 n 6.) Berger offers an even more uncomplimentary assessment in 'Ronald Dworkin's *The Moral Reading of the Constitution*: A Critique' (1997) 72 *Indiana L. J.* 1099, 1102–1103. For a defence of Dworkin's moral, abstract conviction-based reading of the US Constitution (a defence which is candid about the uphill task), see Christopher L. Eisgruber, 'Should Constitutional Judges be Philosophers?', in *Exploring Law's Empire: The Jurisprudence of Ronald Dworkin*, ed. S. Hershovitz (Oxford: OUP, 2006), 5–22. For the argument that Dworkin's reading comes undone in the face of historical evidence, see Keith E. Whittington, 'Dworkin's "Originalism": The Role of Intentions in Constitutional Interpretation' (2000) 62 *Rev. of Politics* 197.

very likely will find—materials that enable them to loosen, possibly even re-move, some of those constraints.

The bulk of this book has been about source-negotiation rather than source-recognition. Lawyers and judges value secondary sources when they help them to get their way with the primary ones—when they help them make the case that a law which appears to bind in a particular instance actually does not, or that it binds even though no-one has realized it yet, or that it binds but not in the way that others maintain, or that it binds but ideally ought to be altered or removed, and so on. Now and again, the secondary sources themselves are for-mally turned into, or are enlisted to serve as surrogates for, primary ones. Some secondary sources—particularly the ones with content resembling applicable holdings or statutory provisions—seem more equipped for the upgrade than others. Scholarship is, as secondary sources go, one of the lesser equipped, more suited to a back-room role: informing and advising, but rarely, if ever, de-ciding. Yet that role, it turns out, has depth to it. Besides influencing—besides occasionally being replicated in—authoritative legal opinion, scholarship sometimes meets with judicial scepticism or criticism yet still has a bearing on how some facet of the law comes to be fashioned by a court. Academic legal reasoning makes its mark on judicial reasoning in all sorts of ways, not all of them obvious or straightforward.

Although this book has engaged with legal philosophy, it isn't an attempt to come up with one. It offers no theory or grand idea but only a collection of findings and claims pertaining to law's sources and the ways in which they bear upon judicial decision-making and aspects of legal practice. One objective has been to project light into crevices, some of them quite obscure (such as pre-scribed custom and the puzzles thrown up by void *ab initio* declarations and by authorities invoked *sua sponte* for the settlement of legal outcomes). But argu-ments have been advanced as well: that primary sources are not originating lo-cations but practices and processes involving tests and thresholds, that statutes have a legal-normative dimension of their own and aren't just legal texts, that judge-made law is a multifarious concept, that the sources thesis is a notably hardy perennial, that secondary sources can be especially wily operators, and that the fragility of the primary-secondary source distinction doesn't mean that it's not genuine.

Readers who have stayed the course may recall that roundabout admission at the end of the Introduction: that primary and secondary sources pose different questions, answers to which might seem more or less intriguing depending on one's own mode of engagement with law. Legal philosophers and legal histor-ians will have spotted traces of their own methodologies and lines of inquiry featuring in the course of this study. And perhaps, with luck, it will have some appeal to these sectors. First and foremost, however, the book is meant to resonate with a different, rather more diffuse constituency: with judges, lawyers, law students, indeed with anyone invested in identifying, and establishing the meaning of, the laws that pertain to what they have to say. Practitioner texts are often derided, and this study hardly epitomizes the genre. Yet it fits the bill, so long as the genre is presumed to accommodate meditations on the sources that make courts' decisions applications of law, as well as the ones that judges—and the people looking to win them over—turn to when they try to establish that what they pronounce the law to be is, indeed, what it is.

Index

Digital users should note that page ranges for indexed subjects may occasionally differ as between the digitized and print versions of the book.

Accursius, Franciscus 49–50
Adler v George (1964) 13–14
advocacy 83–86
Airedale NHS Trust v Bland (1993) 112–18
American Law Institute 58–59, 62, 66–68
   see also Restatements
American legal realism 70–71, 83–84
amicus briefs 35, 41–42, 107
Aristotle 50
Arnold, Thurman 120–21
Atkin, James 39–40
Austin, John 4–5
authority 14–15
   binding 40, 70, 74–75, 130–31 *see also*
   content-independent reasons
   continuum of 53–54, 68–73
   de facto binding 42–43, 44–45, 53, 73
   necessary 50
   optional 56–57
   permissive 40
   persuasive 56–57
   probable 50
   textual 14–15, 60–61, 68–69
   uncanvassed 85–91
   see also sources of law
Azo of Bologna 49–50

Bacon, Francis 3–4
Bacon, Nathaniel 26
Bagehot, Walter 90–91
basic norm 9, 22
Berlin, Isaiah 117
Bingham, Tom 46
Birks, Peter 54–55, 126–27
Blackstone, William 24–25
Breyer, Stephen 95
Browne-Wilkinson, Nicolas 113–14
Burke, Edmund 23–24

Calabresi, Guido 100
canon law 17
'Captain of Köpenick' (Wilhelm Voigt) 80
Cardozo, Benjamin 103–4, 109–10
Carman Tool v Evergreen (1988) 105–6
Cicero 1–3
civil law 47–49
   legal scholarship, and 49–51
Coase, Ronald 110–11
Coase theorem 110–11
Coke, Edward 3
commencement regulations 11–12
common law 18–20, 62–63, 69, 109–10
   legal scholarship, and 51–59
communis opinio 49–50, 62–63
constituent power 22–23
constitutions 21–24
Contemporary Mission, Inc. v Famous Music
   Corp (1977) 57–59
content-independent reasons 51–52, 53–
   54, 60–61, 87
conventionalism 29–32
Corpus iuris civilis 17, 47–48
   Code 47–48
   Digest 47–48, 74
   Institutes 47–48
   see also Justinian; Roman law
Cross, Arthur 108–9
custom 16–21, 24–26, 49–50 *see also*
   prescription

de Maistre, Joseph 23–24
Denning, Alfred 71–73, 90–91
Devlin, Patrick 109
Dobbs v Jackson Women's Health Org.
   (2022) 35, 103–4
Domat, Jean 50–51
Dugdale, William 25–26

Dursht, Jaime 123–24
Dworkin, Ronald 28–36, 37, 46, 87,
    129–31
  euthanasia, on 35, 114–18
  secondary sources, on 34–36
  see also integrity; interpretivism

Eisenberg, Melvin 57–58
ex post facto law 8–9, 67–68, 75, 79–80, 82–83

Fairchild v Glenhaven (2002) 94–95
Farah Constructions v Say-Dee
    (2007) 86–88
Field, Oliver 81–82
Field, Stephen Johnson 80–81
Finnis, John 35
Fitzmaurice, Gerald 63–64
foreign judgments 41–42, 46–47, 55
Frank, Jerome 83–84
Friendly, Henry 110–11
Fuller, Lon 112–13

Gaius 2–3, 48–49
Gardner, John 15–16, 31
Gardner Steel v Sheffield Bros (1978) 71–73
Glorious Revolution 22, 23–24
Glossators 49–50
Goff, Robert 94–95, 104–5, 113, 127
Gray, John Chipman 7–11, 27–28
Green, Leon 8
Greenberg, Mark 14, 32

Hadley v Baxendale (1854) 104–5
Hand, Learned 89
hard cases 30–31, 34
Hart, H. L. A. 8, 9, 27–29, 38–40, 68–69,
    70–71, 73, 75–76, 130–31
Hegel, G. W. F. 23, 120–21
Hershovitz, Scott 32
Hoadly, Benjamin 8
Hoffmann, Leonard 114–18, 120–21
Holmes, Oliver Wendell 74
Hope, David 104–5
Hunt, Thomas 24
Hunter v Canary Wharf (1997) 104–6, 108

In re Owens Corning (2005) 102–3
integrity 28–31, 33, 34–36, 87, 90, 129
  adjudication, in 30

interpretation, in 30
  see also Dworkin, Ronald
interpretivism 29–33, 35–36, 87 see also
    Dworkin, Ronald
ius gentium 46

Jansen, Nils 60–63, 67–68, 70–71
judge-made law 7–9, 54–55, 71–72, 109–
    10, 113–14, 131
jurisconsults 48–49
Justinian 2–4, 47–48, 74 see also Corpus
    iuris civilis; Roman law

Kelsen, Hans 4–5, 9, 16–17, 22, 79–83 see
    also basic norm; legal norms; void ab
    initio doctrine
Kent v Griffiths (2001) 77–78
Kozinski, Alex 106–7

Lambarde, William 25–26
law clerks 92–93, 96–97
Lawrence v Texas (2002) 46–47
legal formants 37
legal maxims 3
legal norms 9–16
  chain of creation, and 16–17
  laws, distinct from 10–11
  sources of law, distinct from 10–16
legal pluralism 37–38
legal positivism xi–xii, 4–5, 6, 7, 16–17,
    27–28, 32, 35–36, 37–39, 87
  inclusive 28–29
legal scholarship xiii–xiv, 37–38, 47–59, 92–94
  judges, and 94–127
  judicial attributions to 118–27
  judicial use of 102–18
  source status of 37–38, 47–59
legislative history 34, 40, 92, 118–19
Lévi-Bruhl, Henri 37–38
Lewis, William Draper 58–59
Lexecon v Milberg Weiss (1998) 106–8
Llewellyn, Karl 83–84
Lloyd, Tony 39–40
Lotus principle 76–77

Macmillan, Hugh 98–99
Mann, Frederick 108–9
Marbury v Madison (1803) 80–81
Marshall, John 80–81

McGregor, Harvey 56
McGregor on Damages 56, 58
Merryman, John Henry 68–69
Miller v Miller (2006) 92–93
Millett, Peter 93–94, 125–26
Munby, James 116

natural justice 87–89
Newark, Francis 104–5
non-legal secondary sources 41–42
non-legislative codifications 14–15, 60–62
   see also Restatements
Norton v Shelby County (1886) 80–81

obiter dicta xi, xii–xiii, 35, 39–40, 42–43,
   44–45, 55, 71–72, 104–5
Oppenheimer v Cattermole (1975) 108–9

parliament 24–26
philosophers' brief 35
Plowden, Edmund 3
Pomponius 48–49
Posner, Richard 88–89, 93–94, 95, 121–23
Pothier, Robert Joseph 50–51
Pound, Roscoe 7–8
Precedent 18–19, 30, 31, 33, 56, 70, 77–78,
   103–4, 109–10
  foreign 41–42, 46–47, 55
  horizontal 45, 106–7
prescription 17–21, 24–25, 48 *see also* custom
Prynne, William 24–25

Quintilian 84

Radcliffe, Cyril 109–10
Rahimtoola v Nizan (1958) 90–91
Rawls, John 34
Raz, Joseph 15, 31
Read v Lyons (1947) 98–99
Reich, Charles 103–4
Reid, James 109
Restatements 58–59, 62–68
  adoption of 63–68
  enactment as law 62–63
  federal common law, and 62–63
  resemblance to statutes 66–68
  see also non-legislative codifications
Roberts, John 95–96
Rodell, Fred 120–21

Roe v Wade (1973) 35, 103–4
Roman law 2–4, 17, 47–49 *see also Corpus
   iuris civilis*; Justinian
Roper v Simmons (2005) 46–47
rule of law 8–9, 67–68, 75, 82–83, 126
rule of recognition 27–28, 29, 31, 33, 42–
   43, 44, 52–53, 62–63, 68, 70–73
  Salmond's anticipation of 5–6
  see also sources of law
R v Barton (2020) 71–72
R v Oakes (1986) 53–54

Sacco, Rodolfo 37
Salmond, John 4–6, 7, 27–28, 130–31
Scalia, Antonin 46–47
scholarship xiv *see also* legal scholarship
Sedley, Stephen 85
Shecaira, Fábio 51–55
soft law 68–69
Sorenson's case 39–40
source-norm distinction 7–21
sources of law xi–xii, 2–6, 34–36
  constitutions as 21–26
  customs as 16–21
  juristic writings as 37–38, 49–59
  law, distinguished from 7–16
  legal origins, explained as xi–xii, 3–5
  precedents as 8, 10, 51–53, 77–78
  primary xi–xii, xv–xvi, 37–40, 70–71
  secondary xi–xii, xv–xvi, 37–40, 69–70, 92
  source of law, distinguished from 1–4
  statutes as 7–16
  tests of legal validity, explained as xi–xii,
   5–6, 27–28, 35–36, 38–39, 131 *see also*
   authority; rule of recognition
sources thesis xii, 28–29
statutes 7–16, 78–79
  constitutional 21–22
  unconstitutional *versus* invalid 80
statutory interpretation 11–16, 30–31, 33,
   66–67, 78–79
Sturley, Michael 105–6
sua sponte reliance 83–91, 120
*Supreme Court of Virginia v Consumers
   Union of the United States* (1980) 77–78

textualism 12–13
*Transfield Shipping v Mercator Shipping
   (The Achilleas)* (2008) 104–6, 108

travaux préparatoires 41–42
treatises xiii–xiv, 14–15, 56–59
Twysden, Roger 25–26
Tyrrell, James 24

United States v Carolene Products (1938) 44–45
unregulated disputes 28–29

verdict safety 89–90
void *ab initio* doctrine 79–83
von Savigny, Friedrich Carl 3–4

Wilberforce, Richard 90–91
Williams, Bernard 114–15
Williston on Contracts 57–59
Williston, Samuel 58–59
Wilson, James 129
Woolf, Harry 77–78
Woolwich Equitable Building Society v IRC
    (1988) 126–27
Wright, Charles Alan 107

Young, Ernest 46–47